Last Exit to Utopia

Last Exit to Utopia

The Survival of Socialism in a Post-Soviet Era

JEAN-FRANÇOIS REVEL
Member of L'Académie Française

translated by Diarmid V. C. Cammell

Encounter Books New York · London

First English language edition published in 2009 by Encounter Books,
an activity of Encounter for Culture and Education, Inc.,
a nonprofit, tax exempt corporation.
Encounter Books website address: www.encounterbooks.com

Originally published in France as *La Grande Parade: Essai sur la survie de l'utopie
socialiste* in 2000 by Plon.

Manufactured in the United States and printed on
acid-free paper. The paper used in this publication meets
the minimum requirements of ANSI/NISO Z39.48-1992
(R 1997) (*Permanence of Paper*).

FIRST AMERICAN EDITION

LIBRARY OF CONGRESS CATALOGING-IN-PUBLICATION DATA

Revel, Jean-François.
[Grande parade. English]
Last exit to Utopia : the survival of socialism in a post-Soviet era /
Jean-François Revel ; translated by Diarmid V.C. Cammell.
p. cm.
Includes bibliographical references and index.
ISBN-13: 978-1-59403-264-6 (hardcover : alk. paper)
ISBN-10: 1-59403-264-5 (hardcover : alk. paper) 1. Utopian socialism. I. Title.
HX630.R4813 2009
335'.02—dc22
2009018978

10 9 8 7 6 5 4 3 2

In memory of Christian Jelen

Nil igitur mors est ad nos neque pertinet hilum,
Quandoquidem natura animi mortalis habetur.

Hence death is nothing to us,
It does not matter in the slightest,
Since the nature of mind
Is understood to be mortal.

—Lucretius

Contents

Foreword

Jean-François Revel's essay on socialist utopianism in a post-Soviet era might have appeared slightly dated and parochial a few years ago, its main subject being French intellectuals' defensive response to the implosion of Soviet Communism during the 1990s. Communism had quickly become something like an item from last year's newspapers that few people cared to discuss anymore. It is understandable, which is not to say excusable, that those on the left preferred to avert their eyes when the Soviet archives were opened, offering up corroboration of what the anticommunists had been saying all along. On the right, many seemed content to let bygones be bygones and move on, satisfied that the dominant ideological fight of the century had ended in a clear victory for the good guys. With some notable exceptions, such as the Annals of Communism series published by Yale University Press, the story of totalitarian socialism was tossed into the trash bin of historiography.

That is not where it belongs, Revel argues. The failure of our cultural elites to appraise the Communist record with the same moral seriousness that is rightly and continually brought to Nazism is one of his central themes. Analyzing this failure takes him far beyond the French intelligentsia and beyond Communism itself.

Revel diagnoses a "voluntary blindness" not only to the criminality of totalitarian socialism but also to the flaws of its more respectable social-democratic cousins. It is not merely an academic or anti-quarian matter, for it results in "an incapacity to learn lessons from history that might help us with the policy decisions that confront us today."

Revel traces this blindness to a utopian fantasy that long pre-dates Karl Marx, a fixture of the human mind that is constantly at war with liberty and with the integrity of the individual. Even so, when he published this book in 2000, Revel probably did not anticipate how soon his latest reflections on the "totalitarian temptation" would acquire an unsettling timeliness for the United States, a country he admired for its resistance to European-style *dirigisme*. True, he was well aware that a Marxist mentality flour-ished on American university campuses and spread through the media, and that Big Government was more intrusive in American life than most Europeans realized. But he noted that collectivism has historically had relatively light public support here. (In fact, attaching the "socialist" label to a left-wing politician elicits cries of foul.) Most likely, Revel would have been startled to see American voters in 2008 elect a president with a thinly veiled collectivist soul, and a major American newsmagazine soon afterward declaring on its cover, without irony, that "we are all socialists now."*

What is more certain is that the statist turn in American pol-itics was dismaying to the translator, Diarmid Cammell, an immi-grant from Great Britain who said that he felt freedom in the air when he first arrived in the United States in the 1970s. He had happily translated Revel's *L'Obsession anti-américaine* into English (as *Anti-Americanism*), sharing with the author a non-native's appreciation for America's singular virtues, as well as a taste for the refinements of French culture and cuisine. Subsequently he

---

* *Newsweek*, February 16, 2009. The article by Jean Meacham and Evan Thomas titled "We Are All Socialists Now," published in the February 7 online edition, includes in its subtitle the assertion that Americans are becoming "even more French." Perhaps Revel would have been amused.

returned to this earlier book, which he had already begun trans-
lating, confident that anything by Revel deserved wide exposure,
and that the subject of socialist criminality and failure—and the
denial thereof—was far from passé. Having lived and worked in
Berkeley for many years, he could not assume that the fundamental flaws of socialism were generally acknowledged or that
utopian fantasies had run their course. Like Revel, he disdained
"ideocracy," the rule of all-encompassing ideology, and abhorred
totalitarian tyranny.

Diarmid passed away before this book was typeset, but he knew
that events were confirming its enduring relevance. The United
States government has been racing down the *dirigiste* path, taking
on unprecedented power over the economy and society. An editorialist for the online English edition of *Pravda* has incredulously
remarked on how fast the United States is sliding into Marxism.*
The socialist president of Venezuela worries, only half in jest,
about ending up to the right of his U.S. counterpart.** And many
American citizens wonder what country they are living in now.

It was not very long ago that the errors of collectivism seemed
to have been so clearly demonstrated that some on the left, staring
at the rubble of the Communist edifice, appeared ready to revise
their ideology. After the Berlin Wall came down, a highly literate
octogenarian, who had earlier expressed the view that Franklin
Roosevelt "saved capitalism" from its own defects, confided to me
her fresh realization: "I guess capitalism really does work better"
than socialism. Around the same time, a leftist professor of mine
seemed to have suddenly discovered that the East Bloc regimes
being cast off by their subjects had been "authoritarian." Revel
comments that the lessons of the socialist experiment should
have been all the more obvious when even the democratic versions of socialism, the "mixed economies" following a Third Way,
were compelled to retreat or transform themselves. At the turn
of the century he observed most of the world moving away from

---

* "American Capitalism Gone with a Whimper," Pravda.ru, April 27, 2009.

** "Venezuela Chavez Says 'Comrade' Obama More Left-Wing," Reuters, June
2, 2009.

statist *dirigisme,* toward free-market democracy—*liberalisme* in the French political lexicon—as the surest formula for prosperity. To his inventory of retreats from statism I would add how President Clinton, seeing his party trounced in midterm elections after he attempted to nationalize the health-care industry, shifted expediently to the center on social and budgetary issues, gaining popularity as result.

The end of history was not upon us, however. There have since been reversals in Latin America, with Daniel Ortega making a comeback to join the far-left club of Chàvez and Morales and the Castros, while Hondurans struggle valiantly to avoid being pulled in with them. Then there is the U.S. government acting in such a way that Russian and Chinese officials see fit to lecture it on the fundamentals of capitalism. While a large part of the American public is horrified, a recent survey found an underwhelming majority persuaded that capitalism works better than socialism.* Man-on-the-street interviews easily turn up young adults who cannot distinguish the ideas of Karl Marx from those of the Founders, if they even know who Karl Marx was. They are products of the left-dominated educational machine along with a popular culture that glorifies Che Guevara and demonizes the McCarthyist Red-baiters who victimized so many well-meaning seekers of justice and equality.

It is amusing but not surprising to hear a nose-ringed clerk at the neighborhood Whole Foods Market (a corporation!) declare that the government cares too much about "business" and thus "we need some kind of social revolution"—perhaps referring to that elusive creature, the "real socialism" that "hasn't even been tried." This line became a convenient response to the growing body of evidence that actually existing socialism has yielded misery wherever it was planted. The argument that flawed application has *always* betrayed a fundamentally good system is a difficult one to sustain indefinitely. What we have seen instead, Revel stresses,

---

* "Just 53% Say Capitalism Better Than Socialism," *Rasmussen Reports,* April 9, 2009.

is the application of bad ideas: the ideas laid out in the founding documents of socialism.

Nonetheless, the collectivist ideologues keep parrying attacks on the failures of socialism by holding up its supposedly noble ideals—the omelet for which the eggs have to be cracked. Socialism promises equality, justice, fraternity. Those who oppose socialism must be hostile to these wonderful things. The collapse of the Soviet empire, Revel suggests, was actually a boon to this line of argument because it allowed the debate to retreat to a more abstract plane, the realm of pure ideas where Utopia resides.

Yet there remained plenty of observable facts that needed to be ignored for socialists to maintain the luster of their good intentions—facts including the consequences of "progressive" policies in the social democracies. In France, for example, the vaunted devotion to *égalité* has yielded no such thing, but rather an entrenched system of state-granted privileges. Revel's discussion of intentions trumping results will sound familiar to American readers. We are accustomed to hearing that seriousness about education is to be measured in tax dollars spent rather than literacy and numeracy achieved. It is likewise with "antipoverty" programs: no matter how much social pathology can be linked to welfare payments that prop up successive generations of single-mother households, it is the *intention* to end poverty that counts.

Today, as the U.S. government engineers a somewhat stealthy takeover of the medical profession, many people are criticizing particulars of the plan or calling attention to the unhealthy outcomes of similar policies elsewhere—to which a common rejoinder is: "Don't you think everyone should have health care?" Only mean people could oppose the *intention* to take care of everybody. Left-leaning politicians apparently believe that ideas with an unblemished record of failure will succeed if only they are put into the right hands—theirs. This might be called a triumph of hope over experience, or more accurately of hubris over evidence.

History shows that raising taxes will slow the economy and decrease revenue and actually hurt the poor, yet "progressives" cling to the principle of raising taxes on "the rich" because "it's fair." Who could be against fairness? Side-by-side comparisons of economic policies are available in the various states: for example, a deeply troubled state like California, with its high taxes and onerous regulations, versus a state like Texas with a friendlier business climate and a more robust economy. A "progressive" can see the two examples and conclude that California's policies, such as an exceptionally strict energy code, are the ones to spread across the nation. The progressives may simply deny a correlation between certain policies and conditions on the ground. Or there is another possibility: that they do not really want progress as most people understand it.

Revel points out that socialists claim to be progressive but build archaic societies, imbued with the anticivilizational spirit of Jean-Jacques Rousseau. He notes the Luddite tendencies that brought together left-wing utopians and environmentalists in the riots against the World Trade Organization in Seattle. Today, powerful figures in the U.S. government consider it good that our electricity prices should "skyrocket," that we refrain from making productive use of our energy resources, that the public's mobility be limited to where the government's transportation system goes, that we expect less medical innovation and perhaps shorter lives, and that we "de-develop" large parts of the country.

The "progressive" label gives cover to a hatred of freedom, a desire to control others or even to be controlled by others. Revel finds a fear of competition and of responsibility, widespread in every society, to be a key to the rise and survival of totalitarian regimes in otherwise civilized countries. He helps us understand why liberty is so readily sacrificed in the name of a Utopia that can never be achieved, for Utopia is always in the future. It is also, therefore, always beyond reproach.

The original title of this book, *La Grande Parade*, does not translate particularly well into English with all the nuances that Revel explains in his first chapter. It highlights the book's retrospective angle, concerning the efforts to evade an honest confrontation with the Communist record. Diarmid Cammell chose the title *Last Exist to Utopia,* which puts more emphasis on the persistence of socialist ideology. This title has an ironic twist, since Revel shows utopians always finding new routes toward their statist vision. But they have been known to press their agenda with the urgency of grabbing the last chance to save the country or humanity or the planet. In the current rush to "reform"—i.e., nationalize—health care in the United States, the president has repeated the assertion that if we don't act immediately, the necessary "reform" will probably never happen. Here is a whiff of the messianic complex, a corollary to the utopian cult of the leader.

In his translation, Diarmid transposed a few paragraphs at the opening of the first chapter and added one appendix to give background for the concept of *la pensée unique.* He also provided numerous explanatory notes for the benefit of American readers. If he determined a book named in the text to be available in English translation, he used the English title so as to bring maximum accessibility to the discussion, including information for both the original publication and the translation in the endnotes. He trusted that the names of French institutions and organizations are generally quite understandable to English readers who do not know French, but chose the English capitalization style as most helpful.

Having followed the writing of Anthony Daniels for many years, Diarmid suggested him as the ideal contributor of a preface. I am grateful to Mr. Daniels for fulfilling Diarmid's wish, and to Roger Kimball for having confidence in this enterprise.

Carol Staswick
August 2009

Preface

ANTHONY DANIELS

One of the abiding myths of the twentieth century is that many Western intellectuals sympathized with the Soviet Union because they were unaware of the true nature of the regime established by the Bolsheviks. According to this mythology, a lack of information allowed or encouraged them to fix their minds on the regime's declared ideals, and to ignore its terrible realities. Their sympathy, therefore, was a manifestation of generosity of spirit; they were guilty (if of anything at all) only of an error of judgment.

Nothing could be further from the truth. The nature of Bolshevism was reported from the very first, immediately after the Revolution and continuously thereafter. Neither Khrushchev's famous speech nor the work of Alexander Solzhenitsyn revealed anything that was not already known. My own small collection of books published in Britain, France and the United States in the 1920s and 1930s contains many volumes that, by themselves, prove beyond reasonable doubt that every class of atrocity, if not every atrocity itself, was made known in the West as or soon after it occurred.

It is worthwhile to compare the concluding words of Theodore Dreiser's *Dreiser Looks at Russia,* published in 1928, with those of Sergey Petrovich Melgounov's *The Red Terror in Russia,* published in 1925 (a year earlier in Germany, incidentally). Dreiser, having just visited the Lenin mausoleum, finishes his book:

> Sleep well, Ilitch, father of a new and possibly—who shall say?—world-altering social force. How fortunate, you, its chosen if martyred instrument. How fortunate indeed.

Melgounov, the frontispiece of whose book is a photograph of the corpses of ecclesiastics shot at Yuriev on January, 1, 1918, and whose claims throughout his book are extremely well documented and attested, concludes:

> Yet though the living may be dumb, it is not so with the dead. They are crying aloud to us from the ravine of Saratov, from the dungeons of Kharkov and Khuban, and from the "camp of death" at Kholmogory. For the dead can never be put to silence!

Putting the dead to silence is what a very considerable proportion of the Western intelligentsia, at least that part of it that concerned itself with political and economic matters, did for at least half a century. They were very successful. When Robert Conquest published his book on the Ukrainian famine, *Harvest of Sorrow,* in 1986, the blurb to the British edition said, "[This book] will register in the public consciousness of the West a sense of the darker side of the history of this century." But did the West really need to wait until 1986 to have its awareness awakened to the scope and moral significance of the Ukrainian famine?

In 1934, the British writer Malcolm Muggeridge published a book, *Winter in Moscow,* that described not only the famine but the means by which Western liberal news media censored reports of it. In 1936, Dr. Ewalde Ammende published a book, *Human Life in Russia,* that begins:

All serious observers of conditions in Soviet Russia are of one opinion as to the causes of the Russian famine. In their view the real cause is to be found not in any natural events, but in the fiasco of the collective system which was introduced with such excessive haste.

Toward the end of the book, the author writes:

It is not my task to controvert the views of Joseph Stalin. It is useless to enter into controversy with people who openly and on principle avow that the annihilation of whole masses of humanity is justified to secure the realization of the Communist ideal.

No subsequent research has cast any doubt on the justice of Dr. Ammende's lapidary conclusions, nor is any future research ever likely to do so. And it is worth adding that his book is interspersed with many startling photographs, including of people walking past corpses in the street. One photograph bears the legend "Mass graves of famine victims, in such numbers that they resemble dunes." Another shows a pile of emaciated corpses, possibly the most startling image of its kind published before the liberation of Belsen, and is captioned "A great multitude which no man could number."

As Jean-François Revel establishes very clearly in this book, the left-leaning intelligentsia's long infatuation with the Soviet Union and other Communist countries was not merely an intellectual error but, if not quite a crime itself, at the very least complicity with crime; and moreover crime on a scale virtually unparalleled in human history before the Nazis came on the scene. With very few honorable exceptions, the whole of the left-leaning intelligentsia devoted a great deal of its formidable powers of sophistry to denying or exculpating the crimes of Communism, thus siding with the mass executioners rather than with the victims in the mass graves.

When the moral, economic, social and philosophical failure of Communism was admitted in the land of its birth, the Western

left-leaning intelligentsia found itself with a serious and embar-
rassing problem. It stood revealed for all to see as having, for
many years, been morally not very different from, and not any
better than, M. Le Pen of the French Front National, who once
famously (or infamously) declared that the Holocaust was nothing
but a detail of history. While it is relatively easy, especially as one
grows older, to admit to having been in error, even in gross error,
it is very difficult to admit to having been a willing accomplice to
evil, and evil of the most obvious and evident kind. As M. Revel
convincingly explains, this accounts for the difference in the
reception in France of two magisterial books about Communism
by French scholars, François Furet's *Le Passé d'une illusion*, and
Stephane Courtois's *Le Livre noire du communisme*.

The first deals with what might be called the fashion for Communism as an intellectual error. Anyone can be mistaken in his
philosophy, and few people never change their philosophy in the
light of experience and further reflection. (An unchanging person
would be suffering from what a medical friend of mine once
called "a hardening of the concepts.") Therefore, however prepos-
terous Marxism-Leninism might be as an intellectual system—"a
farrago of nonsense," as Professor Acton once called it—those
who adhered to it do not stand convicted of wickedness or defect
of character. Hence Furet's book, whose exposure of the errors
of Communist doctrine could hardly be denied, was received
respectfully and even with acclamation.

It was quite otherwise with the *Livre noir.* This book showed
implacably that evil was implicit in both the theory and the practice
of Communism, and that everywhere and anywhere it was tried,
it resulted in the same appalling conduct of affairs, differing only
as to scale. Evil was in Communism's DNA, as it were; and the
crimes of Communist polities were not the result of a perversion
of noble ideals, but were caused by the adoption of evil ideals.

Thus, those who espoused or sympathized with Communist
ideals were convicted of harboring evil within themselves; and this
is not an easy thing for people, especially those without a belief in
original sin, to accept. Courtois's book was roundly condemned,
therefore, by France's left-leaning intelligentsia; and since it could

not actually point to any serious factual errors contained in this massive work of scholarship, it resorted to defamation and the raising of smokescreens, such as that the book would bring relief and comfort to the Front National.

With delicious humor and characteristic forensic skill, as well as erudition, M. Revel recounts the mental pirouettes that the intellectuals performed in the struggle to continue to think well of themselves: the end product, after all, of so much intellectual activity. And although his book refers mainly to France, where the grip on intellectual life of the left-with-a-bad-conscience-about-Russia has probably been stronger than in any other Western country, it is certainly not parochial. I doubt that the inhabitant of any Western country will fail to see the pattern reflected in his own country.

M. Revel's book is, as ever, rich in ideas. He points out that liberal democracy is not an ideology in the sense that Marxism or any other form of utopian political thought is an ideology; liberal democracy does not hold out the hope of a denouement of history in which all human contradictions are resolved, no conflicts can arise and everyone is ceaselessly—and one might almost add remorselessly—happy. It assumes that conflicts, difficulties, problems and dissatisfactions are inescapable characteristics of the human condition, and that the best that can be hoped for is compromise without slaughter, bringing with it some faint hope, though not the certainty, of progress. There is no blueprint.

Those on the left, however, tend to assume that because they are seized by ideology, everyone else is seized by ideology also. Therefore, those who reject their ideology must be in possession of another ideology. They are like homoeopaths, whose practice is based upon a single principle—*similia similibus curantur,* like cures like—who therefore imagine that what they term allopaths, non-homoeopathic doctors, have a single doctrine that covers their practice; or like a purveyor of a quack panacea, in the efficacy of which he persuades himself to believe, who assumes that anyone who denies the cure-all properties of his preparation must have one of his own up his sleeve that he wants to sell instead. In their imagination, if a doctor holds that antibiotics can cure bacterial pneumonia, he must also hold that antibiotics can cure cancer, hypothyroidism and polycythaemia rubra vera as well. The world is not so various that it requires constant flexibility; everything can be known and laid down in advance.

Intellectuals, the justification for whose existence is that they have a superior understanding of the world to that of non-intellectuals, find it hard to accept that all understanding of empirical matters is partial, temporary, subject to revision and doubtful; and that any political system that does not take this into account will end up imposing lies (and worse) upon whole populations. There have been times and places in history, perhaps, when to impose a priori schema on society has not been utterly disastrous; but Europe in the twentieth century was decidedly not one of them.

But intellectuals not only want to think well of themselves; they want to be important. The attraction of ideology is that it offers a simple principle, or a few simple principles, by which to understand the world; and, of course, it offers the prospect of power to those who know and wield those principles with the greatest facility. It seems to me likely that inside every Marxist Western intellectual there has been a Stalin trying to get out.

Reality, however, will not be mocked, even by the greatest possible dictatorial power. Though you pitch reality out with a pitchfork, it will return. You can wish people different from how they are, but that will not make them different from how they are. You might want the price of scarce goods not to rise in conditions of high demand, but that does not mean that the price will not rise, do what you will to prevent it. Among other effects, therefore, ideologies blind us to the difference between what we can and cannot do; they make us voluntarists while denying us the reality of free will.

Like all good studies of intellectual history, M. Revel's book suggests and provokes deep and wide reflection. It is very enjoyable; it often makes you laugh, but with the kind of laughter that is the very reverse of frivolous. He writes in what the French call, with justified national pride in their great philosopher, a Cartesian spirit: that is to say, with the utmost intellectual clarity without descent to superficiality. Needless to say, this is not a spirit in which the contemporary world abounds.

CHAPTER ONE

La Grande Parade*

"Lenin continues to have imperishable value," wrote Ivan Frolov, an advisor to Mikhail Gorbachev. I quoted this pearl of wisdom in 1990 and added the comment: "Mr. Frolov should know that statements like this can only sound farcical in the West today."[1] But I would hardly venture to make the same comment now in 2000, for the rehabilitation of Marxism-Leninism has been proceeding apace, inspiring books and articles that advise us—that *command* us—to return to the True Marx. Some of Mr. Frolov's oratorical flights, preaching "a transition toward a qualitatively new condition, toward a renewed, human socialism," sounded like pathetic gibberish even when he pronounced them. But today such phrases pop up frequently in the musings of

---

* *La Grande Parade* is the original title of this book in French, but the term with its multiple meanings does not translate well into English. See page 2.

1

Western writers, many of whom would not hesitate to endorse another priceless example of Frolov's claptrap: "We are in the process of re-evaluating the dialectical unity of the scientific, revolutionary and humanistic aspects of Marxism."

After the collapse of Soviet Communism, politicians and intellectuals of the Old Left began a vigorous counteroffensive, aiming to erase or invert the obvious conclusions to be drawn from that event and, more generally, from the manifest failures of socialist ideology. What prompted these elites to believe they could extract lessons from history that blatantly contradict what history so plainly says? What arguments have they deployed to shore up their defense of totalitarian delusions and crimes, or at least the motives behind them? How persuasive have these arguments been? Do they have a wide following, or is their influence limited to a powerful but small clientele that regards itself in a flattering mirror, the better to deny its errors and chase away the pangs of remorse?

In short, is this *grande parade* of the left accomplishing its agenda? Or is it merely the final spasm of a criminal aberration, one which later generations that took no part in it will be able finally to reject freely and completely, without duplicity or regret?

The primary meaning of the French word *parade* is shared by the English word "parade": a procession or an attention-grabbing display. The term is also used by fencers to mean the parrying of an attack. Accordingly, the leftists' performance has served a dual purpose, allowing them, on the one hand, to deflect the sword of history that was threatening to cut down their doctrine for good; and on the other, to remain players in the pageant of culture and politics, still marching at the head of the procession. In nautical terms, their *parade* was preliminary to a tacking maneuver, a way of changing course without being too obvious about it. To bring in yet another metaphor, it was a matter of "dressing" (in French, *parer*) Communism in the way a chef prepares meat or fish before cooking a dish, removing the unusable parts while saving as much of the original as possible. Which leads to the question: Is the left just serving up the same old ideological hash, but now relabeled as nouvelle cuisine?

These are far from idle questions, for even in the midst of a global information explosion it may turn out that we understand little or nothing about totalitarianism. If this is the case, then information per se may be of limited value, and those responsible for providing us with information may prove to be useless or even harmful. At a time when "the meaning of history" (*le sens de l'histoire*) is still venerated, to have so poorly understood history's lessons would testify to a crippling cultural failure, or worse, to a troubled relationship with facts—a permanent legacy, perhaps, of ideological indoctrination.

For a while, sensible things were said. Reviewing the journalism of the early 1990s, I am struck to see in the majority of periodicals, even those of the left, how frequently two ideas keep cropping up, presented as empirically derived certainties. The first of these is that we must write off Communism and everything associated with it once and for all—the logical conclusion to be drawn from the pitiless evidence of history. The corollary is that after the Marxist catastrophe, the classical liberal formula has emerged as the *only* solution. Whatever its imperfections, this option alone is economically and politically viable, and it will persist.* Indeed, for something to be imperfect, it must first exist, a condition that command economies do not fulfill.

By now, however, a striking reversal has occurred: these reasonable conclusions are being spurned almost everywhere—in theory at least, for action often flies in the face of theory. Although Communism is no longer put into practice, it is mentioned with growing approval; while the practice of liberalism, though almost universally denounced, is increasingly evident in the realm of action. Thus, the internal antithesis between the ideal and the actual that is a fundamental characteristic of the totalitarian mentality is reconstituted in another vocabulary and, as it were, in a void, since "actual Communism" has all but vanished.

---

* *Translator's note:* Throughout, the author uses *libérale* and *libéralisme* in the sense of "classical liberalism," which is very nearly the opposite of the contemporary American meaning of "liberalism."

A revival of liberalism began prior to the collapse of Communism, preceding it by a good ten years with the leadership of Margaret Thatcher in Great Britain and then Ronald Reagan in the United States. But these electoral victories were not inevitable. It is erroneous to think that classical liberalism—something to which the French genius finds itself miraculously immune—belongs exclusively to "Anglo-Saxon" culture, as through some congenital defect. Since Franklin D. Roosevelt, America had steadily pushed Big Government further into almost every part of economic and social life, while doggedly following the tax-and-spend gospel. But any awareness of such historical realities was brushed aside, either deliberately or unconsciously, in Europe and especially in France.

Likewise, there was widespread ignorance of conditions in the United Kingdom: of how, since 1945, the Labor Party ideology had created the most statist, bureaucratic, highly taxed, unionized and regulated society in democratic Europe. Although the Conservative Party had won several elections during this period, no Conservative government before Margaret Thatcher's had won a sufficiently strong and clear electoral mandate to permit tampering with the fundamental props of the Labor edifice. Economic decline had set in, bringing widespread impoverishment, failure of public services, administrative paralysis—festering sores that had become critically infected by 1977–1978 and threatened to plunge Britain into chaos. And so the electorate chose, not another routine party rotation, but a razing of the very foundations laid down in 1945: it voted for a draconian liberal revolution. Since this turnabout, the British people have not changed their minds; in 1997, Labor could not be sure of victory at the polling booths without disavowing their socialist agenda. Politically, Tony Blair is less the successor of James Callaghan, the last Labor prime minister before the free-market revolution, than of Margaret Thatcher—with all due deference to fabulists of "the left's triumph in Europe" at the century's end.

More astounding still was the tide of liberalism that rushed across continental Europe during the Thatcher and Reagan years. In Italy, Socialists and Communists were professing to be less and

4

less *dirigiste;* in Spain, the Socialist Party let it be known that it had never been *dirigiste;* and in Portugal—where, since the Revolution of the Carnations in 1974, the Socialist leader Mario Soares had been an invincible rampart against all coups d'états on the part of the Communists—the electorate twice, in 1980 and 1985, swept reprivatizing liberals into power.

But it was mainly the abrupt economic and financial crackup of France, after two years of Mitterrand's Socialist regime, that impressed people's imaginations and turned public opinion. Virtually overnight, we began to hear effusions of praise for "enterprise"—*private* enterprise, that is—from every side. Adolescents went so far (and I was witness to one such semicomical scene) as to reproach their civil-servant fathers for "never having established a business." Overnight, the French became fierce critics of nationalization schemes, which they had long mostly favored. Their change of attitude can be tracked through opinion polls, such as the one published by *Paris Match* (April 1, 1983) showing that 59 percent of French people were in favor of more entrepreneurial policies, while only 25 percent wanted more state control of the economy.

The French left, already a national minority since the municipal elections of 1983, became all but marginal when the European elections took place in 1984. Moreover, studies of voters' wishes, analyzed at the time by various polling organizations, show that they were ready to reject not merely this or that governmental team but the left *as such* and its ideological principles, the first of which is reverence for the state. Thus the Communist Party was reduced to 11 percent support among voters and was destined to sink even lower. It had lost half its supporters in five years and would never find them again. Moreover, it refused to form part of the government of Laurent Fabius, which followed and turned its back on that of Pierre Mauroy. So Mitterrand, with a Socialist Party that slipped from 38 percent of the legislative vote in 1981 to 21 percent in the 1984 European elections, led a government that represented barely one-fifth of French citizens until the elections of 1986.

Perhaps still more humbling for the left than its political and economic failures was its philosophical and cultural shipwreck.

It was not only the economic program of the left that began to take a farcical turn—its slogan *"rupture avec le capitalisme!"* sounding risible when all the world's noncapitalist regimes were sinking beneath the waves—but also its other projects for social redemption, each of which seemed leakier than the last as they all crashed in turn on the shoals of public exasperation.

In July 1984, Mitterrand had to withdraw his education plan, a model of socialist anachronism if ever there was one. The protests against Mitterrand's draft bill, aimed at suppressing private instruction, owed something to traditional religious convictions; but that was only part of the explanation. In fact, the majority of the millions who demonstrated all over the country for more than a year, religious believers or not, were mainly protesting against a totalitarian scheme to unify elementary, secondary and university education under the aegis of the state and the Marxist-dominated teachers' unions. The public well understood what was afoot with the bill: the establishment of another hegemony, an ideological monopoly, by the Socialists and Communists. In this matter, as in many others, we witnessed a popular repudiation of the state.

The government had seriously misread the wishes of the society over which it presided. Other examples of its tone-deafness included its law on the press, its exploitation of state television, and its notion that governmental success is primarily a matter of propaganda. Socialists in power had thus unleashed against themselves not only the people but also most of the country's intellectuals.

★ ★ ★

This, then, was the picture midway between 1980 and 1990: Communism had been discredited well before the Berlin Wall came crumbling down and at a time when the approaching disaster was not yet foreseen. Socialism, too, had run into hard times, not just in practice but as an ideal. The setback in France was paralleled by a lengthy exclusion from power of the Labor Party in Britain and of the SPD (Social Democratic Party) in Germany. The finishing touch to a dismal scene was the condition of Sweden's economy:

even this Sacred Grotto of Miracles—for forty years a realistically managed social-democratic welfare state—was moribund.

An assault had to be launched against this tentative resurgence of classical liberalism. The incipient success of free-market themes, along with the manifest contradictions of socialist ideology and Communist regimes, filled the sectarians with fresh ardor to beat back the dissidents—employing, naturally, the time-honored weapons of leftist "debate."

Thus, when the celebrated Mexican writer Octavio Paz, in a 1987 speech delivered in Frankfurt, compared the Nicaraguan Sandinista regime to Castro's tyranny and dared to mention that Moscow was financing and equipping it—an obvious and proven fact by now—he found himself greeted with the fine courtesy that characterizes left-wing discourse. Among Mexican intellectuals, the Marxist left, a veritable museum of mummified political thought, exploded with rage. For a week, newspapers and magazines vented their anger with articles and cartoons and polls, culminating with a manifesto signed by 228 professors of "every scientific and cultural discipline, from thirteen countries and five institutions." These pro-Communist shamans were exemplary manifestations of the classic personality type that has been dubbed "the perfect Latin American idiot."[2]

Octavio Paz's name was summarily erased from the program of a choral concert featuring his poems, and an actor slated to introduce the performance with a reading of the poems backed out. The Frankfurt speech was unanimously condemned despite the fact that no one in Mexico could possibly have read it, for the simple reason that, with the exception of a few words quoted in the German press, it had not yet been published. In his speech, Paz dealt with many topics other than Nicaragua, and his overall account of the political landscape seems quite self-evident today. Nevertheless, elements of the heroic left (typically informed and tolerant, and bursting with antifascist zeal) went so far as to demonstrate before the United States embassy in Mexico, where Octavio Paz—that "traitor to Mexico"—was burned in effigy to the accompaniment of chants by the student crowd: "Rapacious Reagan, your friend is Octavio Paz!"[3]

Let's never forget that in Europe as in Latin America you can be a card-carrying member of the left with one simple qualification, well within the reach of anyone, however slow of mind: to be reflexively anti-American, at all costs and in all circumstances, whatever the event or the issue.

It is quite possible, indeed not unusual, for a person to be politically obtuse while being brilliant in other respects. Examples abound, but Harold Pinter is typical. The English dramatist explains NATO's intervention against Serbia in April 1999 with the assertion that the United States follows but one principle in international politics: "Kiss my ass or I'll beat you up."[4] Evidently, talent for theater does not inoculate one against profound idiocy and vulgarity when it comes to venting political opinions. One of the mysteries of politics is its power to induce such befuddling in otherwise intelligent people. How would Harold Pinter react if drama critics allowed themselves to fall so low in abusive imbecility while critiquing his plays?

When the French, of both the right and the left, awoke to the reality that the United States had emerged triumphant from the Cold War, they began to focus their animosity on the economic arrangements of the one remaining superpower, their anti-American animus rising to a peak of frenzy in the last decade of the century. The antiliberal crusade was launched with the Socialists' two-year struggle against Jacques Chirac's government, in 1986–1988. Although the privatizations actually carried out by this government concerned only a few nationalized enterprises, and although none of its reforms made any substantial reduction in public expenditures or in the tax burden, the left did not relent in its bombardment of Chirac's team, routinely stigmatizing it with the charge of "*ultra*-liberalism"—the shameful prefix having become *de rigueur*—and accusing it of antisocial perfidy.

But to get an idea of how far the "liberal" reformers, throughout continental Europe but above all in France, were from being real free-market reformers, and how deeply they were stuck in the old mold of centralized planning, consider how much of Europe's economy continues to be state-dominated ten years after the so-called "liberal wave" began and despite substantial privatizations.

8

The state-owned proportion of the national product in European countries went, on average, from 15.4 percent in 1920, to 27.9 percent in 1960, and to 45.9 percent in 1996. And in France, ever eager to tax and to regulate, the public-sector share in 1997 rose to a staggering 54.5 percent.[5] Despite the half-heartedness of liberal reforms, the campaign against the free-market idea was marvelously successful, since Mitterrand, who in 1984 had been the most unpopular head of state in the entire history of the Fifth Republic, managed to get re-elected four years later.

To pad their propaganda, the Socialists set up Reagan's United States and Thatcher's United Kingdom as cautionary tales of "savage capitalism." Here was the origin of that prolific tradition in which these advanced nations are castigated as vast camps for the indigent, where weary hordes of diseased and hungry homeless people fill the streets. A literary genre like this had no basis in reality, of course; it was a fruit of fantasy, inspired not by liberalism's failures but by socialism's need to conceal its own shortcomings. The campaign was nevertheless effective because the mass media and a large part of the so-called quality press, mostly but not only of the left, bought into the credo. The political leaders of the French right came to be branded as doctrinal allies of the demonic Reagan and Thatcher. The left's winning strategy was to make classical liberals fear the consequences of their own devotion to their philosophy, and to pressure them eventually to abjure it altogether. The battle was decided in those years.

Meanwhile, the European left put its condemnation of the anticommunists on the back burner, feigning indifference to attacks on Marxist regimes. The reason was that it had invested its emotional capital in Mikhail Gorbachev, convinced that he at last was constructing a Communism compatible with liberty—that rare bird awaited in vain for seventy years. Why get irritated with the stale vociferations of the anticommunists when the messiah of "socialism with a human face" was coming soon to shut the mouths of the crypto-fascists permanently?

After the failed (or apparently failed?) Moscow putsch of August 19, 1991, and despite the brief return of Gorbachev to the Kremlin as a lame duck, the international left correctly intuited that Communism this time around was well and truly finished. The last lifeboat had capsized.

Outwardly, the edifice still stood. The abortive coup against the misconceived policy of perestroika had apparently left the citadel of Communist power intact. But it was a mere façade, behind which lay a mass of rubble. The left immediately got the picture, months before the official crackup of the Soviet Union on December 25, 1991. It was thus fully prepared to launch an ideological counteroffensive by summer of the next year, with a torrent of articles—signed for the most part by authors who were not actually Communists and hence were in a better position to rev up the engines of postmortem justification. Their under-taking grew in scope and intensity over the following years, and although theirs was necessarily a defensive operation, they went on the attack straightaway. An event that should have tolled the hour of repentance for those who had indulged Communism mutated into a brief against those who had descried in Commu-nism's crimes and failures proof of its toxicity. The refrain went: Communism is finished, but what wonderful people it inspired to action! And how can we get by without that ideal? In any case, liberalism is obviously worse. And do we really have to sacrifice the sublime vistas of revolutionary hope and resign ourselves to the grim pragmatism of managerial politics?

We have to admire the agility with which the left uprooted the debate from down-to-earth realities and ensconced it in that empyrean of pure ideas where well-intentioned ideologues can never be wrong. They were making a U-turn back to the emer-gency exit: to the early days of Marxism-Leninism, that pristine age before the Fall when the doctrine still shone with every per-fection, for the simple reason that it had not yet been put into practice.

Here is a tasty paradox: The ferocity of the Marxist legions redoubled in the very same year when history had finally put paid to the object of their sacred cult. Marx's disciples, betraying the master's analysis, refused to bow down before the criterion of *praxis,* choosing instead to retreat into the impregnable for-tress of the ideal. As long as they had been obliged to drag around the ball and chain of actually existing socialism, they could not avoid facing up to criticism. Their solution to the imperfections of socialism in practice had always been to tout the infinite perfectibility of the as yet unachieved revolution. But once the Soviet system had disappeared, the mirage of a reformable Communism vanished along with the object to be reformed, and so too did the painful servitude of having to argue the cause in terms of tangible successes and failures. Released from importunate reality—which they would henceforth blithely dismiss as inconsequential—the faithful could return to the roots of their fanaticism. They felt free at last to restore socialism to its primordial state: Utopia.

After all, socialism incarnate was always vulnerable to criticism. Utopia, on the other hand, lies by definition beyond criticism. Hence the rage of Utopia's haughty champions could again become boundless, since there was no longer, anywhere, any embodiment of their vision.

CHAPTER TWO

Evasion . . .
Then Counterattack

When disaster struck, the response at first was hushed and plaintive. There were grudging acknowledgments of Communism's failures and even of its crimes. But this was little more than rhetorical posturing, the better to lament the loss of that supreme good which Communism alone would have brought us, and which will now be forever beyond humanity's reach. It all added up to a timeworn subterfuge, designed to challenge the essential lesson—which was not merely that the Communist experiment had failed (a fact that no one in 1990 dared deny anymore), but that failure had occurred on such a scale and in such a manner as to condemn the Marxist principle itself. Therein lay the new historical fact. After so many unmerited reprieves, the hour of judgment had finally tolled for the Communist doctrine.

Everything else was archaeology. We had long been accustomed to the disasters of socialism, since it had never managed to produce anything but disasters anywhere. What had now become obvious was that it *could not* produce anything else. A liberating truth had emerged: Marxism had suffered from defective DNA all along.

It was a truth that many a marginalized observer had pointed out. The left—even of the non-Communist variety—had routinely pigeonholed such dissidents as reactionaries. But in 1990 the dissidents' insight came to be shared by the entire world. The underlying logic, the very idea of Communism lay exposed; it was not merely unlucky circumstances and contingent betrayals that had spawned such an engine of injustice, misery and massacre. After a respectable interval of post-Soviet grieving, however, the left was soon to reassert a postulate that amounted to a sweeping rejection of this conclusion. Lacking any factual foundation, their thesis was really no more than a superstitious attachment to the notion that under some distant skies could be found a perfect society of perfect justice, prosperity and happiness, as sublime as Plato's supernal world and as unknowable as Kant's Thing in Itself. Communism, you see, is the only conceivable means of realizing the ideal on this earthly plane; and with its exit from the stage, any possibility of the just society is gone. So the defeat of Communism, despite all the evil done in its name, is also a defeat of the Good.

This argument is vacuous, however, for it purports to demonstrate precisely what experience has refuted. It is also an evasion, a replay of an old sophism tirelessly drummed into the ears of dupes rushing to empty the garbage cans of history: "We don't deny the disastrous results and atrocities of Communism," the socialists will periodically admit when they are in tactical retreat. "On the other hand, we *do* deny that such regrettable outcomes represent the essence of socialism. *This* remains inviolate and immaculate, and is destined soon to be reborn!"

By this line of reasoning, the horror of the outcome proves the excellence of the principle. Appealing to a perfect (because unrealizable) prototype, Communism cannot be reactionary no matter how monstrous its practical consequences, whereas those who insist on judging Communism by its consequences are ipso facto reactionaries. For when an ideal is being championed, it is intentions—not actions—that count. The Kingdom of Communism, in the eyes of its devotees, is essentially not of this world, and its failure here below is imputable to the world's failure, not to the concept itself. Those who challenge the doctrine by citing mundane facts clearly have an ulterior motive: a secret hatred for Communism's purported goal, the realization of social justice. Thus, while Communism's balance sheet may be in the red, it is anticommunism that remains darkly reprehensible.

The subterfuge of salvation through intention was to be seen in numerous texts that surfaced while the Soviet Union was in the process of decomposing, or just afterward. One example is this passage from a paper delivered by Lily Marcou, pondering the winding-down of the Communist experiment, for which she had been making more optimistic prognostications over the years:

> Outside the countries of "actual socialism," and not only among Western Communists, how many there were who believed in the experiment. "Imbeciles" are what they are called today. But they are imbeciles for whom I feel great affection: they had faith, and they fought with and for that faith, and they were mistaken; but at least their commitment came with a generosity and an altruism that don't exist anymore at the end of the century. . . . Yes, we should put aside the behavior and attitudes that were appropriate during the first half of the century, but the fact remains that they exemplified the powerful emotional charge and strength of conviction of the Communist project.[1]

Here, Marcou is unequivocal: the first half of the century was morally superior to its last decade for the reason that Communism was ascendant, and its withdrawal from the scene is therefore a retreat, not a step in the direction of progress. Those who served it, even at the price of a lifetime spent in imbecilic enthrallment to the lie, were more "generous" than those who attempted to use their intelligence in the service of truth. In this view, the "altruists" were the calumniators who strove furiously to denigrate and discredit anyone trying to give an accurate account of the Communist imposture. Of course, Mme Marcou concedes, socialist sins are unquestionable, but they are pardonable because the perpetrators of the twentieth century's most protracted and widespread crime against humanity—and their accomplices or dupes—were bearers of an "emotional charge" and "strength of conviction."

Coming from a Marxist, an absolution of this sort, rooted in a subjectivity that borders on solipsism, is a comical contradiction. Assessing the soundness of political *praxis* exclusively on the criterion of inward conviction and sentimentality—what a strange avatar of historical materialism! I always feel a little uneasy when I hear someone eulogize a political figure with the vague phrase: "He (or she) is a person of conviction." What conviction, exactly? Or convictions? They can be anything at all, it seems to me. Hitler was a man of conviction, and how much better for the world if he had believed in nothing.

You will find similar appeals to affectivity in every retrospective apology for Communism. In the gospel according to Marcou and many another true believer, any hint of a connection between the noble convictions of militant Communists and the terrible consequences of those convictions is severed. And this voluntary blindness and moral irresponsibility are praised as crowning virtues *in the realm of political action!* Conversely, anyone who has managed to open her eyes and look unblinkingly at the real nature of Communism is guilty of egotism and mean-spiritedness: she is a right-winger or a reactionary, a hypocrite who, behind a mask of honest impartiality, is concealing a "visceral" aversion not just toward Communism as it actually was (which must be quietly consigned to the closet) but *toward the just society that Communism aimed to create.* Here is another curious corollary of this redemptive version of historical materialism: History has no objective meaning or direction. Or if there is a trajectory, it is defined by a subjective starting point, not by the actual destination.

Marcou's diligent piling-up of sophistries prepares the ground for the next step: claiming that, at a time when "the great light from the East" is extinguished, those who suffer the most and deserve the most pity are not Communism's victims past and present, but rather its old enthusiasts, now sorely tried by its demise. Danièle Sallenave was among the choristers who intoned this *De profundis*, developing the theme with such tearful brio and shattering effect that she could almost have inspired a group of former gulag *zeks* to pool their resources and buy her a consolatory gift.*

The title of Sallenave's article, "The End of Communism: Winter of Souls,"[2] has an obvious implication: If Communism's end inaugurated winter, then Communism at its apogee presided over summer. Naturally, the souls in question, those who are worthy of our compassion, are not the tens of millions of "dead souls" that the Communists have "disappeared," but the wounded souls of Western leftists who, safely enjoying the comforts of our democracies, gazed from afar—with interest, altruism and generosity—on the executioners' hard task.

Mme Sallenave's funeral oration, reduced to its logical underpinnings, rests on the self-contradictory intellectual *démarche* that we have already seen at work. Communism, she admits, was "a hateful tyranny" and "a pernicious economic model"; and yet it is the only system that could save us from "enslavement to consumerism," from unrestrained liberalism and the reign of money, from domination and contempt. The author adopts almost verbatim the sweeping condemnation of capitalism voiced by the early proponents of socialism in the mid-nineteenth century, and denunciations of democracy made by Communists during the 1920s. With a sovereign tear she erases half a century of history during which there were ample opportunities for socialism to prove itself, while capitalism did not develop in the ways predicted by Jaurès or Marx or Lenin. The Communist prescription wrecked the societies upon which it was forced—intellectually degrading, enslaving and murdering entire populations. Nonetheless, it remains the only way to go, while liberalism is to be greatly feared as an illness that can never be cured after Communism has departed from the scene. Sounding for all the world like some stalwart Communist Party official of the 1950s, Sallenave finds nothing else in the Western democracies but "domination and contempt."

---

* *Translator's note: Zeks* were inmates of the Soviet labor camps.

Sallenave's psalmodizing embodies further logical contradictions. Throughout history up to the present day, humanity's ruling obsession has been to eliminate poverty. This indeed was the goal that the Communists said they alone could achieve. As we know, their program was mostly a factory of famines, but abundance nevertheless remained the ideal toward which their system aimed. Why is it, then, that when abundance *does* arrive but happens to be the fruit of capitalism, suddenly "consumption" becomes a curse?

The rest of Sallenave's literary menu consists of invitations to chew on rotten scraps of post-Communist dialectic. Communism was good because it corresponded to the "dream" of so many fine people; but there is not the slightest recognition in her piece that those fine people might have been cat's-paws and indentured servants of intellectual shysters, propagators of a universal lie. No, according to Mme Sallenave, what we should do—it's only decent, after all—is shed a tear for those whose hopes were betrayed. Her tone rising upward in a crescendo of supplication, she pleads that we "extend more *piety*" to the "magical vanishing" of the Communist project. (Why "magical"?) "The Soviet Union's disappearance ought first and foremost to have disposed us toward a mood of remembrance, meditation, *piety*." Reading Sallenave, one understands how Communist-style personality worship can be likened to a "cult."

To get a better appreciation of the enormous cynicism involved, let's imagine for a moment that the Nazi chiefs on trial for their crimes at Nuremberg had addressed the tribunal in terms like these: "Your Honors, you certainly have the right to reproach us for particular actions. Moreover, we'll be the first to deplore them. But might it not be more appropriate here to have a pious thought for the grief of all those fine folks—believers in National Socialism—who now have been forced to abandon hope? Today they are condemned to 'live without promise,' to borrow Edgar Morin's phrase. Let's just observe a moment of silence, contemplating the winter of their souls." It's true that Mme Sallenave and her Western intellectual clones, whether Communists or sympathizers, have no blood on their hands; but their pens are dripping with it.

All the more so in that here, as in the lachrymose outpourings of other sentimentalists, Sallenave's lamentations quickly turn to accusations. Mastering her softer emotions, she opens fire on the gloating anticommunists, those "for whom Communism was necessarily bad, of course, because it strove for the ideals of equality, justice and fraternity."

The underlying postulate remains unchanged: Although Communism has never done anything but magnify injustice, if you oppose Communism you oppose justice. The greatest danger is still capitalism. In a book published a year after the article discussed here, Sallenave deplores the reunification of Germany: "Did we have to move ahead so quickly? Who is pushing for it? The Western industrialists, avid to open new markets, even if it means personal ruin and suffering for individuals."[3] I have often been intrigued by the studious indifference to elementary economics displayed by so many Marxist intellectuals, whose master nevertheless was, as I recall, an economist who actually did some work in the field. Anyone who has bothered to read a newspaper couldn't fail to know about the gigantic cost of reunification for West Germany, amounting to hundreds of billions of marks and necessitating a special "solidarity" tax, as well as taxes on the profits of private companies.[4] Yet it is the industrialists of the Federal Republic, not the Stasi operatives, who are summoned to appear before Sallenave's tribunal.

We would like to know: Why is it a crime to open new markets? Isn't it obvious that the successful creation of markets in a region with a low standard of living goes hand in hand with increased purchasing power? Why exactly is this bad? Perhaps it's because capitalism is intrinsically bad even if it promotes "solidarity," while socialism cannot be anything but good, even if it brings poverty.

So, between 1990 and 1993, the left's initial reaction to the fall of the Soviet Union constituted a double denial: a failure to make realistic assessments of the reasons for the collapse, and a failure to confront questions of moral responsibility. After a few unrepentant gestures were made toward critical reappraisal, the door on intellectual honesty, momentarily ajar, was peremptorily slammed shut.

One such gesture was a colloquium, billed as "international" but with a strong French coloration, held in December 1991 at the National Assembly and at the Sorbonne—that is, at taxpayers' expense—and under the patronage of the Maison des Écrivains, which is also supported by public funds. Since the leftist intelligentsia operates on the principle of a guilt-free conscience fed by public subsidies, progress requires that the left's remorse should likewise be subsidized, although indications of remorse at this colloquium were few indeed. Another piquant feature was the conspicuous absence among the speakers of those observers who had marshaled evidence condemning Communism ten or twenty or thirty years before the system passed judgment on itself by collapsing under the weight of its victims. Authors who for decades had been uncompromising witnesses for the prosecution, and who moreover had frequently debated the colloquium's participants, were not invited. The only anticommunists on the roster were a handful of foreign writers who, patchily informed or entirely ignorant of the French intellectuals' past commitments, were ill positioned to call them to account. Only a tiny minority of the French invitees represented a moderate left that—without going so far as to "perpetrate anticommunism"—had managed to retain a modicum of liberty and dignity during the years of ideological intimidation; and these people did nothing to upset the seminar's ceremonial self-justification. So, even after the fall of the Berlin Wall, the left evaded any exercise in self-knowledge and shunned encounters with thinkers who had set forth the terms of a fundamental disagreement during the Cold War when everything was at stake.

A third point concerns the colloquium's title. Some possibilities come to mind: "The Left: Intentions and Illusions," or "The Left: Naïveté or Complicity," or the straightforward "The Left and Totalitarianism." But of course these wouldn't work, because it was out of the question for the title to hint at the slightest intellectual or moral shortcoming, even with regard to the most recent past. The left is never mistaken. Or at least it can be mistaken only in relation to itself. Contradictions may be internally thrashed out by mutually respectful peers, but never under conditions that might allow their adversaries a chance to speak, much less to prove a case. Uncompromised, the left's intellectual creativity and redemptive vocation march triumphantly on. The title actually chosen to be posted at the entranceway of the conference hall, *Les Métamorphoses de l'engagement* (Metamorphoses of Commitment), was a tour de force of self-absolution, suave and elegant indeed. But the high-toned phraseology deserves to be called what it is: sheer hypocrisy.

It is true that two of the speakers did summon enough nerve to ask: Is *shame* something we should feel? But this provocation was, of course, merely a sort of rhetorical trampoline, enabling the orators to bounce back to a resounding No! and then expatiate on the absurdity of even asking such a question. It should be pointed out that the non-Communist left were in the majority at the conference on "Metamorphoses of Commitment," since former Communists have often been less inclined to deny their errors and betrayals and to assume airs of innocence than the assorted fellow travelers. Paul Noirot's confession was honorable:

> Rationality is the last thing to ask of all those—and I was one of them—who took part in that chimerical enterprise. At the end of the day we built nothing that lasted: no political system, no economic system, no communities, no ethic, no aesthetic. We wanted to realize the highest human aspirations and we ended up birthing monsters.[5]

Why, in this opening phase of the post-Communist era, were so few voices of similar honesty to be heard? After all, nobody was insisting on public self-flagellation. What's more, the task of frankly dissecting the past, of dismantling the mechanisms that lured someone into making the wrong choices, need not be humiliating; for even the best and brightest of us are not exempt from error.

Courageous lucidity like Noirot's does a service for humanity. Equal candor is to be found in the memoirs of such former Communists as Arthur Koestler, Sidney Hook and Pierre Daix, men who with perspicacity and probity analyzed the political and ideological factors that led them astray and that might have done the same to anybody. Are the pilgrims of the non-Communist left unable to be so forthright for the reason that they are painfully aware of having been the manipulated and not the manipulators?

Sincerity, or Hunger for Justice, or Hope to Change the World—none of these vapid platitudes excuses anything, especially not in the mouths of intellectuals. It won't do to deploy, as proof of a political system's presumed orientation toward justice and liberty, the delusions of the dupes and the lies of the beneficiaries.

The phenomena I am drawing attention to belong principally to the so-called Western world, to countries that have never been under the yoke of the Communist totalitarian system, even if the ideology has left its mark. Countries where Communism has actually ruled must confront far more formidable difficulties, for they are prisoners not only of passé ideas but of past realities. I must add that among nations that have managed to escape Communism but where totalitarian ideology continues to have a powerful influence, both in theory and in practice, France holds a leading place—perhaps *the* leading place. France is a sort of Eurolab for the development of cutting-edge means of discarding or inverting the lessons of experience, or of reluctantly accepting those lessons only after such delays as to nullify the benefits.

The practical advantages of conceding the truth would have been far greater had it been done at an earlier date, for then it would have led to the shortening of Communism's life. The symbolic event that marked the failure of Communism was not the fall of the Berlin Wall, but its construction more than twenty years earlier, in 1961—a watershed event in that it dramatically demonstrated how actually existing socialism had already reached an advanced state of breakdown: its subjects had to be literally walled in to prevent them from fleeing. Unfortunately, this stunning admission of defeat was understood by only a minority of Westerners. For a much larger number, the two decades that followed the Wall's construction were a golden age of Marxist parties and fashions, leftist terrorism both criminal and intellectual, and the spread of revolutionary ideologies. And for liberal parties they were decades of timidity: blushing rapprochements, détente, *Ost-politik,* Eurocommunism, Italian "historical compromise." To the West's dishonor, the Berlin Wall was finally torn down not by the democracies in 1961, as could easily have been done, but by the subjugated people themselves nearly thirty years later.

The authors of all those panegyrics to Communism—regarded as the only conceivable vector that could possibly lead to pros- perity-plus-solidarity—are careful to withhold comment about surviving remnants now that Communism has almost vanished. In North Korea, for example, in the last decade of the century, famine wiped out between 1.5 million and 3 million inhabitants out of a population of 22 million. The life of the survivors has been, in their own words, "worse than a pig's life in China." But if you mention North Korea to socialists, they will come back with the standard rejoinder that your example is not conclusive. No Communist disaster—nor even a failure of so-called moderate socialism—can ever conclusively refute the model's validity, because exceptional circumstances can always be invoked to dis- prove specific cases. You might suggest to Mme Sallenave that if she wishes to experience again the "summer of the soul," she can go live in Pyongyang, but by doing so you reveal your own sordid *mauvaise foi.* North Korea can never "kill hope." The place is a terminal ward, doubtless, but the ideal of "fraternity" that origi- nally inspired the Democratic People's Republic remains morally superior to the cesspool of liberalism. Utopia is not under the slightest obligation to produce results: its sole function is to allow its devotees to condemn what exists in the name of what does not.

The suppression of the Soviet past is as prevalent in America as in France, and perhaps even more successful precisely because Communism has been less of a factor in America's political history and therefore less culpable. The United States has never had a Communist Party capable of electing anyone to the Senate or the House of Representatives. Americans who actually want to see the Soviet system transplanted to their own country have never constituted more than a negligible and unrealistic minority, composed mainly of intellectuals. American labor unions, while predominantly Democratic, have had a long tradition of anticommunism and have often been more uncompromising than the big capitalists in this regard. In 1959, for instance, rightly pointing to the absence of unions in the USSR, American labor unions refused to receive Khrushchev when the jubilant Soviet premier was touring the United States and being showered with ovations by CEOs.* To be sure, the Communist Party of the USA, although minuscule, had played a subversive role of appalling effectiveness during the 1940s, becoming an operational base for Soviet espionage. But collectivism never achieved the same level of public support in America as it did in Italy, France and Spain. Consequently, the funeral knell never rang, as it did in Europe, for the death of Communism as an ideal cherished by large numbers of people, an ideal that would have to be painstakingly restored. In the political imagination of the American people, it had never occupied the important place it had in Europe, where the idea of socialism had informed our worldview and our sense of belonging for generations.

Nevertheless, American "liberals" after 1990 felt compelled to put any serious discussion of the Soviet tragedy off-limits, and likewise any reappraisals of Western misconceptions about the USSR. In the United States, the word "liberal" is often used to describe the left wing of the Democratic Party. The American left wields a dispersed yet dominant influence thanks to its strongholds in American culture—in academia, publishing and the media. The American use of "liberalism" is quite clearly the opposite of Europeans' classical understanding of the word, which Americans, to avoid confusion, logically enough call "classical liberalism."

---

* Here I would like to mention a personal experience. When my book *The Totalitarian Temptation* came out in the United States in 1977, it was heartily supported by some union bosses, who on numerous occasions invited me to speak before union members. On the other hand, the book found a decidedly cooler reception in university circles, which were then imbued with a spirit of "détente" vis-à-vis the Soviet Union and a lively admiration for Communist China.

The hostility that the American left expresses toward any effort to inventory the Soviet past or to analyze post-Communist problems has its roots in the Cold War. Over several decades, informed opinion in the United States was essentially divided between the hawks and the doves, with the latter in control of the principal media outlets. According to the doves, Soviet aggression did not spring automatically from the very nature of the Soviet system: it was but an anguished response to the hawks' policy of "containment." Western diplomacy should therefore have consisted of relieving the Soviets and other Communist governments of their feelings of insecurity by offering more concessions and aid—and above all by refraining from responding, even verbally, to any attacks.

When the Red Army invaded Afghanistan in 1979, the American liberal press—the organs with the largest circulation, the most prestige and the greatest influence—rushed to condemn those insane cold warriors, the Americans, in many an editorial, analysis and opinion piece. The incorrigible warmongers in the White House, they warned, would not fail to exploit the situation (so poorly understood) as a pretext for demanding a toughening-up of the Atlantic alliance's posture and an end to détente. Such a reaction, and not the Soviet action, was the real danger. Invasion or no invasion, the West was the aggressor. The most urgent task of the day, therefore, was to frustrate the advocates of "confrontation," who doubtless would seize the occasion to spread the dangerous idea that ten years of diplomatic and strategic concessions to the Soviet Union had failed and that a reversal of policy was necessary.

The fanciful notion that Soviet diplomacy was oriented toward peace rested on the assumption that the regime was domestically progressive. According to the majority of American Sovietologists, the USSR had long ceased to be totalitarian: having succeeded in creating a modern industrial base and reforming agriculture, it was slowly moving toward political pluralism more or less along Western lines. This seraphic vision, dependent as it was on crude ignorance of readily available facts, gave proof that although the

United States has never had a politically important Communist Party, she had (and still has) an ample share of Marxists. It was their version of the USSR that prevailed in American universities during the 1960s and 1970s.

A corollary of the American left's thesis was that confrontational policies on the part of the West could only slow down or compromise the process of Soviet democratization. Thus the Sovietologist Stephen F. Cohen, a university professor and regular editorialist for the *New York Times,* made repeated attacks on what the left referred to as "the Cold War establishment." He claimed that the Soviet political monolith was subdividing into various crypto-parties and that an overly rigid Western stance would undermine the reformist and conciliatory factions. Therefore, even when challenged by Soviet actions that were—or gave the appearance of being—expansionist, we ought to remain calm and refrain from precipitate reaction.

The opposition between hawkish cold warriors and their dovish critics continued to be the main criterion of political classification and the leading theme of historical thinking even after the Cold War's end. When political stakes were not so critical, any attempt to assess Communism's past calmly and objectively, any analysis based on researching East Bloc archives, even any book focusing on post-Communism—that is, on the difficulties encountered by societies re-emerging from decades of debilitating totalitarian oppression—was put down to "nostalgia for the Cold War" disguised as scholarship. "Why drag out that old stuff?" was the refrain. "Haven't we heard it all before? Let's move on!" It was repeatedly suggested that the hawks' fixation on the history and prospects of Communist states sprang from bitterness at having lost the object of their hatred and thus being deprived of their cultural vocation. And from this point of view, the real winter of the soul was being felt by the old anticommunists, even more inconsolable than the old Communists.

In the United States as in Europe, at a time when the full extent of the Communist horror was exposed for all to see, it was the anticommunists who were put in the dock. Meanwhile, the former Reds proudly assured themselves that their choices had been correct, that they had never been in error, and that it was their adversaries whom history had refuted. In what way, exactly? Above all, because the hawks had characterized Communist totalitarianism as irreversible; but Communism had evaporated, thus proving them wrong.

Now, insofar as it relates to my own work, I have already replied at length to this contention.[6] So here I will be as concise as I can: I have often written that Communism is irreparable, in the sense that it cannot be made to work. But I have never said that it could not be toppled, and in fact I have always maintained that it could be. The left's dream, always and everywhere, has been to perfect the Communist enterprise—to humanize it, make it more efficient economically and less repressive politically, while retaining the basic structures of socialism. And always, everywhere, the dream has been shipwrecked on the shoals of reality. A totalitarian system cannot reform itself. Its choices are to survive at all costs, or to collapse.

In *The Totalitarian Temptation* (1976), I wrote, "The only way to reform Communism is to get rid of it."[7] That is exactly what the subject peoples of the Soviet Union and its colonies in central Europe understood and acted on between 1989 and 1991. How could I possibly have believed in Communism's imperishability when I wrote in *Without Marx or Jesus* that already by 1970 it had utterly failed in every domain, that it had never been viable, and that its longevity was an anomaly owing entirely to the effectiveness of its repressive machinery combined with the paradoxical indulgence of the democracies?[8] And in 1983, in *How Democracies Perish,* I argued that it would suffice for the West to abandon its complacency in order for the inherent fragility of Communism to become manifest and lead to total breakdown—an inevitability that the West had persisted in staving off from 1921 onward, at great economic cost to itself.

In making these observations, I must ask for the reader's indulgence; but since accusations have been made in the American press that *Democracy Against Itself* contradicted the position I argued in my previous books, I think it appropriate to set the record straight here.[9]

However much light was shed on Communism's shadowy history by its epilogue, from the left's point of view, in America as in Europe, nothing had really changed: the good remained the good and the bad remained the bad. In America, the latter were those whose nostalgia for the Cold War was incurable. In Europe, they were the right-wing holdovers, those reactionaries who could critique Communism only by rejecting social progress out of hand. But for leftist intellectuals the world over, the idea was the same: Those who had been intellectually mistaken and morally compromised with regard to the socialist phenomenon had nothing to regret—or hardly anything—and nothing to repent; for at the end of the day, the Seekers of Justice had not been wrong and had done no evil.

Worse still, leftists very soon sensed that they were once again in a position to point the finger. Among the victims of the counterattack was the naïve Cardinal Decourtray, the late archbishop of Lyon and Primate of the Gauls, who was unfortunate enough not to have realized that the wind had shifted. The January 5, 1990, issue of *Le Figaro* published an interview with the cardinal wherein he discussed the ongoing meltdown of Communism, which, with the veil of censorship torn asunder, stood so charmingly revealed. Referring to left-wing Catholics, the cardinal cautioned, "We must admit that, in their concern to maintain good relations with the most politically *engagés*, they have allowed themselves to be drawn into something like connivance." These are very moderate words, since Decourtray qualifies his critique with reassurances about purity of intentions and the limited nature of the compromise. But his remarks were nevertheless too much for Christians who had been fellow travelers of totalitarianism, and brickbats began to rain down on the imprudent prelate.

"Are suspicions being cast on those who struggle against injustice?" demanded the secretary-general of Action Catholique Ouvrière (Workers' Catholic Action).[10] Again we see the typical question-begging maneuver of taking as proven what history has specifically refuted, namely Communism's utility as an instrument for combating social injustice. Added the secretary-general, "This is a slap in the face to many men and women, Christian believers or not, fighting for the liberation of humanity." Apparently this inquisitor still, in 1990, harbored no doubts that Communism had actually been fighting for humanity's liberation. The usual evasions are trotted out once again in defense of that shopworn thesis: The crimes and injustices of totalitarianism have nothing to do with "real" Communism, and economic catastrophes can have no bearing on the truth of Marxism. Decourtray was interdicting the "missionary dynamism of the Church from the world of the working classes." Which comes down to asserting that the only way for the aforesaid missionary dynamism to operate is in connivance with Communism, even after it has cracked up.

Many indictments in the same vein were flung at the Primate of the Gauls, until this hapless individual was driven to retract. Contrite, he wrote to the bishops that his words had been "too hasty" to get his meaning across and that he hadn't had a chance to "verify the interview's contents." Coming from a priest who had an opportunity to offer us an example of courage, this climb-down nicely illustrates Communism's ongoing capacity for ideological terrorism. Those who have been active accomplices or silent witnesses of its crimes, the moment they come under the slightest suspicion of disloyalty, will promptly do what is necessary to fall back into line and march valiantly onward.

CHAPTER THREE

The Real Culprit

The posthumous defense of Communism went hand in glove with an indictment of classical liberalism. To rehabilitate Communism as such was a difficult task, if not impossible, so a strategy was devised to plead its case indirectly by painting its opposite as even worse. In addition to the nobility of intentions that inspired it, the argument went, Communism had the merit of being able to stand up against the triumphal progress of liberalism and limit the damage it could do. But with the Communist levee swept away, the tide of liberalism and globalization was free to spread everywhere, and it would inevitably plunge humanity into a sea of misery, or at least injustice.

Soon after the collapse of Communism in Europe, an alternative *pensée unique** began to crystallize: an orthodoxy according

---

* *Translator's note: La pensée unique,* literally "unique thought" or "single thinking," is employed as a political pejorative whose meaning cannot easily be conveyed in English. Analogous to the phrase *bien pensant* in the sense that it refers to an orthodoxy, *pensée unique* is generally used as a code phrase to imply an uncompromising approach to policy based on free-market liberalism. See Appendix A for Ignacio Ramonet's coinage of the term.

to which, in the words of a Socialist in Lionel Jospin's government, "the twentieth century will witness the collapse of liberalism." Some naïfs might be excused for having gathered the impression that the century had, on the contrary, witnessed the failure of planned economies. Hadn't it been firmly established, by eye-witnesses and historians alike, that the century's most tragically failed economies were Russia's under Stalin and Brezhnev, and China's during the Great Leap Forward? And in the developing world, weren't the most miserable countries those that had most slavishly followed the Soviet and Maoist recipes? It would seem, at first glance, that life since 1945 has been altogether more bearable in Holland and France and Italy than in Bulgaria or Romania or Poland; and, indeed, better in India than in China. Well, these superficial assessments are merely a trap, insist the *bien pensants*. What the breakdown of Communism actually proves is that liberalism is not viable!

In France, the term *pensée unique* generally refers to the outlook of those who favor the European currency and globalization, hence an outlook rooted in liberalism. But isn't the notion of a single dominating system of thought, a *pensée unique,* more fittingly ascribed to the foes of liberalism, given the weight of public opinion-making that leans in their direction? Rarely have we seen such a deluge of antiliberal propaganda as during the years following the bankruptcy of actually existing socialism and collectivist *dirigisme.* Yet never before had a social experiment resulted so rapidly in such a complete crackup, owing entirely to its inherent defects and independent of extrinsic pressures such as natural disaster, epidemic or military defeat.

The reason for the collapse of the socialist experiment seemed all the more evident in that even the democratic versions of socialism had either failed or been forced to undergo drastic makeovers. Such was the case for British Labor Party socialism after 1980, for the "rupture with capitalism" *à la française* after 1983, and for Swedish-style social democracy between 1985 and 1990. Nevertheless, twenty years after China's turn toward the market, ten years after the dismantling of the Berlin Wall, eight years after the USSR's closing act, apparently the major lesson to be drawn from twentieth-century history was not the bankruptcy of collectivism but the bankruptcy of liberalism.

Hence the systematic adoption—in the media, in politics and among intellectuals—of the term *ultraliberalisme,* along with references to "savage" or "unbridled" liberalism. Even in traditional right-wing circles one heard the cliché of liberalism as a "jungle," an epithet that Alain Juppé, prime minister in Jacques Chirac's government, blithely used in a 1997 statement on RTL radio. The French politicians most faithful to free-market ideas dared not claim allegiance to Margaret Thatcher, preferring to place themselves under the banner of Tony Blair. The physician-pundit Jean-Christophe Rufin saw nothing ridiculous about titling one of his books *La Dictature libérale* (The Liberal Dictatorship).[1] This nonsensical phrase was to be turned around and aimed at the Socialists by the Gaullist Philippe Séguin: it was they, he thundered, who had unleashed *"la dictature du libéralisme."* In another speech, Séguin warned against a threatening European *"capitalisme totalitaire."*[2] The Catholic Church, including the majority of bishops, likewise bought into a similarly censorious vocabulary. In the cultural domain, it's the same old story: the free market reeks of evil. In the pages of *Le Monde,*[3] Philippe Dagen called Marc Fumaroli, the greatest living historian of seventeenth-century art and literature, essentially a Nazi for daring to raise objections to the notion that cultural activities should be entirely directed and subsidized by the state.

It is not only in France that such absurdities prevail. The German minister for labor Norbert Blüm declared, "The market economy is acceptable only if it brings about equilibrium between competition and solidarity."[4] Which is to forget that the *only* countries that have had the will and the means to create effective welfare states with social security, family allowances, unemployment compensation, pensions and so on—in short, the full menu of substantive benefits—are those with capitalist economies. Liberal societies are essentially not "savage." On the contrary, they are the only societies governed by the rule of law, the only societies where economic activities follow strict legal principles that are actually enforced.

The historical ignorance of our contemporaries sometimes borders on abysmal. The American multibillionaire (and Hungarian immigrant) George Soros likes to issue sweeping critiques of free-market capitalism.[5] He has claimed that during his childhood in Europe he saw how market capitalism gave rise to unemployment and how unemployment in turn gave rise to totalitarianism. But unemployment was not a causal factor in the 1917 Bolshevik revolution nor in the 1922 Italian Fascist takeover. It did play a part in Hitler's ascent in 1933, but only as one among many more important factors. In two countries, France and America, the economic crisis and unemployment of the 1930s provoked reactions not toward the extreme right but toward the left: Léon Blum's Popular Front and Roosevelt's New Deal. Finally, this was a time of general retreat from true economic liberalism, as the advanced nations cowered behind thick protectionist barriers. Despite his adoption of United States citizenship, Soros's argument shows that intellectually he remains more European than American.

What is the reason for this phobia against liberalism that, with the exception of the United Kingdom and Ireland, torments the European Union? The explanation may lie in the fact that European countries, in varying degrees but with France the most hidebound, blame "excessive liberalism" for evils that in reality derive from excessive regulation, taxation, redistribution, protectionism and state intervention generally. It's rather like an overweight couch potato blaming her lethargy on too much physical exercise. For example, in *L'Horreur economique*[6]—a book whose enormous sales figures indicate how much the public shares its bias—Viviane Forrester maintains that the ongoing process of liberalization and globalization is destroying jobs. But the truth is that, since 1980, this advancing wave has created hundreds of millions of jobs all over the world, *with the exception of Europe*. It's in Europe that average unemployment levels have been the highest and job creation the most anemic. Why so?

Instead of asking such an excellent question, Europeans prefer to retreat into fantasy, opting to make up stories about American and British jobs being the dead-end variety (*petits boulots*), which they themselves would never dream of taking. Well, it's better by far to buckle down to poorly paid work, in the hope of finding something better later on, than to be an unemployed outcast, sinking to the bottom of the social ladder. There are millions of such *exclus* in Europe. And the Europeans' argument about the U.S. economy doesn't stand up to scrutiny, anyway. As Alain Cotta points out, the American unemployment rate dropped from its high point of 7 percent in 1991 (which was nonetheless 5 percentage points lower than the French level), to less than 4.5 percent in 1998 and to 4.1 percent at the end of 1999.[7] At healthy levels like these, the supply of jobs actually exceeds demand and the worker tends to rule the labor market. This achievement was all the more remarkable given that the working population had meanwhile increased by ten million.

The worst form of blindness is willful blindness. European governments—in a nice example of antiphrasis—like to talk about "employment policies." But the policies in question resemble nothing so much as an unhinged shipbuilding company's insistence on launching vessels too heavy to float. After the inevitable comes about, the mad designers proceed to bankrupt themselves with salvage operations, struggling to raise their sunken boats and compensate the victims. Likewise, European governments in their blindness ignore the successes of liberalism and blame it for reverses that it did not cause. Even such an astute man as Hubert Védrine, the foreign minister in Jospin's cabinet, on a visit to Moscow in 1999, attributed the Russian crisis of the previous summer to "the abuse of ultraliberal 'gadgets.'" To detect ultra-liberalism in a massive state juggernaut—packed with Brezhnev-appointed apparatchiks and thieving rogues who expeditiously funnel monies loaned by the International Monetary Fund to secret Swiss bank accounts—reveals a disturbingly askew reading of the contemporary world, and of history and economics, on the part of a highly placed politician whose job it is to have a handle on international affairs. But Hubert Védrine was far from alone in his misperception of the 1998 crisis, or more generally in his faulty assessment of Russia and its satellites' capacity for surmounting the crippling legacy of their past.*

It is a good and useful task to criticize democratic capitalism for its defects, for its failures and injustices, but it is a futile one if the purpose is to rehabilitate socialism. The latter has foundered, and remedies for any social, economic or political afflictions that liberal societies suffer from will not be found amid its wreckage, but only within liberalism itself. At the century's close, Socialist parties are socialist in name only, apart from a certain knack for stunting economic growth. They have been compelled to renounce any ambition of implementing socialism in the exact sense of the word: a nineteenth-century invention that was put into practice in the twentieth. This socialism—the only authentic kind—is dead. Left standing today are only various ways of practicing capitalism, with varying mixes of market freedom, private ownership, taxation, redistribution and regulation.

Here is a savory paradox: The left has adroitly used antiliberalism so as to maneuver the right into a suicidal repudiation of its liberal convictions, whereas the left itself, when in power, has managed to tiptoe away from socialist dogma while surreptitiously adopting the principles of a market economy. Granted, this progress has always been slow. Statist interventionism, based on confiscatory taxation and deficit spending, was allowed to persist for too long. But still the left, compelled by circumstances, took the liberal path—while the terrorized right kept on mouthing denunciations of the "Anglo-Saxon model."

For example: "You can't call yourself a Gaullist if you defend unbridled liberalism," proclaimed Charles Pasqua, a Gaullist politician who, for the 1999 European elections, formed a list of candidates who had broken away from the official Gaullist Party.

---

* The extreme difficulty experienced by countries struggling out from the straitjacket of Communism is a theme of *Le Regain démocratique* (1992), in which I warned against the excessive optimism that in 1990 predicted a rapid climb toward capitalist prosperity and democratic polities.

And François Bayrou, whose name headed the list of centrist candidates (Union for French Democracy, or UDF), had this to say: "In alliance with a conservative liberal party,* we are going to take possession of the vast center ground, with a party—finally—that is European and progressive, and has *solidarity* as a main plank." Here the word *solidarity* implies the opposite of classical liberalism and, yet again, the wrong-headed notion that societies committed to liberty are somehow incompatible with social solidarity.

Another defense of Communism is based on the historical error of ascribing to it a positive role as a spur to social progress in non-Communist societies. The argument boils down to this: Even if every single Communist state has proved to be a failure, Communism as an opposition force in democratic societies has functioned as an engine of social justice.

Such is Jean-Denis Bredin's thesis in an article that appeared a few days after the failed coup d'état against Gorbachev. Regardless of whether it was a genuine putsch or merely political theater, many observers rightly sensed, often with chagrin, that the affair presaged the imminent dissolution of the Soviet Union. Bredin's title is: "Are We Permitted?" The implicit following clause is: ". . . to Mourn Communism?"[8] The text elaborates: "Are we allowed, diffidently, to suggest that Communism, so detestable when it held power, has performed a useful service for some of the democracies, those that never make much progress without being shaken up? . . . In an old, conservative country, social progress owes much to Communism." And further: "Without Communism to give it direction, socialism in France would perhaps have been just another form of radicalism." Here we see at work the Marxist imagination and ability to rewrite history. The idea is that only through "struggle"—strikes, seizure and occupation of factories, riots, and so on—can there be social progress, and only by wresting the means of production from the owners. The facts, however, show something very different.

---

* Bayrou is referring to the coalition of RPR, the Gaullist Party, and Alain Madelin's Liberal Democrats.

Decades before the appearance of the first Communist parties and even the first socialist theoreticians, it was the nineteenth-century liberals who first posed what was then called "the social question," and who answered it by working out several of the founding laws of modern social rights. It was the liberal François Guizot, minister for King Louis-Philippe, who in 1841 put up for vote the first law aimed at regulating child labor in factories. It was Frédéric Bastiat, that economist of genius who today would be branded an "unbridled" ultraliberal, who in 1849, as a deputy in the Legislative Assembly, was the first Frenchman to set forth the principle and call for legal recognition of the right to strike. It was the liberal Émile Ollivier who in 1864 convinced Napoleon III to abolish the "crime of coalition"—that is, the ban against workers organizing to defend their own interests—thus opening the way for the trade-unionism of the future. It was the liberal Pierre Waldeck-Rousseau who in 1884, at the beginning of the Third Republic, proposed a law granting full legal status to trade unions.

Are we permitted to point out that the socialists of the time, in accordance with revolutionary logic and well before the appearance of any Communist party whatsoever, displayed violent hostility toward this last law? The reason, according to Jules Guesde,* was that "under the pretext of permitting workers' organizations, the new law has but one goal: to prevent our workers from organizing politically." Subsequent events refuted this perspicacious prognostication, showing that the freedom to form professional organizations is entirely compatible with the freedom to vote. For a long time the big workers' unions were the political base and main source of financial support for Britain's Labor Party, for the Democrats in the United States, for the German Socialist Party and for various Scandinavian reformist parties. The most powerful unions emerged and flourished in these countries almost entirely without Communist prodding. On the other hand, where Communist parties achieved substantial political weight, in ideol-

---

* *Tanslator's note*: Jules Guesde (1845–1922) was a Marxist politician and theoretician, as well as a government minister, 1914–1916.

ogizing the unions they succeeded only in weakening them. This is what happened especially in France, where union members today constitute but a tiny percentage of the voting population. What's more, the trade-union movement in France—whatever the political orientations of its various groupings—quickly degenerated into organizations devoted to defending the interests of public employees only, although these were already privileged in comparison with private-sector workers. It has been a long time since the unions stopped meeting the requirements, established by law in the early 1950s, to represent all their members fairly and above all to subsist exclusively on members' dues. They have come to depend on direct and indirect state subsidies levied from taxpayers, the vast majority of whom belong to no union.

So the thesis that Communist parties have been spurs to progress seems untenable. In many instances the presence of a strong Communist party in the political arena has served to retard social progress rather than accelerate it. For example, the French Communist Party, in the late 1950s and early 1960s, fiercely defended the stupid theory that the working class was being "completely pauperized"—during an unprecedented economic boom that would enable French workers to enjoy a standard of living they would not have dared dream about during the Popular Front era twenty years earlier. In fact, the only twentieth-century examples of workers' "complete pauperization" were produced in countries under the shadow of socialist ideology.

Thus I cannot quite agree with Jean-Denis Bredin, a writer whom I respect and regard as a friend, when he writes that those who rejoiced at the fall of Communism were only those "who, fearing the armed might of Communism less than they did its ideology, trembled at the thought that somewhere, on some sinister evening, the oppressed of the world would take power into their own hands." Whatever Bredin thinks about the matter, many of those who celebrated Communism's collapse did so out of solidarity with the working class, out of compassion for the legions of the persecuted who were finally delivered from one of the cruelest and most absurd despotisms ever to afflict the human race.

Are we allowed to point this out?

★ ★ ★

The path was thus cleared for less subtle spirits to rush into the fray. Abandoning careful language altogether, these people were prepared to assert that they had witnessed the exact opposite of what had actually occurred. Only naïfs (the argument went) were led to believe that after 1989 we had entered the post-Communist era. They must be disabused of this error. So we saw the well-timed publication of a book with the title *L'Après-libéralisme* by Immanuel Wallerstein.[9] The back cover informs us that the author is a professor of sociology at Binghamton University (SUNY), where he directs the Fernand Braudel Center, and he also teaches social science at the École des Hautes Études in Paris.

What does Wallerstein teach? That what we have lived through with the collapse of the Soviet Union, though we may not have been aware of it, is "the implosion of liberalism" (which is the title of his third chapter); and that 1989, "the year of the so-called end of the so-called Communisms," actually marked the end of liberalism. Implicit in Wallerstein's phrase is a predictable evasion: the Communism that failed was not *real* Communism. To the end of time, real Communism will remain both irreplaceable and never to be found, anywhere. It is thus immunized from all criticism.

The urgent task, so clearly necessitated by socialism's failure, became critiquing liberalism, and numerous intellectuals of the Old and the New Left, moderate or extreme, applied themselves tirelessly to this project. These intellectuals comported themselves like victors, for hadn't events proved them right? As for the others, the so-called liberals, they had to appear before the tribunal of History and be summarily indicted by investigating magistrates who were thoroughly steeped in the defunct ideology.

Some months after my memoir, *Le Voleur dans la maison vide* ("Thief in an Empty House"), was published in 1996,[10] I was visited by a talented young writer, Frédéric Martel, whose groundbreaking book on the gay liberation movement since 1968 had been stirring lively debate and deservedly selling well.[11] He had asked me for an interview about my memoirs for *Politique internationale,* a journal founded and edited by Patrick Wajsman. I accepted with pleasure, out of sympathy alike for the interviewer and the publication.

What struck me from the outset was the political slant of Martel's questions. My autobiography is essentially a personal narrative, recalling events of my private life and individuals who for the most part were not public figures. Nevertheless, my interrogator's probes were relentlessly political. Obviously, where my life concerned politics, I had written about the circumstances and sketched portraits of the players involved. But even then I had taken great care to remain faithful to the narrative style, avoiding theoretical analysis—something I had dealt with in so many previous books. And yet, the one time I had produced a book as far removed as possible from political debate, here they were trying to drag me back into the fray.

Martel had no intention of listening to me talk about my life. What he wanted was a confession regarding my ideological itinerary. I quickly grasped the assumptions dominating his outlook and the agenda informing his line of questioning. They added up to the following propositions: To defend liberalism—if you really have to—is permissible only so long as it remains no more than a tactic to expose the weaknesses of collectivism. But with the Communist adversary defeated, hasn't the time come to discard such a strictly polemical posture? It is no longer useful, and shouldn't liberals now think about submitting to self-criticism and recognizing the inadequacy of liberalism *considered as such?* The argument here comes down to that perennial sophism: The end of the Cold War has effectively deprived anticommunists of their argument, and isn't it high time for them to start beating their breasts and denouncing liberalism, the real danger, too long masked by the anticommunist obsession? Obsession: this was the mental malady that my inquisitor diagnosed in his eventual review of *Le Voleur dans la maison vide.*[12] My six hundred or so pages were, he said, a recital of "fifty years of face-saving, intense reflection about an obsession: Communism."

Martel's statement is materially false, as my memoirs make clear. I have never belonged to the Communist Party, never approved of or supported it. But like many intellectuals of my generation in the years following World War II, I subscribed, at least to some extent, to the Marxist interpretation of history and of class warfare within capitalist societies. Martel's assertion demonstrates how far the Stalinist vocabulary has inserted itself into the best minds of the non-Stalinist left. Stalinists have always subjected authors who publish critiques of Communism to ad hominem attacks, labeling them "simplistic" or "obsessive" or "visceral" anticommunists, the object being to discredit them as paranoids incapable of objective thought. Epithets like these were cooked up more than a half-century ago in the backrooms of the totalitarians' thought police, yet the non-Communist left, with pathetic servility, still uses them in their strivings to marginalize the heterodox.

When I was elected to the Académie Française in 1997, the daily paper *Libération* mentioned the fact with the comment: "In his seventies, he remains reactionary and abrasive, a paladin of anticommunism." Conversely, to have been pro-Communist is, for the left, to have been progressive. Despite claiming independence from the Stalinist intellectual straitjacket, the left is loath to abandon its system for tagging potential candidates for the abattoir. In its heart of hearts, the left still thinks of anticommunism as a sin, the symptom of a predisposition toward fascism aggravated by a shade of mental disorder.

As the twentieth century wound down, anticommunism was still to be discriminated against—which is an indication of how slow progress is in the domain of intellectual freedom. The majority of intellectuals continue to be more concerned with what others think about them, than with what they themselves should think.

Concluding his review, Frédéric Martel charitably asks, "What will become of them, these antitotalitarians—of whom Revel was one of the most active and clear-headed—now that their great adversary has vanished?" Then he delivers stern counsel of the type that has since become routine: "Better than anyone else, perhaps,

Revel knows that liberals henceforth must reposition themselves and show that they are capable, in their turn, of inventing a post-antitotalitarian paradigm." In short, now that liberals have been deprived of justification for a show of liberalism, they must toe the line.

I mentioned to Martel that since our conversation seemed quite irrelevant to *Le Voleur dans la maison vide,* I hoped it would not be published. But the interview did come out, and at the end of the day it is not without interest. I have kept a copy. It could almost have functioned as an appendix to a book I wrote five years earlier, in which I attempted to do precisely what Martel recommended—that is, invent "a post-antitotalitarian paradigm."[13]

Alain Touraine, in a lucidly argued book that came out in 1999, focused on the misinterpretation—or hallucination—that leads people to castigate as "liberalism" what is in fact its opposite. Exposing the inherent contradictions of the French left, he owns up to "not really being able to see how defending the state as prime economic player, and tax-immune categories of employees, can help the unemployed or assist in the creation of new jobs." The support granted to public-sector jobs—the consolidation of privileges—has become the principal rallying cause for what the left still dares to call "social" movements, whereas they are actually antisocial. Touraine shrewdly notes the duplicity of the organizers and the naïveté of their victims: "Those who see a renewal of class warfare and union activism in the massive public support for the December 1995 strike [of public employees] are simply taking their desires for reality." Here he is following the sensible advice of Karl Marx (rarely if ever followed by Marxists) to refrain from confusing reality with the *idea of reality* that the dominant society would foist upon us. Touraine has fun at the expense of those who are fixated on the notion that the French economic model is "ultraliberal": "Isn't it ridiculous to hear talk about extreme liberalism in a country where the state commands half the national resources, either through social welfare programs or by economic regulation?"

Unfortunately, by a printer's error, the title that appears on the cover of Touraine's book, *Comment sortir du libéralisme?* (How to Leave Liberalism?), was clearly intended for another of the publisher's productions.[14] For the text brilliantly demonstrates that at least three-quarters of the world's countries, France conspicuously among them, have not yet even *entered* liberalism. So how could they possibly leave it? We are "*étatiste* to an extreme degree," writes Touraine, "especially since 1995, when defense of the public sector became a democratic duty—the better to resist the attacks, it is asserted, of a civil society (and more importantly an economy) dominated by the selfish pursuit of private interest. What a grotesque misrepresentation!"

Frédéric Bastiat himself could not have put it better. Like him, and in the great tradition of French liberalism, Touraine convinces us that the state is the principal creator of injustices and privileges rather than the best instrument for combating them— which makes the mysterious typographer's blunder of the title all the more odious. It is appalling that an eminent French sociologist could fall victim to such a trick. Was the author lied to? Was he drugged? Tortured, even? Did he cave in to threats? Was he afraid of something? Having always enjoyed very cordial relations with Alain Touraine, I hereby offer my services as founding member of a society for the defense of his individual rights and freedom of expression. But the antiliberal "resistance fighters" are actually capable of worse in their struggle to fend off the danger of *la pensée unique*. Didn't a certain Nicaraguan gentleman go so far as to "strangle his wife because she sympathized with the liberals"?[15]

Obviously, Touraine has been co-opted, by devious means and against his will, into the plot to discredit liberalism and thus indirectly rehabilitate Communism. To besmirch liberalism naturally entails retrospective indulgence toward Communism and a discrediting of the right, accused of having failed to notice the collapse of capitalism—which, as every good Marxist knows, has been in a state of putrefaction since the middle of the nineteenth century.

If capitalism has brought only injustice, penury and despotism in those parts of the world where actual socialism has not reigned, logically it must do the same in those countries that were engaged in dismantling their command economies. From the first years of the post-Communist era, a favorite theme of Western antiliberal *pensée unique* was denunciation of capitalism's chaotic ravages in countries that hitherto had enjoyed the reassuring, stable structures of actually existing socialism. Imprecations rang out from every side condemning the criminal haste with which the sectarian "ideologues of neoliberalism" had inflicted massive—indeed, lethal—doses of free-market economics on those unhappy lands.

These were cries of joy as much as distress, for weren't they heralding one more proof, if any further proof were needed, of the market's poisonous character? Unsurprisingly, though, such prophetically inspired utterances sprang from a twin error of observation. First, critics willfully ignored the fact that the return to the market, within the limits allowed by the existing structures, had not everywhere yielded bad results. Aside from the success story of East Germany—for no other ex-Communist zone could dream of such colossal aid as it received from the West, showered on a population of barely fifteen million—it quickly became apparent that Poland, Hungary and the Czech Republic were not completely botching their transition to liberal democracy. The fact that their adjustment was generally on track was actually confirmed when some elections were won by ex-Communist bosses; although a divine surprise for Western Marxists, this development had no effect on the overall course of affairs. Where it occurred, the return to power of Communists did not mean the return to power of Communism. The former apparatchiks renamed themselves "social democrats" or otherwise tricked themselves out, as did their confreres in Italy. But political transsexuals of this type never for one instant expected a return to one-party regimes with collective ownership, cultural dictatorship and all the rest. They had left this program for their mentors in the French ultra-left. Likewise there were Stalinist renegades, ever extending the limits of perversity, who took to reading *The Economist* instead of *Le Monde diplomatique*. The new president of Poland, elected in 1995, was a scion of the old nomenklatura, but he was also a suave opportunist who hurried to declare allegiance to the market economy and privatization. He never turned his back on the "shock therapy" that had been administered by the reforming neoliberals, architects of an economic restructuring that was a brilliant success—whatever Western nostalgists choose to think.

The second mistake that is made with regard to the post-Communist economic cataclysms is to blame them on the free-market system as such, rather than on a failure in applying it. You would have to be hallucinating to discern market discipline in the current Russian economy, where normal exchanges have been utterly distorted by a nomenklatura-turned-mafia, an oligarchy of political racketeers who have exercised a ruthless grip on society. A genuine free market presupposes the rule of law. So are we dealing with a free market when monies generated by the International Monetary Fund, the World Bank, the European Bank for Reconstruction and Development, along with private banks in generous donor countries such as Germany—all earmarked for Russia's economic recovery and deposited in Moscow—are instantly rerouted, to the tune of billions of dollars, to secret private accounts in Switzerland or other shelters? Or when foreign investors are held for ransom, and if they don't pay up, are liable to be murdered by hired thugs?

The inability of Russia and the newly independent republics of the former USSR to create vital economies is not caused by too much liberalism. Rather, it stems from the fact that *liberalism has not even begun to be applied*. For liberalism to work, there must be a legal framework, political structures, and a fund of economic know-how—all of which the peoples of that part of the world have not been able to rebuild under the thumb of corrupt governments who perceive such an evolution to be against their interests. Communism in a state of breakdown must not be confused with democratic capitalism. Boris Yeltsin tacitly acknowledged this in his television address of December 31, 1999, announcing his resignation from the presidency. He asked for the Russian people's "forgiveness" for what had happened since his accession to power in 1991, admitting that "what seemed simple to us then has turned out to be arduous and painful."

To summarize: The cause of Russia's malady, which in August 1998 became agonizing, was not the market but the absence of a functional, legitimate market. And this was a result of continuing dominance by the old political class. Under these conditions, international aide proved to be futile; and fantasies of a Marshall Plan for Russia could only founder on the realities of an economy quite incapable of creatively turning to good account the resources thrown at it. To extend limitless credit to a nation lacking in viable economic, political and legal structures is like pumping gasoline into the tank of a motorless automobile. Tripling the amount of fuel will not make it start up again. The development aid, squandered and hijacked, has served only to delay the hour of truth; it hasn't stopped the knell from sounding.

The same verdict will sooner or later come down with respect to China's "commercial communism" (to use Zbigniew Brzezinski's term). For more than twenty years now, the leadership cadres of China have gone as far as possible in their attempt to introduce capitalism into the heart of the economy without blowing up the despotic one-party system. But they will assuredly not succeed in raising the living standard of the vast majority of the population, four-fifths of whom are still left behind in the midst of a boom that, despite impressive growth rates, is superficial. Real progress in this regard will need a total restructuring—a transition toward the rule of law, openness to the outside, freedom of information, and democratization. The crisis that China will have to endure when the bill comes due will not be caused by the free market (which socialists won't fail to blame); it will flow from incompatibility, beyond a certain point, between the market and a monolithic, corrupt totalitarian state.

When the Asian crisis suddenly erupted in 1997, the ecstatic foot-stamping to celebrate "the end of capitalism" was scarcely more prophetic than the other examples of clairvoyance we have looked at. For neither Indonesia, where the economy was monopolized for thirty years by the racketeering Suharto family and their pals, nor Malaysia, which has been under the *dirigiste* control of that autocratic megalomaniac Mahathir bin Mohamed since 1987, is a shining example of economic liberty within a legal framework. In these countries there was no commercial law, nor any law at all worth mentioning—or at least any law from which the potentates did not consider themselves exempt. By blaming "speculators" for troubles that should with more justice have been laid at his own door (a 45 percent crash of the Kuala Lumpur stock exchange in January 1998, and a 46 percent fall in the value of the Malaysian monetary unit, the ringgit, in six months), Mahathir proved himself to be a brilliant virtuoso of *la pensée unique*. In other Asian countries—Korea, Thailand and, above all, Japan—the crisis was the result of the major companies' excessive indebtedness to financial institutions. The banks, obedient to directives from political interests not untainted by corruption, had for years been granting loans and overdrafts beyond any reasonable limit. For private banks to disburse credits recklessly is no way to be obedient to the market. The Mitterrandian Crédit Lyonnais "model" is not liberalism. It is corrupt statism through and through.

The Japanese economy has long been structured around an organic deformation. Except for some brilliantly performing multinationals, pumped up by the banking dementias, Japanese companies were as fossilized as Communist conglomerates. This contradiction, which gave a deceptive appearance of modernity to Japan's economy, was lucidly analyzed in 1989 by Karel von Wolferen in *The Enigma of Japanese Power*.[16] The author's thesis, which at the time seemed like an amusing paradox, was borne out when growing pressure from the ever more interlinked global economy pricked the bubble of an essentially autistic and protectionist system, albeit one whose financial practices were wildly extravagant and imprudent.

But two years later, the socialists' enthusiasm for the Asian crisis and their funeral oration for capitalism turned out to be premature. At the century's end, if the situation in Asia has not completely turned around, it seems nevertheless well on the way to recovery—in contrast to Russia's agony. The collapse of global capitalism did not transpire. However anguishing the thought, the post-crisis global economy is even more open than before. Lessons have been learned from the mishap. New laws and more transparent practices will allow markets to function with fewer hiccups. But rest assured: the guardians of political orthodoxy—of the real *pensée unique*—will never waver from their antiliberal *idée fixe*.

CHAPTER FOUR

A Rigged Match

A perennial misapprehension distorts virtually all discussions about the competing merits of socialism and liberalism: Socialists like to imagine that liberalism is an *ideology*. Reared on ideology themselves, they cannot imagine that any other form of intellectual activity exists, so they constantly detect in others the same propensity toward abstract and moralistic systematizing by which they themselves are possessed. Socialists are convinced that opposing doctrines are an inverted imitation of their own, and that these opposing doctrines must likewise be promising absolute perfection, albeit by a different route. And liberals, reflexively compliant as always, have too frequently accepted this grossly mistaken view of their own position.

If a liberal asserts, "In practice, the market seems to be a less inefficient means of allocating resources than top-down, planned distribution," a socialist will immediately shoot back, "The market is not a solution to every problem." Of course not. Who has ever maintained such an absurdity? But since socialism was conceived in the delusion of being able to resolve *every* problem, its partisans project the same ambition onto their opponents. Fortunately, not everyone shares their megalomania. Liberals have never aimed to build a perfect society. They are content to compare the various types of society that exist or have existed, and to draw appropriate conclusions from studying those that have functioned the least badly. But many liberals, hypnotized by the socialists' moral imperialism, fall into the trap of debating on the socialists' terms. "I believe in market laws, but they're not enough," writes the American economist Jeremy Rifkin.[1] "The free market can't solve everything," concurs the speculator George Soros.[2] These lame truisms emanate from a rigid hermeneutical system that reads capitalism as theoretically opposed to socialism but identical in its mechanics.

Liberalism has never been an ideology, by which I mean a theory based on a priori concepts; nor is it an unchanging dogma divorced from the course of events and outcomes. It is merely a set of observations on facts. The general ideas derived from these observations do not constitute a global doctrine aspiring to comprehensiveness, but rather a series of interpretive hypotheses concerning real-world events. Adam Smith, when he undertook to write *The Wealth of Nations,* noticed that some countries were richer than others. He attempted to locate in their economic arrangements the features and practices that could account for such disparities, with the practical goal of being able to recommend prudent policies. His method is the same as that of Kant, who in the *Critique of Pure Reason* told his philosophical colleagues: For two thousand years, humanity has labored to develop theories of the Real that are valid for all time. These are no sooner created, however, than they are rejected by succeeding generations for want of conclusive evidence. But for a century and a half now, Kant continued, we have had right before our eyes a new discipline that has finally succeeded in reliably establishing at least *some* laws of nature: namely physics. We should emulate the physicists' methods instead of persisting with our sterile metaphysical dogmatism.

As an a priori construction, formulated without regard to facts or ethics, ideology is distinct from science and philosophy on the one hand, and from religion and ethics on the other. Ideology is not science—which it pretends to be. Science accepts the results of the experiments it devises, whereas ideology systematically rejects empirical evidence. It is not moral philosophy—which it claims to have a monopoly on, while striving furiously to destroy the source and necessary condition of morality: the free will of the individual. The basis of morality is respect for the person, whereas ideology invariably tramples on the person wherever it reigns. Ideology is not religion—to which it is often, and mistakenly, compared; for religion draws its meaning from faith in a transcendent reality, while ideology aims to perfect the world here below.

Ideology—that malignant invention of the human spirit's dark side, an invention which has cost us dearly—has the singular property of causing zealots to project the structural features of their own mentality onto others. Ideologues cannot imagine that an objection to their abstract systems could come from any source other than a competing system.

All ideologies are aberrations. A sound and rational ideology cannot exist. Falsehood is intrinsic to ideology by virtue of cause, motivation and objective, which is to bring into being a fictional version of the human self—the "self," at least, that has resolved no longer to accept reality as a source of information or a guide to action. When an ideology has died, it is nonsensical to think that another must promptly be found to take its place. So you replace one aberration with another aberration: what is this but surrender to yet one more mirage? It matters little what mirage you choose, since it is not the content of an illusion that counts so much as the fact that it *is* an illusion.

The confrontation between socialism and liberalism is not a confrontation of ideologies. Liberalism is not upside-down socialism; it is not a totalizing ideology governed by intellectual rules equivalent to those it criticizes. This is the misunderstanding that can make dialogues between socialists and liberals sound so absurd. Thus, in my exchange with Frédéric Martel (related in Chapter 3), the sympathetic interviewer was captive all along to the idea that my only reason for combating Communism—diehard *"viscéral"* that I am—was to promote liberalism. The end of the Cold War having made my warrior's panoply look superfluous, it was incumbent on me to question my now pointless adherence to fanatical liberalism. Well, aside from the fact that liberalism was never just another brand of fanaticism launched against an adversary, I for one have never fought against Communism in the name of liberalism alone, but for the sake of human rights and human dignity. Granted, the perpetual failure of managed economies is clearly a significant fact for liberal economists, but it hardly constitutes the crux of the matter.

When you stand before a combination prison, lunatic asylum and base of operations for a gang of murderers, you don't ask yourself whether it should be destroyed in the name of liberalism, or social democracy, or the Third Way, or market socialism, or "anarcho-capitalism." Pettifogging of this sort would be unconscionable. Only in a free society can there even be debate between liberalism and statism. For my part, I took up arms against Communism inspired by the same "obsession" that years ago made me battle against Nazism: a "visceral" *idée fixe* of respect for the human person. Who wins the economic policy debates—Margaret Thatcher or Jacques Delors, Alain Madelin or Lionel Jospin, Ronald Reagan or Olaf Palme—is a secondary issue that presupposes the re-establishment of a free civilization.

Contemporary socialists—"light" totalitarians in mindset and vocabulary—go wrong when they imagine that liberals are busily planning the perfect society, the best that is possible in the world, but *of opposite sign to their own.* Therein lies the essential futility of post-Communist debate. Consider, for example, how a socialist would interpret the following statement: "Cultural liberty is more propitious for literary and artistic creation than state *dirigisme.*" An empirical observation like this, supported by vast experience, obviously does not imply that *everything* created under conditions of liberty (or, contrariwise, by dissidents living under totalitarian conditions) has been or always will be a masterpiece. Yet this, evidently, is what socialists think it means! For they will scurry to point out that thousands of books and paintings and plays and movies produced in a free context are mediocre or worthless. The socialists, having proprietary rights on a system that resolves all conceivable problems, including problems of aesthetics, cling to the idea that eliminating the market will eliminate ugliness.

Needless to say, cultural totalitarianism has never produced anything *but* ugliness—a fact that doesn't bother its overlords in the
slightest. Didn't the socialist powers systematically strangle capitalist art in the cradle? If they were destroying art in the process
of reforming it, wasn't this simply the price that had to be paid for
aesthetic purification?

Artists, of course, have always known times when the market
was not sufficient to provide them with a living and when they had
to rely on subsidies from princes or republics or private patrons.
There have also been many creators whose favor with the general
public was quite enough to keep them alive, even to enrich them.
But neither market forces nor state support can guarantee the
presence of talent. The market can rain fortunes on a Carolus-
Duran or a Picasso alike, while the state can just as readily bestow
financial security on a genius or on some hack whose principal
talents are for toadying up to well-placed bureaucrats, political
logrolling and public relations chutzpah. So, when virtuosos of
the public treasury decree that the market per se is reactionary
and that state subvention is intrinsically progressive, they are not
merely being simplistic but reeking of self-interested parasitism
and jobbery.

During John Paul II's visit to Poland in June 1999, I heard a
radio journalist on France-Info "inform" his listeners by saying,
in substance, that the Pope knew the Polish people's return to
capitalism had brought them a certain prosperity, but to the detriment of social justice. The implication was that Communism
had brought them social justice, although numerous studies have
exposed the humbug behind this myth. To be sure, capitalism does
not bring equality, but Communism does so even less—and only
in the form of general impoverishment. Here again, socialism
was being judged by what it is intended to bring, and capitalism
by what it does bring.

But what does it bring, in fact? In 1989, the last year of Communism, a laid-off worker in the West received compensation
between five and ten times as much, in real purchasing power,
as the earnings of a worker with a so-called "job" in the East Bloc.
The capitalist democratic societies implemented by far the most

effective social welfare systems as protection against the economic uncertainties of life. You can reject this well-established fact only if you insist on comparing the perfection of what doesn't exist with the imperfection of what does.

★ ★ ★

The fight between socialism and liberalism is evidently rigged, and the more so in that it is dominated by confusion between a true market economy and capitalism per se, between laissez-faire policies and the lawless "jungle." It is disturbing, for example, that even a Nobel Prize winner in economics, Maurice Allais, can commit the spelling mistake of *laisser-faire,* with the infinitive, while inveighing against what he calls *"laisser-fairistes* perversions."[3]

Everyone knows, or ought to know, that the celebrated words of Turgot and the physiocrats—*"laissez faire, laissez passer"*—are synonymous with free enterprise and free trade. They are imperatives with an active connotation, quite unlike the indifferent apathy of a substantivized infinitive linked by a hyphen. *Laisser-faire* soon degenerates into *laisser-aller.** It is said that the expression *laissez faire* comes from a merchant, François Legendre (or Le Gendre), who was asked by Louis XIV's minister Colbert how best the king's government could aid commerce, and he replied, *"Laissez-nous faire."* ("Let *us* do it.")[4]

It is possible to have capitalism without free enterprise. A private sector without an open market—a private sector protected from competition by a compliant, paid-off political power—is the dream of many a capitalist. This was the system practiced for decades in Latin America, a form of capitalism called "savage" even though it was admirably organized to profit the ruling cliques. Thus in Chiapas, Mexico, we saw "Subcomandante Marcos" puffing out his chest as he nominated himself "leader

---

* *Translator's note: Laisser-aller: s.m. inv.* 1. unconstraint, free-and-easiness; abandon. 2. carelessness, slovenliness. (*Harrap's New Standard French and English Dictionary,* 1981).

in the global war against neoliberalism," which he described as a "crime against humanity." Actually, he was voicing the interests of an oligarchic capitalism bereft of a true market and closely tied to the monopoly of the Institutional Revolutionary Party that for forty years—*in the name of socialism*—systematically perpetuated the poverty and backwardness of the Mexican people.

For a long time, an antiliberal form of capitalism has been a specialty of Japan, and also of France. In my country, liberalism's enemies are mixed up in a potpourri that includes Communists, Trotskyists, right-wing extremists of the National Front (with an admixture of various socialists and another of Gaullists), lots of neo-Keynesians, cultural commissars and elites of the public sector: an ideological harlequinade of rainbow hues. Multifarious in motivation, they are united in self-interest. French capitalism for more than half a century has been, and remains today, in large part a *closed capitalism,* in direct reflection of our political arrangements. Any large-scale business transaction—such as the amalgamation of so-called "private" companies or a contract that affects both publicly and privately owned enterprises—is concluded only after consultation with and approval by the government, and often the president of the Republic himself. This tradition of closed capitalism has been shared by both ends of the political spectrum, justified either with appeals for social solidarity or on grounds of national autonomy. Both left and right have engaged in social engineering by legislation and have massively increased the tax burden. We owe one huge increment to Alain Juppé's center-right government. As Nicolas Baverez pointed out, this 1995 measure struck as hard a blow to our economy as did the 1973 oil crisis.[5]

I have already alluded to the unconscionable editing trick played on the author Alain Touraine with regard to his *Comment sortir du libéralisme?* Here I'd like to point out that someone interpolated the following statement into his essay: "The end of the liberal illusion has weakened and disoriented the right, which has been soundly rebuffed at the ballot box." In the first place, the right was less soundly rebuffed in the 1997 legislative elections than was the left in those of 1993. Second, we can safely say that neither the right nor the left in France has succumbed to any "liberal illusion" whatsoever. And even if it were an illusion, it would be one that the European Union has bought into: for Europe is dragging us, slowly but inexorably, out of the stagnant pond of "social statism" (to use Guy Sorman's phrase).[6] What *has* been rejected, in practice if not in principle, is the statist illusion shared by all French political parties.

The real situation has been astutely analyzed by Jacques Lesourne.[7] Former editor-in-chief of *Le Monde* and president of Futuribles International (an organization founded by Bertrand de Jouvenel, the famous author of *L'Économie dirigée*), Lesourne is an economist and sociologist who can hardly be characterized as a bloodthirsty ultraliberal. With a soupçon of provocation—and, I think, a degree of oversimplification—Lesourne advances the thesis that France from the Liberation to the late 1970s, economically speaking, was a Soviet Union that succeeded. This outcome was achieved under the aegis of the state through a compromise between the Marxists and the Christian socialists. It was characterized by a vast public sector, by state control of prices, salaries, exchange rates and capital circulation, and by credit restriction and regulation of the labor market. The application of this model coincided with a thirty-year boom that is sometimes dubbed the "Trente Glorieuses." Despite some gigantic errors, the system worked thanks to the efficiency of the French administrative bodies and an appreciable margin of initiative allowed to private businesses. But today, says Lesourne, the model is dysfunctional, broken down, out-of-date. The reason? Because it has proved incapable of adapting to the two great innovations that are transforming the world: globalization and the technology revolution. The historic changes unfolding before us constitute the death pangs of sovietism *à la française*.

When the national secretary of the French Communist Party, Robert Hue, hopes that the "plural" government of the left, in which Communist ministers play a part, will extricate itself from the "liberal ascendancy," he is perhaps looking too far ahead; for the current ascendancy is still of the statist kind.[8] But perhaps, on the other hand, M. Hue is venting well-founded fears, since the erosion of French-style sovietism has become irreversible, despite the bastions of privilege that give it shelter.

Only the market economy, based on free enterprise and democratic capitalism—that is, private-sector capitalism divorced from the state but wedded to the rule of law—can claim to embody liberalism. And this is what is being implemented in the world, often without the awareness of those who in practice are consolidating and extending it. Here the question is not whether it is the best or the worst system, for there is simply no other system, except in the imagination.

Such was Francis Fukuyama's thesis in his "End of History?" article of 1989, where he described "the end point of mankind's ideological evolution and the universalization of Western liberal democracy as the final form of government."[9] Fukuyama was expressing a truth at once self-evident and scandalous; and his book of the same title, after the initial worldwide success it enjoyed, became an object of opprobrium for the defenders of the defunct ideology once they were able to rally. Functioning totalitarianism doesn't have to be existent for those who hate liberty to persist in their efforts to abolish liberty. Even when the totalitarian world has been largely engulfed, even when its abettors find themselves embracing a void, their thirst to destroy liberty remains unquenched—as though its opposite were still a realizable program and a feasible eventuality.

CHAPTER FIVE

From Illusion
to Accountability

The *Passing of an Illusion* by François Furet enjoyed excellent sales when it was published in 1995. More remarkably, it was reviewed favorably by almost the entire intellectual and journalistic left. There had been other books highly critical of Communism that met with approval from the "masses," but these had been dismissed out of hand by the leftist elites.

So when *Le Monde*'s book section greeted Furet's work as a "masterpiece"—a title it rarely awards—this was cause for optimism: after all, didn't the book take issue with the political line followed by *Le Monde* for half a century? Perhaps the lesson to be drawn from the Communist aberration had finally been absorbed. Only a hardcore rearguard, entrenched in a handful of journals such as that veritable medieval fortress *Le Monde diplomatique,* saw fit to defend the fossilized ideology, issuing soothing dismissals and decreeing that Furet was a notoriously incompetent historian whose book was totally devoid of substance. But such exceptions may be put down to simplicity rather than malice, and those who applauded Furet came in large part from the ranks of readers whom the author, in effect, was telling to revise their convictions and commitments drastically.

At the time, I thought this unprecedented chorus of approval could be attributed to the ending of the Cold War: ideological combat had lost its central importance when so much less was at stake politically. It is true that I was underestimating the ability of ideologies to survive contact with more reality-based perspectives— a potential for expanding into the void, as it were. Even so, the Sartrean *mise en situation* in which *The Passing of an Illusion* made its appearance was very different from the historical context that had inspired similar books before the demise of Communism; these had been published in an era when there were still two opposing camps and when debates could have concrete consequences by influencing public opinion and elections in the free countries.

Unlike its predecessors, *The Passing of an Illusion* dealt not with the present but with the past. It was not politics that Furet addressed, but history—which perhaps goes some way toward explaining the weak-kneed resistance his book initially met. With his customary lucidity, Furet frankly confessed in an interview, "I could no doubt have written the book twenty years ago, but then it would have been virtually unpublishable. It would have stirred up a frightful controversy. Ideological intimidation was unrelenting in those days, and in France it was inconceivable that you could be leftist *and* anticommunist."[1*]

In addition to the protection afforded by the retrospective if not benign character of his analysis, Furet was shielded by his having remained "a man of the left"—certainly in socialist eyes and most probably even in the Communists' estimation. (In

---

* *L'Événement du jeudi*, February 9, 1995. Having published *The Totalitarian Temptation* twenty years earlier, I can confirm the accuracy of Furet's diagnosis. I experienced such annoyances and gave a full account of them, with documentary evidence, in my book *La Nouvelle Censure* (The New Censorship). Here I would like to take the opportunity to thank François for his friendship and encouragement during this episode; he used to congratulate me heartily for having been promoted to the rank of guinea pig in "an unparalleled sociocultural experiment."

his early days he had been a Communist Party member.) One of the symptoms of how intellectual debate has degenerated in France is that "where you're coming from" (to use that horrible expression) counts for more than what you are actually saying. François had accomplished the tour de force of continuing to be regarded as "on the left" by a left that he was criticizing as much as I was—and even more, for he had deprived it, in masterly fashion, of its founding myth: the French Revolution. In the above-quoted interview in *L'Événement du jeudi,* which he gave a short time before the 1995 presidential election, he took care to mention that he would have "no problem voting for Jospin." And with paradoxical illogicality, of which he was certainly aware, he added, "When I meet the leading people of the left, I am pained by their lack of historical understanding." An unimpeachable reason to vote for them, clearly!

A little more than two years after the appearance of Furet's book, in October 1997, *The Black Book of Communism* came out.[2] This massive (eight-hundred-page) compilation of data about Communist crimes, covering all Communist systems past and present, was the work of a team of historians under the direction of Stéphane Courtois. The book enjoyed even better sales than *The Passing of an Illusion,* but its reception by the intelligentsia was quite different: immediate and unrelenting fury. Even before the book went on sale, all the artifices, stratagems, deceits and frauds from the old Stalinist arsenal were deployed in attempts to discredit it. The non-Communist left joined in this campaign of defamation with a shrewdness in subterfuge, ardor in calumny and exuberance in vulgarity that often surpassed the excesses of the Communists themselves. And university authorities, with the means at their disposal to damage the careers of some of the book's authors, notably Nicolas Werth and Jean-Louis Margolin, pressured and intimidated them into disavowing the work they had contributed to.

Why the completely different reactions to the two books? Their subject was the same, albeit approached from different angles, and the plan was for François Furet to supply a preface to *The Black Book,* which only his sudden and tragic death in July

1997 prevented him from doing. Here were two fundamentally identical assessments, one of which was calmly if not enthusiastically received, while the other was peremptorily and angrily dismissed.

A plausible explanation for the disparity, it seems to me, is that people will sometimes acknowledge that they have succumbed to the seductions of an "illusion," but almost never will they admit to having been complicit in a crime. Furet treated Communism as an intellectual error, giving his book the subtitle "The Idea of Communism in the Twentieth Century." Courtois and his team, in contrast, were making the macabre inventory of the eighty million deaths that—in addition to the violent deaths incurred in wars and other "normal" catastrophes—may be directly imputed to the very logic of the system in question. To repeat my point: while error can be admitted, it is usually with much less grace that someone will confess to a crime, or to having been an accomplice to it, or to having looked away in full knowledge of what was going on.

It is true that Communists in the West, having never come to power, did not match their foreign exemplars in evil deeds. They were not guilty of crimes like those of the Soviet Union, or those perpetrated in China, in Cuba, in Vietnam, in Cambodia, in Ethiopia and other earthly paradises. But today we have innumerable proofs that they knew about them, for the most part—or could have known, if they had not cultivated the art of voluntary blindness.

Didn't Jean-Paul Sartre, one of the postwar period's great preceptors, inculcate the intellectual left with his theory of responsibility? Didn't he instruct us that it isn't necessary to have committed a crime personally in order to be responsible for it? That it suffices to have stood back, to have failed to search for some way to prevent it, if only by denunciation? And that if we have turned a blind eye, it is because we have *chosen* to let the crime be perpetrated? Commitment, according to Sartre—the *engagement* of existentialism—is not just a philosophical possibility; it is an inescapable fact of life. To be confronted with inescapable facts is not pleasant when, with regard to radical

Communist criminality, we have been enthusiastic supporters or sympathizers, or simply indulgent onlookers. Hence the bitter animosity focused on *The Black Book,* in contrast to the melancholy confessions that were reluctantly murmured in the wake of *The Passing of an Illusion.*

Here I will merely gesture toward the intellectual and historical riches within Furet's great book, to which I paid tribute on its first printing.[3] I will confine myself to summarizing, for readers concerned about the "illusion" and its continuing legacy, the two principal lines of argument that the author develops.

The first of these arguments throws us back on the central role of the "revolutionary passion" that was ignited by the 1789 Revolution in France and swept across other European countries—most importantly Italy, Germany, Spain and Russia—and then across the entire world. The idea that it is impossible to improve societies through a process of gradual reform, that progress requires all existing societies to be completely swept away and replaced with clean slates, as it were—this redemptive political vision allows us to understand how the proud thought of placing oneself in the service of a "radiant future" has been able to strangle the critical spirit and the moral sense of so many people, the deceived and the deceivers alike.

Furet's second argument—and for him doubtless the central one, the most pertinent for the century of actually existing Communism—consists in showing how, from the 1930s on, the sacred duty of antifascist struggle spawned a Holy Alliance of combined left-wing forces that the Communists cunningly manipulated to their advantage. Furet exposes the Comintern's strategy of "exploiting the accusation of fascism against all enemies, whether from the left or the right."[4] Before 1934, the Communists had been labeling as "fascists" not only Italian and German ideologues but also liberals and socialists of the democratic countries. Subsequently they made a concession: you could be sincerely antifascist even without being a Communist. But to qualify as an antifascist, you could not be tainted with anticommunism.

The ultimatum delivered to the left, and to all democrats, came in these terms: "You don't have the right to criticize Hitler unless you stop criticizing Stalin."* Which reduces to this: Being anticommunist makes you a fascist, or at the very least a reactionary. With this rule of thumb, the Communists handcuffed the entire left, and every democrat, right up to and beyond the 1939 Nonaggression Pact between Hitler and Stalin. This rule crystallized into a lasting taboo. Twenty years later it would find memorable expression in Jean-Paul Sartre's shattering assertion: "Every anticommunist is a dog." Even as late as 2000, despite actually existing Communism's collapse into infamy and ridicule, those who fought against it in its heyday are still tarred as "reactionaries." Over half a century after the disappearance of Nazism, over a decade since the fall of Communism, the propaganda machine perfected by the Comintern during the 1930s keeps on grinding away.

Upon the publication of *The Black Book of Communism*, accusations of fascism came quickly and proliferated on every side. The journal *L'Histoire* noted that the book's publication coincided with a National Front convention whose main agenda item was to put Communism on trial.[5] The same tip-off was made by *L'Humanité*, but this journal can claim the excuse of being true to form.[6] For a long time, *L'Humanité* has served as a useful device for establishing the truth or falsity of any proposition, since everyone knows that when something appears in its pages, you have only to take the opposite position to get the best possible approximation to the true state of affairs. Very handy indeed.

L'Humanité's line was followed, alas, by *Témoignage chrétien* and *Le Monde*.[7] In the latter, Patrick Jarreau fulminated the fateful anathema: "The reference [in *The Black Book*] to crimes against humanity and to the Nuremberg trials recalls the remarks made on several occasions by Jean-Marie Le Pen, president of the National Front." What is intriguing about this reflexive, ritual eructation is its intellectual poverty. How is it that for eighty years now the left

---

* Regarding these developments, see *Hitler ou Staline* (Flammarion, 1988), by Christian Jelen, who quotes Furet. It is symptomatic of the tenacity of the ideological lie that, even while glasnost was in full swing, this illuminating book was attacked by the French left, including non-Communists, in pure Stalinist style.

has never come up with anything better? Anyone who dares to confront the left with its real curriculum vitae, or even ventures to disagree with the left's judgments on literature, philosophy, economics or art, is automatically dismissed as "fascist." For *Le Monde*'s editor, Jean-Marie Colombani, *The Black Book* served as "an alibi for those who want to prove—one crime canceling out the other—that the last barriers protecting us from legitimization of the extreme right are obsolete." Here Colombani is manifesting a strange, utilitarian concept of what scholarly research is all about. How, by way of analogy, could historians' findings vis-à-vis the crimes committed by France in her colonies conceivably excuse those of Spain or England?

According to Madeleine Rebérioux, honorary president of the French Human Rights League, the ulterior motive lurking behind *The Black Book* was Stéphane Courtois's project to clear, "in a way" (what way, *s'il vous plaît?*), the name of Maurice Papon, the Vichyist prefect who was on trial in Bordeaux when the book was published.[8] There is no point in telling us over and over again that we must distinguish between Communism and Stalinism—the latter being a perversion of the former—since the nastiest kind of Stalinist low blows continue to be delivered on a daily basis by the Parisian intellectuals, both high and low, and their political clones.

The historian Pierre Vidal-Naquet detects, on the part of the devilish *Black Book*'s authors, the will to "substitute, in lieu of the crimes of Nazism, not just those of that universal foil, Stalinism, but those of Communism."[9] May we be permitted to observe that, until now, it is the crimes of the Nazis that have been systematically "instrumentalized" in order to occlude, minimize, even justify those of the Communists? May we also be allowed to register some astonishment at the notion that a tableau showing one set of totalitarian crimes could somehow attenuate the grievous crimes of the competition? An exhaustive, exact description of the one does not absolve the other. The converse is also true. Do sectarians who adduce arguments of this sort—who censor knowledge in accordance with the effect it might have on their cherished cause—deserve to be called seekers of truth?

Yet the sociologist Annette Wieviorka hauls up the flag of such a methodology: the banner, as it were, of a historico-sociological Lysenkoism. According to her, *The Black Book*'s real purpose was to "substitute Communist criminality for that of the Nazis in the collective memory."[10] What fantastic sleight of hand! How on earth could the study of one historical phenomenon be substituted in the collective memory for the study of another historical phenomenon? You have to smile indulgently when some political huckster tries to pull off such transparent tricks, but it's hard to do so when the swindler is someone with scholarly credentials. The key to the enigma is that these people are accusing others of a strategy that they themselves consistently resort to; but in their case, Nazism is the smokescreen used to prevent the real history of Communism from seeing the light of day.

In December 1997, I took part in an edition of Jean-Marie Cavada's television series *La Marche du siècle,* this one devoted to *The Black Book of Communism.* I recall how Robert Hue, the national secretary of the French Communist Party, made a highly revealing gesture: holding aloft a copy of Le Pen's journal, *National Hebdo,* he loudly accused Stéphane Courtois, also a guest on the show, of playing into the hands of the extreme right, who were agitating "to put Communists and Jews in the dock again." That tactics like these are still tolerated, that they do not permanently discredit those who employ them, and that the leading figure of a party that has representatives in parliament and participates in government can use them on a public television channel—while passing himself off as a "moderate" Communist, a Marxist thinker of a "new type"—proves that the French left is very far from having set the record straight about its contemporary history. This is the left, mind you, that aims to put history itself on trial rather than its own sorry record. Hasn't history been mistaken in giving Communism the sack, they ask, since Communists were and still are on the correct path? At the East-West colloquium I mentioned above, I heard a woman cry out, "Have we made mistakes? Never! It is history that has changed direction."[11]

Here let me hasten to exonerate a section of the intellectual and journalistic left—happily for France, an important section with the most authority—who proved themselves equal to the question posed by *The Black Book*, or more exactly, to the *answer* given by the book on the matter of Communist criminality. They rose to the occasion and saved the honor of their political family. In this they were quite unlike Pierre Bourdieu, who in a piece published in *Le Monde* wallowed in the sort of rubbish you find only among the "left of the left" (Bourdieu's own gem of a phrase, indispensable from now on).[12] According to him, our "ultraliberal" (bravo! a fine term!) society has been tormented by a "lurking, or openly declared *fascisation*."

Jean Daniel and Jacques Julliard in *Le Nouvel Observateur*, Jacques Amalric and Laurent Joffrin in *Libération*, and André Glucksmann are among those resolved to undertake the intellectual and moral duty of acknowledging the facts and then drawing appropriate conclusions. It is a duty that Jean-François Bouthors, in an article that appeared in *La Croix*, has beautifully expressed in lapidary fashion:

> Page by page, that's how this book should be read. Before launching into polemics, let us respect the victims whose fate it lays bare. Let us read every page, from first to last. And with each page turned, maybe we will say to ourselves: That was but one step—just one—of all the steps made by the deportees. And still we will be far from comprehending the drama, the suffering. . . . When we have made it all the way to the last page, then we can talk about it, debate it. Thus we can fulfill the duty of remembrance and pay honor to the victims. We must put them before ideology, before political intentions.[13]

★ ★ ★

Journalists often showed themselves to be more scrupulous with regard to historical truth than did certain academics ensconced in institutions of high learning and low deeds. I have already alluded to the treatment bestowed on two of the contributors to *The Black Book*: Nicolas Werth, author of the chapter on the

Soviet Union, and Jean-Louis Margolin, the China expert. Pressured by their superiors with what amounted to blackmail, these scholars, their careers in jeopardy, felt constrained to make public retractions, which they did on Bernard Pivot's *Bouillon de culture* program of November 13, 1997.

This abuse of power illustrates the ravages that the deadening hand of academic centralism inflicts on French intellectual life. In countries where teaching and research are disseminated across dozens of independent universities, scholars may find themselves at odds with the ideological coloration of their particular institution without therefore being impeded in their work or deprived of their livelihood. If their research has value, a rival university will want to hire them regardless of possible hostility toward their results. It is quite otherwise in France, where each area of research comes under the control of some potentate at the top of the hierarchy, the absolute master of appointments and grants, to whom a groveling intellectual and personal servility is indispensable for those who wish to survive. Nicolas Werth's boss, by forcing him to "retract," revealed the sorry state of his scholarly conscience; for an opinion can be retracted, but a fact cannot. To compel retraction on the part of a historian who has asserted, for example, that "Napoleon lost the Battle of Waterloo" is an act of totalitarian buffoonery, not legitimate historical controversy.

Such petty-minded vendettas should not be allowed to distract us from the essence of the problem. If *The Black Book* well and truly stirred up the "frightful polemics" that François Furet congratulated himself on managing to avoid with *The Passing of an Illusion,* the reason should be clear: by making a full inventory of Communism's crimes, by simply letting the facts speak for themselves, *The Black Book* amounts to a far more damaging indictment of Communism—and of those who cheered it on or came to terms with it—than does Furet's subtle work of the previous year.

The "revolutionary passion" invoked by Furet can, like all passions, be blind; and if it succumbs to belief in Communism, it is a weakness to be regretted. But it is not a crime. Antifascist solidarity could function as a trap for the unwary, but falling into

70

it was not necessarily dishonorable. The naïfs who did so were guilty of an error of judgment rather than a moral transgression. It wasn't pleasant to be reminded by Furet that you had been duped, but that didn't make you a criminal.

With *The Black Book,* we go from paternal admonitions to the court of assizes. The legions of Communist criminals file past, inventoried and gathered for the first time in an exhaustive synthesis. Of course, each of the dossiers contains information known for a long time, if only in part. But since the facts had reached the West usually in isolated dribs and drabs—sometimes about one Communist country, sometimes another—they had been relatively easy to contest, or ignore, or bury as quickly as possible. The story of the West's propensity to misinform itself had been amply documented even while the Cold War was still in progress.[14] *The Black Book*'s novelty, the reason why it made such a smashing impact, lay in its comprehensiveness. Moreover, it added new information to what was already available, the fruit of research by eminently qualified historians who tested, verified, corroborated and supplemented. A conclusion leaps out from the pages: Communism was something far worse than an "illusion." It was a crime. To have been a Communist was to have been an active participant or accomplice in a colossal crime against humanity.

The "connivance," to quote Cardinal Decourtray's unfortunate choice of terms to describe the attitude of large segments of the non-Communist left,* can be explained to some extent by the imperatives of the antifascist struggle. But this justification ceased to be pertinent after World War II, right up to the 1970s (an objection I raised with François Furet in my review of his book and in several public debates and private conversations I had with him). During these years, in the absence of any serious fascist threat in Europe and when Francoist and Salazarist remnants were fading, we saw socialists returning to Marxism and drawing closer to the French Communist Party and the Soviet Union, while those stubborn souls who insisted on looking at Communism without

---

* See Chapter 1, pp. 28–29, for details of Cardinal Decourtray's misadventure.

rose-tinted glasses were promptly hurled into that everlasting hell reserved for reactionaries. Furet goes a little too far when he suggests that socialists have always been respected by Communists on account of the famous precept "No enemies on the left!"

We don't need to go back as far as the Congress of Tours in 1920 and the immortal words of the all-too-mortal Louis Aragon: "Down with Léon Blum! Down with social democracy!" We have only to recall that the Second International, and in France the SFIO,* renewed their antitotalitarian tradition during the Resistance and after the war. The Socialist Jules Moch, interior minister from 1947 to 1950, was evidently not paralyzed by fear of seeming anticommunist when he unfeelingly cracked down on the insurrectionist strikes of winter 1947–1948, nor when he revealed before the National Assembly the secrets of the Soviet bank in France and the extent of its involvement in Moscow's financing of the French CP. And it was a Socialist prime minister, Paul Ramadier, who in May 1947 booted the Communist ministers out of the government. This was a time when the favorite saying of the SFIO was: "The Communists are not to the left, they are to the east." By then, the 1930s left-wing taboo against anticommunism and anti-Sovietism had been shattered, and it disintegrated completely after the 1953 popular uprising in East Berlin and those in Poland and Hungary in 1956—revolts that were crushed by the Soviet occupiers with customary savagery.

During the 1940s and 1950s, then, the old relation between the two lefts had been restored. Far from submitting obsequiously to the blackmail of "If you're an anticommunist, you must be a fascist," left-wing democrats turned the tables and became prosecutors: it was their turn to interrogate the Communists, challenging them to justify the Soviet Union's unspeakable actions in central Europe. Then Nikita Khrushchev's famous "secret" report of 1956 compromised the Communists' claim to be paladins for

---

* *Translator's note:* SFIO was the "Section Française de l'International Ouvrière" (French Section of the Workers' International). It was a predecessor of the Socialist Party.

liberty, a pretense that was further discredited five years later with the erection of the Berlin Wall.

The restoration of roles was a healthy development that made what followed all the more astonishing to behold: how during the fateful decade of the Sixties and beyond, the taboo placed on anti-communism by the left—and even by the right—was reinstated; and how in France the Socialist-Communist "Common Program" was adopted.* Far from being an outcome of electoral decisions by the majority, the Common Program represented a revival of deep Marxist-Leninist conviction among the new generation of socialists. Willy Brandt in Germany, Olaf Palme in Sweden, Kalevi Sorsa in Finland also understood social democracy in the pro-Soviet sense; and under their influence the Socialist International, for the first time in its history, began to pay court to Moscow. Only Portugal's Mario Soares and Spain's Felipe Gonzalez, among the social-democratic leaders in Europe, resisted this trend.

Although by this time it had become impossible to ignore the irredeemably despotic character of all the Communist regimes and their chronic cultural and economic failure, Western progressives were copying Communist doctrine more eagerly than ever. Thus in 1977 the Socialist Party brought forth a *Petite Bibliographie socialiste* for the theoretical edification of its members. This booklet was embellished with a preface by Lionel Jospin, the Socialist national secretary and future party leader, who was later to become minister of education and then prime minister of France. The list of "socialist classics" recommended for the avant garde consists almost exclusively of Communist productions. With the exception of Jaurès and Blum, who would have been difficult for French Socialists to purge, the *Petite Bibliographie* follows a pure Leninist logic, not mentioning the most important authors of the reformist Marxist tradition—Karl Kautsky, Otto Bauer or Edouard Bernstein. In lockstep with Bolshevik sectarianism, it consigns

---

* *Translator's note:* The "Programme commun" was signed by the Socialist Party, the Communist Party and the Radical Party of the Left in 1972. It was partially implemented after Mitterrand's presidential victory in 1981, leading to capital flight and economic malaise.

Lenin's bêtes noirs to oblivion. Prominent in the list of socialist classics are Marx and Engels, obviously, and Lenin himself, along with such luminaries as Rosa Luxemburg, Antonio Gramsci, Mao Zedong (whose crimes had been amply documented and the inanity of whose "thought" had been exposed for all to see by Simon Leys) and Fidel Castro, another virtuoso of the firing squads, whom even the Soviets had never elevated to the status of a thinker. The reader can only regret that the Socialist Party didn't see fit to exhort its activists to soak themselves in the works of those intellectual titans Kim Il Sung and Enver Hoxha.

To make the excommunication of anticommunists contingent upon the necessity of countering fascism smacks of the sort of argument that Furet himself, in his *Interpreting the French Revolution*,[15] censures as an empty "justification from circumstances"—in this case, imaginary circumstances.

Let me add, by the way, that *The Passing of an Illusion* already contained everything needed to silence *The Black Book's* critics. And Furet would not have agreed to add a preface to the Herculean labors of Stéphane Courtois and his team if he hadn't been convinced that their findings were solid. The public's simplified image of Furet's essay was based on the twin notions of "illusion" and "antifascist front"—just as any intellectual analysis that manages to gain a mass audience will ipso facto be reduced to a few simple ideas.

The mystery surrounding the reactions to *The Black Book* resides in the strange fact that the pharisaic pleading for Communism and the sly rage directed against the anticommunists has survived not only the passing of the fascist threat but also the vanishing of hope for Communism. Furet eloquently clarified this paradox in the epilogue to his book, where he wrote about how, "On the eve of the implosion of the regime founded by Lenin, anticommunism is without a doubt more widely condemned in the West than it was in the fair-weather days of victorious antifascism."

Since 1917, none of the arguments advanced in favor of actually existing Communism have stood up to reality and none of its vaunted objectives have been attained: not liberty, not prosperity, not equality, not peace. And so it sank under the weight of its own vices rather than the blows of its adversaries. Yet perhaps never before has it found so many ferocious defenders willing to twist the facts so unscrupulously.

What self-abrogation, to take up arms valiantly for a political and ideological system devoid of a future, even a present, and with a past so sterile, bloody and grotesque! Voluntary sacrifice of one's intellect, pushed to such an extreme, commands a certain respect, but it remains an enigma—one that dwells within the very heart of humanity.

CHAPTER SIX

Panic among the Revisionists

Pro-Nazi revisionists are few in number; the Communist variety are legion. In France, there is a law that provides for sanctions against the lies of Holocaust deniers.* Yet Communists are permitted to lie with impunity about the crimes of their chosen camp. Here the word "camp" may be taken as referring not only to a political position but to all that the word implies in its plural form: the Soviet gulag of yesterday as well as China's network of concentration camps, the Laogaï, which is in full swing today, with thousands of summary executions every year. These are but the most notorious examples of a type of institution endemic to all Communist regimes.

Accustomed to a double standard that let Communism off the hook, its apologists were dumbfounded by the mass of evidence presented in *The Black Book of Communism* that convincingly

---

* *Translator's note:* The Gayssot Act, named after the Communist deputy who proposed it—evidently someone who gazed upon crimes against humanity with one eye shut.

77

supports a two-part verdict: Communism always and necessarily engenders criminality, and in this respect it is indistinguishable from Nazism.

The blasphemers who made this case were met with a torrent of imprecations. *Le Monde's* editor rolled out the accusation of *amalgame,* or mixing things up. Lily Marcou was completely unaware that she committed precisely that sin when, with similar poverty of imagination, she anathematized this "gift offered to the National Front while the Papon trial was in progress."* Here Marcou exemplifies a favorite trick of the pro-totalitarian left, namely refusing to take the facts into consideration, even if they are admitted to be true, under the pretext that the moment is wrong to talk about them because it might help the fascists. For the Communist Gilles Perrault, the book amounted to an "intellectual imposture," and for the Trotskyist Jean-Jacques Marie it was a "fraud." The intellectual poverty of such invectives is staggering. They have been repeated without change in every decade following the Russian Revolution, heaped on such figures as Panaït Istrati, Boris Souvarine, Victor Serge, André Gide, Arthur Koestler, David Rousset, Victor Kravtchenko, Robert Conquest—the list goes on. Identical abuse was hurled at *The Gulag Archipelago* almost twenty years after Khrushchev's confessional report. If you want to study a mental system that functions altogether outside the realm of facts and that automatically rejects any data contradicting its worldview, you can do no better than contemplate the Communist enemies of a scientific history.

Card-carrying Communists or their sworn protectors in the media may turn out to be more adept in the art of evasion than their clumsy fellow-traveling allies. They may even concede that "it is not a question of denying the crimes reported in *The Black Book,*" in the words of Régine Deforges in her *L'Humanité* column.[1] So what is it a question of, then? Simply to maintain that those crimes are in no way representative of Communism.

---

* *Translator's note:* In 1998, after a controversial six-month trial, Maurice Papon was sentenced to ten years in jail for ordering the deportation of 1,600 Jews to Nazi Germany.

This is the strategy that the national secretary of the French Communist Party, Robert Hue, would unflappably deploy during the *Marche du siècle* television broadcast that I took part in, along with Stéphane Courtois, Andrei Gratchev (former spokesman for Gorbachev and author of *L'Histoire vraie de la fin de l'URSS*),[2] the cabaret star Jean Ferrat and the former Communist International member Jacques Rossi, who was nearly ninety years old. Like many good and faithful servants of the Soviet regime, Rossi had been arrested in Moscow on trumped-up charges and sent to the gulag, where he spent nineteen instructive years. Thus he was amply qualified to write his *Gulag Handbook,* where he demonstrates, as an experienced patron of this type of holiday facility, that it was much more than a repressive system of labor and death camps. The gulag "served as a *laboratory* for the Soviet regime in order to create *an ideal society:* to compel obedience and indoctrinate." (My italics.)[3] For the Communists participating in the TV debate, these were unpleasant words to hear.

Throughout that evening, Robert Hue stuck to his two-stage plan of battle: We admit (he said) the reality of the abominations described in *The Black Book*. But these abominations have *nothing to do with Communism*. They are a perversion. They don't follow from Communism; they betray it.

One can only admire the ingenuity of "scientific" socialists when they argue that historical phenomena—phenomena that, moreover, display the irksome habit of repeating themselves with the regularity of astronomical rotations—have no cause. Incarceration camps and prisons, show trials, murderous purges and deliberately induced famines have accompanied each and every Communist regime from beginning to end, without exception. And this unvarying pattern is fortuitous? The true essence of Communism lies in what it has never been and what it has never produced? What, then, is this system, which we are told is the best ever conceived by mankind but which comes with the added supernatural property of never implementing anything, anywhere, but its own opposite, its own perversion?

On another television program a month earlier, *Bouillon de culture,* apologists had already mounted the same defense: that the history of Communism as it really was had nothing to do with Communism. If that is so, why persist in denying the deeds of totalitarian regimes that supposedly were not Communist? If these remain so dear to your hearts, they must in fact have been Communist, or at least somewhat. But if they were not, we are left with, on one hand, a set of causes capable of producing the most sublime perfection, and on the other, a set of effects that are among the most execrable in human history. Here we are dealing no longer with historical materialism but with black magic. Despite the implausibility of their frenzied sophistry, the ideologues on this occasion achieved their aim, which was to interrupt their historian opponents constantly so that the viewers had little or no chance of learning what *The Black Book* was actually all about. As a parting shot, one Communist even contrived to brand Stéphane Courtois an anti-Semite.

In the *Marche du siècle* program, Robert Hue dished up the same sort of cant: Communism was a marvelous fruit-bearing tree that, by some incomprehensible stroke of bad luck, had produced only poisonous mushrooms. As accompaniment to this powerfully argued piece of reasoning, the singer Jean Ferrat put on a show of whining sentimentality: he was moved by Communist generosity, fraternity, hope and so forth. Hue had come to hem and haw, and Ferrat to weep and wail. The duettists got well into gear, leading up to a grand finale where they reprised the little trick employed by the worthy comrades on *Bouillon de culture*. This was the moment, which I have already described, when the CP secretary tugged a copy of Le Pen's journal *National Hebdo* from his sleeve and brandished it before the camera, accusing Courtois, Rossi and me of playing into the fascists' hands. In our despicable Gang of Three conspiracy, Jacques Rossi's ingenious ruse must be considered particularly reprehensible, for hadn't he pushed reactionary vice so far as to be locked up in the gulag for nineteen years, with the sole design—plain for all to see—of playing to the anticommunist propaganda of the yet to be established National Front?

But who is not "fascist" at one time or another, in Communist eyes? No one has been exempt. Before the creation of the Popular Front in 1936, when the slogan of the day became "united action," socialists were routinely labeled "social fascists" by the French CP and the Communist International.

Another lesson that emerged from *The Black Book* was even more difficult for the left to digest: the kinship of Communism and Nazism. This is what Jacques Rossi points to when he writes, in *The Gulag Handbook*, "It is pointless to debate which of the totalitarianisms in our century was the most barbarous, when both of them enforced ideological conformity (*la pensée unique*) and left mountains of corpses." The close relationship between the two systems is a recurrent theme of writers on the left, but it is periodically and adroitly buried from sight. Romain Rolland, a relatively lucid supporter of the Bolshevik revolution prior to the disgrace of Stalinism, wrote in 1922, "On the subject of Bolshevism, I have never wavered. A bearer of noble ideas (or rather, since ideation has never been its forte, a promoter of a great cause), Bolshevism has ruined these ideals with its narrow intolerance, stupid intransigence and cult of violence. It gave rise to fascism, which is the mirror image of Bolshevism."[4] François Furet, who quotes Roland's remark in *The Passing of an Illusion,* gives other examples of democrats who, even when the quasi-inviolable taboo against criticizing Communist-antifascist solidarity was in force, had the courage to keep reminding us of the cousinship between the competing totalitarianisms.

In June 1935, when Stalin had just dispatched the dissident Victor Serge to Siberia, an Italian antifascist professor, Gaetano Salvemini, exiled by Mussolini, stepped up to the rostrum in a room almost entirely under the thumb of the Comintern and its delegate, Willy Münzenberg, and dared to say, "I wouldn't feel I had the right to protest against the Gestapo and against the Fascist

OVRA* if I tried to forget that a Soviet political police also exists. There are concentration camps in Germany and prison islands maintained by the Italians. In Soviet Russia there is Siberia. . . . It is in Russia that Victor Serge is held prisoner." Serge himself, in 1944, would write that "Stalinist totalitarianism is the terrible successor to Nazi totalitarianism." And in January 1940, Léon Blum wrote in *La Populaire,* the Socialist Party organ, "For a long time now, Stalin has apparently been demonstrating a pronounced predilection for the German-Soviet alliance. We have often been alerted to this penchant of Stalin's, along with his hatred and scorn for the Western democracies, by our Menshevik comrades or by disillusioned Communists such as Boris Souvarine." Note here *en passant* how an untouchable like Souvarine has again— provisionally, of course—become mentionable. In 1935, only with great difficulty could he find a publisher for his *Staline,* a monument of historiography on Bolshevism. After the war, relegated once more to the lower depths of "visceral anticommunism," his book became virtually unobtainable until its republication over forty years later.[5] Doubtless Blum's article was dictated in part by the terrible blow dealt to the left in the preceding summer of 1939 when the Nazi-Soviet Nonaggression Pact was consummated.

But this is not the whole story, for a tradition of socialist antitotalitarianism goes back as far as the 1920 Congress of Tours. Many other documents could be adduced in support of this thesis; the parallel between the two totalitarianisms long predates the publication of *The Black Book* in 1997 and was often pointed out, despite the intellectual terrorism that reigned when these violent regimes coexisted. If this parallel subsequently became subject to an ever sterner interdict, two reasons were proffered as justification. The first was that the Soviet Union joined in the war against Hitler. The second was the unique, incommensurable character of the Shoah.

---

* *Translator's note:* OVRA stands for Organizzazione di Vigilanza Repressione dell'Antifascismo (Organization for Vigilance Against Antifascism), Mussolini's secret police.

In objection to the first argument, it has often been remarked that Stalin found himself in the Allied camp against his will. He could not have asked for more than to relax in peace, quietly digesting the territorial gifts conferred on him by Hitler in 1939 in order to buy his neutrality. It was Germany that launched a surprise attack on Russia, after all, not the other way around. The Soviet leadership was caught unprepared and was seized with panic. Moreover, the argument that Communism was essentially democratic because it warred against fascists is no more acceptable than its obverse: that Nazism was democratic because it joined the fight against Stalinism. We have not absolved, on the pretext of an anti-Bolshevik crusade, the French *collabos* who fought side by side with the Nazis or who gave them ideological support, even if we share their view that Communism is unacceptable. Nor should we dignify with the label "democrat" those Communists who fought against fascism. Tyrants may wage war on each other. Saddam Hussein and the Ayatollah Khomeini may be locked in mortal struggle without either of them on that account turning miraculously into democrats.

Real democrats who find themselves by force of circumstance on the same side as totalitarians must never forget that their provisional allies have very different motives from their own. Unfortunately, the democracies have only rarely evinced a clear understanding of this point.

The argument emphasizing the exceptional character of the Holocaust, on the other hand, is entirely valid and must be acknowledged as such by any honest observer of good faith. But it does not follow that the extermination of the European Jews must be regarded as the only crime against humanity ever perpetrated, or even the only genocide. In 1945 the French public prosecutor at Nuremberg, François de Menthon, stressed the ideological motivation for the Nazi crimes: "We are confronted here not with accidental or incidental criminality; we find ourselves facing a systematic criminality deriving directly and necessarily from a doctrine." This definition of a crime against humanity is precisely applicable not only to the Nazi crimes but also to those of the Communists. Even clearer, the French Criminal Code (*Code pénal*) of 1992 corroborates this equivalence when it includes in the concept of a crime against humanity "deportations; forcing into slavery; extensive and systematic summary executions; arrests followed by disappearances; torture; politically, philosophically, racially, or religiously motivated acts of an inhuman nature executed as a concerted plan of action against a group within the civilian population." In fact, systematic massacres and deportations of social and ethnic groups—on account of what they *are* and not what they *do*—punctuate the entire history of Communism. For example, on December 27, 1929, Stalin announced "a policy of liquidating the kulaks as a class."[6]

Again, according to our Criminal Code, any crime "committed in the name of a state practicing a policy of ideological hegemony" and "in the execution of a concerted plan aiming at the partial or total destruction of a national, ethnic, racial or religious group, or of a group defined by any other arbitrary criterion," is a crime against humanity. Here we might be reading a thumbnail sketch of the histories of the principal Communist regimes. It is all documented in *The Black Book*. For instance, the method followed in Russia by the GPU, forerunner of the KGB, was that of quotas: each region had to arrest, deport or shoot given percentages of people belonging to specific social, ideological or ethnic groups. What mattered was not the individual nor the individual's possible guilt (with respect to what?), but the group to which he or she belonged.

But periodically, the suggestion that Communism and Nazism are comparable is suppressed, so that whenever a new author brings it up the left regurgitates the same tiresome quibbles in the effort to bury it once again.

Thus, when in November and December 1996 the television channel France 3 broadcast a well-documented miniseries about the Hitler-Stalin collaboration,[7] which focused particularly on the fact that the political complicity and mutual admiration of the dictators long predated their 1939 alliance, the response was a withering silence. A year later, the success of *The Black Book* caused the silence to be broken, although elements of the left did what they could to discredit it. Some of the book's contributors were induced to retreat and in the pages of *L'Humanité* to state the opposite of what they had set forth in their essays. For her part, Madeleine Rebérioux, honorary president of the Human Rights League, argued that Communism and Nazism cannot be compared because the former, although it was responsible for murdering at least a hundred million people, did not act on grounds of racial discrimination—a statement that is not altogether true.[8] But what her argument ignores is that the massacre of any human group, however defined, because of what it is and for no other reason, is a totalitarian crime whose essence is the same regardless of who are the perpetrators.

With regard to the Human Rights League: on the request of its president, Victor Basch, this organization in 1936 set up a commission to enquire into the purge trials that were then going on in Moscow. Both Basch and the league lawyer Raymond Rosenmark were members of the commission. After a trip to Moscow, Rosenmark concluded that the accused were in fact guilty. To excuse the rigged trials, he relied on a sublime argument of Émile Kahn, the league's secretary-general: "If Captain Dreyfus had confessed, there would have been no Dreyfus affair." Invoking Dreyfus to justify the judicial murder of innocents is a tour de force of cynicism and hypocrisy. Indeed, it caused astonishment among some naïfs. The league quickly shut them up. *Les Cahiers de la Ligue* censored letters of protest from some members and rejected an article by Magdeleine Paz criticizing the Rosenmark report. After the second trial in January 1937, the league dismissed a motion demanding that it make an appeal to the Soviet embassy. After this, the so-called commission of enquiry disintegrated into the nothingness from which, truth to tell, it had never really emerged, for it had never been anything but a mouthpiece for the vicious state prosecutor Andrei Vyshinsky. The memory of such complicity in crimes against humanity ought to have inspired in Mme Rebérioux a little more repentance on behalf of her predecessors and a little less pride in herself. It is hard to see how revisionism and denial are criminal offenses when they concern the Nazis but perfectly acceptable with respect to the Communists.

Or maybe it is not so hard. I tried to frame this problem and propose a solution in *The Totalitarian Temptation*. The key to these stupid debates resides in an easily observable phenomenon: in every society, including democratic societies, there is a sizeable proportion of men and women who hate liberty—and consequently truth. The aspiration to live in a tyrannical system, whether as a participant in the exercise of power or, more strangely, as a slave to it, serves to explain the otherwise inexplicable rise and longevity of totalitarian regimes in countries that are among the most civilized on earth, such as Germany, Italy, China—or Russia at the beginning of the twentieth century, which was not at all the nation of savages depicted in Communist propaganda.

Communism's stroke of genius was to authorize the destruction of liberty in the name of liberty. It allowed liberty's enemies to carry out their work of annihilation, or to exonerate those who carried out the work, under a "progressive" rationale. As soon as historians and political philosophers, staying within the factual record, reject this rationale and acknowledge the morphological and behavioral identity of the two systems, the subterfuge of the "progressive" enemies of liberty promptly collapses. Which explains why the ideologues struggle against recognizing the family resemblance in question with such tenacity, tirelessly recycling their threadbare sophisms.

These vacuous arguments, always the same, consist of denying the intrinsically criminogenic nature of Communism or loudly call for the opening of a Black Book of Capitalism. Well, it is impossible to deny that the capitalist states have committed crimes; every state in history has. But apart from the obvious fact that the democracies' crimes have been far less constant, less massive in scale and fewer in number, the fundamental difference lies elsewhere. It is qualitative: the capitalist democracies don't *need* to commit crimes in order to survive, while the totalitarian states have no alternative. The question is not whether capitalism, Christianity, Islam, monarchies or republics have or have not committed criminal acts. We know the answer, and the answer is Yes. The question should be: Are their acts always and necessarily criminal? And here the answer is No. Conversely, criminality is an intrinsic condition of Communism and a necessity for its survival.

As for the objection that the carnage was less extensive in Hungary and Czechoslovakia than in the USSR and China, this is scarcely a loophole. The rigged trials and judicial murders so dear to the Human Rights League flourished (as they do in Cuba today) in those peripheral colonies, where Red Army divisions were based in camps within striking distance so that rebellions against the regime could be bloodily put down. According to its apologists, although Communism everywhere and always engendered crimes, it was not criminogenic—a rather curious application of the causal principle.

If one must concede that crimes against humanity were committed, another defensive stratagem is to deny that the regime responsible for those crimes was *really* Communist. The trophy in this domain goes to Jean Lacouture, who in his book *Survive le peuple cambodgien*,[9] after admitting (to his credit) that he was wrong to praise the Khmer Rouge, goes on to deny flat-out that Pol Pot and his accomplices were guided by Communist ideology. According to Lacouture, Pol Pot's regime was a "tropical fascism" and a "rice-paddy social nationalism." Just so, when it is beyond dispute that a Marxist ideologue in the purest Leninist tradition has behaved like a Nazi executioner, the explanation is simple: Clearly, he wasn't a Communist—he was a Nazi.

So today the battle to deprive liberty's enemies of their sordid subterfuges continues to be just as urgent as ever. First, this is because Communism, with its fraudulent ideological props, continues to kill. In Tibet, for example, at least 1.2 million people have lost their lives on account of China's occupation. The Communists have perpetrated not only the physical liquidation or enslavement of the Tibetans, but also the annihilation of an entire culture, including the destruction of almost all its monasteries and libraries and a ban against speaking and teaching the Tibetan language. Tibet presently has eight million Chinese colonists, forcibly transported, as against six million Tibetans.

The second reason we must continue without letup to oppose any attempt at obscuring Communism's inherent tendencies and kinship to Nazism is that the ideology, while it has retreated considerably since the Soviet Union's collapse, remains a source of hope for the enemies of liberty, always avid to install oppressive hierarchies on the pretext of defending the oppressed. Two academics—one a philosophy professor at the University of Paris VIII and the other a political scientist at the Lyon Institute of Political Studies—put their names to an interminable article in a recent issue of *Le Monde,* in which the following stands out: "Contrary to what François Furet seems to think, the history of social liberation is not simply a story of ineluctable totalitarian catastrophe. From the struggle of the oppressed rise images of an emancipation that could be *actualized in new contexts.*" (My italics.)[10] This is an exemplary declaration since it contains both a lie and a threat. The lie skirts the fact that Communism has nothing whatsoever to do with "the history of social liberation": in practice it has been liberation's worst enemy. The implicit threat is the disquieting promise to work toward another "emancipation" by gulag within some mysterious "new contexts." What's more, whoever points to the equivalence of fascism and socialism is right-wing, and whoever is right-wing is, deep down, on the extreme right and therefore a fascist!

Nothing has changed since those days when, in 1975, Bernard Chapuis could write in *Le Monde,* "Aleksandr Solzhenitsyn regrets that the West came to the aid of the USSR against Nazi Germany. . . . Before him came Westerners like Pierre Laval who thought no differently, and people like Doriot and Déat who greeted the Nazis as liberators." The author of *The Gulag Archipelago* was no better served by the Spanish left. In March 1967—six months after Franco's death and when King Juan Carlos's democratic reforms were under way—after giving a television interview in which he asserted that there were far more liberties in Spain than in the Soviet Union, he found himself the target of this blunderbuss assault by the left-wing but non-Communist author Juan Benet: "I firmly believe that as long as types like Aleksandr Solzhenitsyn exist, concentration camps will continue to exist. Perhaps the camps ought to be a little better guarded, so that the Solzhenitsyns of this world can't get out."[11] M. Benet remains, nonetheless, a "respected" intellectual.

In summary, then, an element of the left, more numerous than might be thought, needs to think that anyone who isn't a socialist must be a Nazi. That is why they fight so savagely to block realization of a truth: the fundamental, concrete identity of the two totalitarian systems. The controversies surrounding this posited equivalence will remain unintelligible and irresolvable as long as one has lost sight of the tendencies that unite them—how in fact they operate; and of what separates them—their ideologies.

There are two sorts of totalitarian systems. There is the kind whose ideology is what I would call *direct,* and which is readily decipherable: Hitler and Mussolini always made it plain that they despised democracy, freedom of expression and culture, political pluralism and independent unions. Long before his accession to power, the Führer painstakingly set forth his racist and, more specifically, anti-Semitic ideology for all to see. Supporters and adversaries of this category of totalitarianism find themselves right from the start on one side or another of a clearly drawn line of demarcation. No one was "deceived" by Hitlerism, for Hitler only carried out what he had promised all along; and he was brought down only by external forces.

Communism differs from direct totalitarianisms in that it has recourse to ideological dissimulation: it is *mediatized by Utopia* (to use a little Hegelian jargon). A detour via Utopia allows an ideology (and the power system that it purports to legitimize) to proclaim one success after another without interruption, while in reality its results are diametrically opposed to the vaunted agenda. Communism promises abundance and engenders misery; it promises liberty and imposes servitude; it promises equality and ends up with the most inegalitarian of all societies, with a nomenklatura class that is privileged to a degree unknown even in feudal societies. It promises respect for human life and then perpetrates mass executions; it promises access to culture for all, only to lay waste to culture; it promises the creation of a "new man," but instead it fossilizes him. Yet many believers will persist in accepting the contradictions because *Utopia is always located in the future.* The intellectual trap of a totalitarian ideology "mediatized" by Utopia is therefore much more difficult to foil than that of direct ideology because, to utopian believers, actually occurring events can never prove their ideology false.

France had already experienced, had even invented, this politico-ideological configuration with Robespierre and the Jacobin dictatorship. The subtle stratagem in question—the conjoining of totalitarianism with utopianism—was unmasked with merciless precision by Russian dissidents writing from the depths of the labor camp system. These Eastern intellectuals became our instructors in the West—masters who were often ignored, misrepresented and slandered, because Western intellectuals, having never lived under actually existing totalitarianism, clung obstinately to its utopian façade.

Right at the beginning, Nazism let the cat out of the bag; but Communism concealed its true nature behind Utopia. It allowed for satisfaction of the appetite for domination and for servitude alike under the mask of generosity and love of freedom; for inequality under the mask of egalitarianism; and for deception under the mask of sincerity. This most efficient form of totalitarianism, the only socially presentable kind and the longest lasting, was not the kind that worked Evil in the name of Evil, but the kind that worked Evil in the name of Good. This is what makes it *even less* excusable, for its duplicity enabled it to ensnare millions of worthy people who were taken in by its promises. We cannot really hold it against them that they were deceived. But the same cannot be said of their deceivers: the prominent politicians and intellectuals who knowingly escorted them down the garden path—and still do today. They know what they are doing. And when they invoke good intentions, they are consciously exploiting the perennial utopian drive.

I can still hear the great orchestra conductor Sergiu Celibidache as he strode along the rue Saint-Jacques in Paris, where he lived, angrily expostulating against *"Les intentions! Les intentions! Les idéaux! Les idéaux!"* Sergiu was of Romanian origin and had known Communism from up close. It is not advisable to form your opinion about a political system by taking at face value the deceptions of those who have profited from it or by sheepishly following credulous dupes in all their credulity. Utopian totalitarianism's infinite capacity for self-justification, in contrast to direct totalitarianism, explains why, even at this late date, so many of its servants go about unscathed by feelings of shame or regret. Perched in their immaculate Utopia, they absolve themselves of crimes to which they were the angelic accomplices, in the name of ideals they have shamelessly trampled underfoot.

That is why the slightest reminder of Communism's historical record, of the reality that threatens to expose the utopian camouflage, instantly throws its minions into paroxysms. This sort of convulsion afflicted the Socialist prime minister of France, Lionel Jospin, in the autumn of 1997 when a deputy for the opposition at the National Assembly was allowed to ask him what conclusions the Socialist Party would draw from the facts contained in *The Black Book,* which had just come out and which everyone was talking about. Beside himself with irritation, Jospin began his retort with the irrelevant charge that the liberal opposition in the nineteenth century had been in favor of slavery and against Dreyfus! Overlooking how utterly beside the point his muddled (to say the least) diatribe was, we should nevertheless note that the prime minister evidently was unaware of the Socialist Party's ambiguous posture in the Dreyfus affair. As for slavery, Victor Schoelcher, who in 1848 brought about its final abolition in the French colonies, was not a socialist but a bourgeois liberal. Moreover, the "Nation of the Rights of Man" was preceded in this respect by England: Viscount Castlereagh outlawed the slave trade at the Congress of Vienna in 1815. Then, in 1833, slavery was finally abolished throughout the British Empire by an act of Parliament—fifteen years before France emancipated her own slaves.

It is instructive to see how the left manages with such a clear conscience to suppose that none of the good deeds that have improved humanity's lot could have emanated from any other source than the Socialist or Communist parties. What Jospin, leader of the "plural" but not coherent left, was careful not to say was that slavery was *re-established* in the twentieth century in the Soviet Union, Communist China, Cuba, North Korea and Vietnam. His version of the Communists' record is altogether fanciful: he depicts them as incorruptible defenders of liberty, unstained adversaries of Nazism, faithful allies of the socialists. Obfuscations like these show to what extremes of absurdity an intelligent and moderate man will go when he falls prey to ideological passion. How can you keep harping so insistently on the "duty of remembrance" and yet so easily forget?* How, after everything we have seen and learned, could a Socialist prime minister have aligned himself so completely with the farcical Communist account of history, the lies made up wholesale after World War II by the CP and the International? François Furet put it well: "Socialists have something of a Bolshevik superego, and for this reason they greeted the fall of the Berlin Wall with dismay."[12]

But does this excess of emotion, this "Bolshevik superego," stem solely from a sense of guilt over the fact of Communism's criminality, the realization that it betrayed Utopia? Or does it rather arise from the awful suspicion that the criminality in question has philosophical roots that are deeper and more ambiguous than can be admitted? That Communism's ideological origins are in fact too close for comfort to those of Nazism?[13]

---

* See Appendix B for an interview I gave to *Le Figaro* on the subject of the prime minister's outburst.

CHAPTER SEVEN

The Intellectual and Moral Origins of Socialism

Can Communism be compared to Nazism? After the publication of *The Black Book of Communism* in 1997, the perpetual sparring over this question degenerated into a vicious brawl, not only in France but in a number of other countries—particularly in Italy and Germany. The non-Communists on the left, who often seem more eager for witch burning than the Communists themselves, were convulsed with anger against the profaners. They hurled onto the bonfire both Stéphane Courtois, guilty of sacrilegiously linking "the two totalitarianisms," and Alain Besançon, who (in a 1997 lecture at the Institut de France) had likewise violated the taboo against putting them on the same plane.[1] Many a fundamentalist, you see, still bows down before the mummified corpse of Communism.

Throughout the row, however, the left's argument had little to do with the facts of Communist criminality, now impossible to deny. Invoked instead was the old line about purity of intentions. Ever since the early days of the Bolshevik revolution, we have been served enough of this insipid yet noxious potion to induce nausea. The standard evasion goes like this: the abominations of actual socialism are characterized as deviations, or treasonous perversions of "true" Communism, which can only emerge strengthened from beneath the deluge of calumnies heaped upon it.

But this account of redemption through good intentions is undermined by an impartial and, above all, comprehensive exploration of socialist literature. Already among the most authentic sources of socialist thought, among the earliest doctrinarians, are found justifications for ethnic cleansing and genocide, along with the totalitarian state, all of which were held up as legitimate and even necessary weapons for the success and preservation of the revolution. Socialism's canonical principles were not at all violated by Stalin or Mao when they implemented their murderous policies; on the contrary, Stalin and Mao were scrupulous in applying these principles with perfect fidelity to the letter and the spirit of the doctrine—as has been rigorously established by the Cambridge scholar George Watson in his treatise on *The Lost Literature of Socialism*.[2]

In the modern hagiography of socialism, an essential part of the theory has been quite effectively suppressed. The true believers, while claiming socialism's founding fathers as their mentors, very early on dispensed with any thorough study of them, even of Marx himself. And today, the key texts seem to enjoy the rare privilege of being understood by everyone, without actually having been read in their entirety by anyone—not even by socialism's adversaries, who for fear of reprisal are likely to quell their own curiosity. (History for the most part is a selective rearrangement of the facts, and the history of ideas does not escape this general law.)

Study of the unexpurgated texts, writes Watson, shows us that "Genocide was an idea unique to socialism."[3] Friedrich Engels, in an article penned in 1849 for the *Neue Rheinische Zeitung*, a periodical edited by his friend Karl Marx, called for extermination of the Hungarians, who had risen up against Austria. He had a low opinion also of Serbs and other Slavic peoples, and of the Basques, the Bretons and the Scottish Highlanders—all problems that needed to be eliminated. Three-quarters of a century later, in his *On Lenin and Leninism* (1924), Stalin would recommend study of Engels' influential piece. Marx himself, in "Revolution and Counter-Revolution in Germany," published in the *Neue Rheinische Zeitung* in 1852, asked how "those moribund peoples, the Bohemians, the Carinthians, the Dalmatians etc.," might be disposed of.

For Marx and Engels, race mattered. The latter wrote in 1894 to one of his correspondents, one W. Borgius, "For us, economic conditions determine all historical phenomena, but race itself is an economic datum." This was the principle that Engels relied upon when (again in Marx's journal, February 15–16, 1849) he denied that Slavs had any capacity to attain civilization:

> Apart from the Poles and the Russians, and perhaps the Slavs of Turkey, no Slavic nation has a future, since all the other Slavs lack the historical, geographical, political and industrial bases that are necessary for independence and survival. Countries that have never had their own history, that have hardly achieved the lowest level of civilization . . . cannot survive and can never achieve the slightest autonomy.

Admittedly, Engels attributed Slavic "inferiority" partly to historical contingency, but he considered race to be a more important factor, and one that would make any change for the better impossible. Imagine the outcry today if some "thinker" were to make a similar diagnosis concerning, say, Africans. Yet according to the founders of socialism, the racial superiority of whites was a "scientific" fact. In the preliminary notes to his *Anti-Dühring*, the evangelist of Marxist philosophy wrote:

> If, for example, in our countries, [the basic] mathematical axioms are self-evident even to eight-year-old children, with no need for empirical demonstration, then this is but the result of "accumulated heredity." On the other hand, it would be very difficult to teach such fundamentals to a Bushman or an Australian Aborigine.

In the twentieth century, socialist intellectuals such as H. G. Wells and George Bernard Shaw, great admirers of the Soviet Union, claimed for socialism the right to liquidate the social classes that opposed the revolution or held it back. Shaw, concerned with finding an efficient way to purge the enemies of socialism, displayed a fine talent for prognostication in the BBC's highbrow periodical *The Listener* in 1933, when he urged chemists to devise a "humane" gas that would cause an "instantaneous and painless death"—a civilized sort of gas, lethal of course but not cruel. It may be recalled that the Nazi mass murderer Adolf Eichmann, at his trial in Jerusalem in 1962, invoked in his defense the "humane" character of Zyklon B, the chemical used to exterminate Jews in the Shoah.

Both Nazis and Communists aimed to achieve a metamorphosis, a "total" redemption of society—indeed, of humanity. Hence they felt justified in annihilating all the racial or social elements they regarded as resistant, even if only on an involuntary or unconscious level ("objectively," in Marxist jargon), to the sacred enterprise of collective salvation. So if the Nazis and the Communists committed genocide similar in extent if not with the same ideological pretext, it was not at all because of some anomalous convergence or fortuitous coincidence resulting from aberrant behavior; on the contrary, the similar results stemmed from identical principles rooted deeply in their respective convictions and modes of operation. Socialism is neither more nor less "of the left" than Nazism. If this fact is too often forgotten, it is because, as Rémy de Gourmont says, "a misconception that has become conventional wisdom is never corrected. Opinions are transmitted hereditarily, ending up as accepted history."

And if a whole socialist tradition dating from the nineteenth century advocated methods that would later be Hitler's—as well as Lenin's, Stalin's and Mao's—the converse is also true: Hitler always considered himself a socialist. His disagreements with the Communists, he explained to Otto Wagener, were "less ideological than tactical." The trouble with the Weimar politicians was that they "had never read Marx."[4] Hitler preferred the Communists to the insipid Social Democratic reformers; and the Communists returned the compliment by voting for him in 1933. The focus of his differences with the Bolsheviks, Hitler went on to say, resided in the racial question. In this he was mistaken. For the Soviet Union was always anti-Semitic, although the "Jewish question," despite Marx's pamphlet on the subject, never became a leading priority for the Marxist-Leninists as it did for the Nazis. Meanwhile, the German dictator's "anti-Bolshevik crusade" was largely a façade, masking a connivance with Stalin that considerably antedated (we now know) the Nazi-Soviet Pact of 1939.

Let's not forget that German National Socialism, like Italian Fascism, thought of itself—following the Bolshevik example—as a *revolution,* and specifically as an *antibourgeois* revolution. "Nazi" is an abbreviation of the German pronunciation of *Nationalsozialist.** Ludwig von Mises, one of the great Viennese economists who were forced to emigrate on account of Nazism, noted sardonically that the ten emergency measures proposed by Marx in his *Communist Manifesto* closely paralleled Hitler's economic program: "Eight out of ten of these points were carried out by the Nazis with a radicalism that would have delighted Marx."[5]

Another Viennese economist, the Nobel Prize–winning Friedrich Hayek, devoted a chapter in *The Road to Serfdom* (1944) to "The Socialist Roots of Naziism." He observed that the Nazis were "not opposed to the socialist elements of Marxism, but to its liberal, international and democratic elements." With accurate intuition, the Nazis had grasped that complete socialism entails total political control.

Louis Dupeux, a specialist in German history, has likewise shed light on the Communist-Nazi affinity in his 1974 doctoral thesis, *German National Bolshevism in the Weimar Republic,*[6] supplemented in 1998 with an article that he eloquently titled "Reading Russian Totalitarianism via German National Bolshevism (1919–1933)."[7] Writing to Dupeux in 1996, François Furet said he was "astounded that your contribution is not better known: the reason, evidently, is that you are touching on a taboo."[8] What

---

* *Translator's note:* The full name of Hitler's party was the Nationalsozialistische Deutsche Arbeiter Partei (National Socialist German Workers' Party).

taboo, exactly? There are at least two that Dupeux transgressed: first, pointing out the intrinsically criminal propensities of Communism; and second, highlighting the similarities between the two ideologies—the supreme sacrilege.

The National Bolsheviks, whose most illustrious representative was Ernst Jünger, contributed to the development of the Hitlerian ideology while embracing the Leninist model. Another intellectual of this stripe, Friedrich Lenz, also made note of Lenin's virtues: "All observers are aware that with Lenin came a head of state who in theory denied the concept of the state but in practice realized it with unprecedented decisiveness and ruthlessness. He linked the destiny of Russian Marxism to the destiny of her state." And Ernst Niekisch—like all "thinkers" of this group—approved of the forced-march collectivization undertaken by the Russians, for he understood that collectivization is the fastest means of creating the Total State, something these German philosophers considered essential for the revival of their country. Niekisch adds:

> Russian Bolshevism is so far the most radical revolt against the ideas of 1789. Russia is not individualistic. She is not liberal. She sets politics above economics. She is not parliamentary, not democratic and not "civilizing." Bolshevism is the repudiation of humanism and of "civilizing" values; its outward forms, often with a Western veneer, cannot deceive as to the "barbarous and Asiatic" content.

As with Communism, the Total State was based on the elimination of private capitalism. In Point 11 of the National Socialist program of 1920, Hitler announced "the abolition of all income acquired without labor and effort." (One can almost hear François Mitterrand stigmatizing those who "enrich themselves while they are sleeping.") The theoretician Hans von Hentig, conjoining National Socialism and Communist Bolshevism, fulminated against what set them irreconcilably apart from the Social Democrats: "What we need in Germany is a savage and brutal form of spiritual and material rearmament. . . . Not a socialism of petit-bourgeois businessmen, but a profound, engaging, armored

socialism bestowing savage energy on the nation and the people."
Professor Paul Eltzbacher, yet another bright star of this pleiad,
added further illumination: "Bolshevism means a powerful
state. . . . It fully understands that the state is coercion: it is emancipated from excessive respect for individual liberty and the senti-
mental weakness from which social democracy suffers."

Enough quotations. By now it is obvious that the claim that
adherence to Communism was justified by the necessity of fighting
Nazism was nothing but an imposture. One cannot understand
the dispute over the kinship between Nazism and Communism if
one loses sight of their resemblances not only in criminal consequences but in ideological origins as well. Intellectually they are
first cousins.

What all totalitarian regimes have in common is that they
are "ideocracies": dictatorships of ideas. Communism rests on
Marxism-Leninism or Mao Zedong Thought, National Socialism
on the criterion of race. The distinction I outlined in the previous
chapter between *direct totalitarianism,* which openly advertises its
intentions, and *totalitarianism mediatized by Utopia,* which proclaims the opposite of what it will actually do, turns out to be secondary, since the results for those who are subjected to them are
the same in both cases. The fundamental feature of both systems
is that the rulers, convinced that they possess the absolute truth
and are guiding the course of history for all humanity, believe
they have the right to destroy dissidents (real or potential), races,
classes, professional or cultural categories—anyone and everyone
they see as obstacles, or capable one day of being obstacles, to the
supreme design.

That's why it is very strange for "socialists," who should have
read Marx more carefully, to think they are justified in distinguishing between the totalitarian systems by stressing the diver-
gences in their ideological superstructures, while they overlook
the close parallels in actual practice. For you don't judge a society
by the ideology that serves as its pretext, said Marx, any more than
you would judge a person by the opinion he has of himself.

With fine connoisseurship, Adolf Hitler was among the first to
grasp the affinities between Communism and National Socialism.

For he understood that a political system must be evaluated not by its philosophical décor and oratorical embellishments, but by its deeds and methods. To Hermann Rauschning, who quoted him in *Hitler Speaks*, the Führer said:

> I am not merely the vanquisher of Marxism, I am its implementer—of that part of it that is essential and justified, stripped of its Talmudic dogma.
>
> I won't conceal that I've learned a great deal from Marxism. . . . What interested me about the Marxists, and instructed me, were their methods. The difference between them and myself is that I have really put into practice what these peddlers and pen-pushers have timidly begun. The whole of National Socialism is contained in Marxism. Take a close look at it: the workers' athletic societies, the industrial cells, the mass demonstrations, the propaganda material specially formulated to reach the masses. All these new means of political struggle were almost entirely invented by the Marxists. I had merely to take them over and adapt them to our purposes.[9]

Ideocracy's level of censorship goes far beyond the routine sort exercised by run-of-the-mill dictatorships. The latter engage mainly in political censorship, or in censorship of what could have political consequences. Even democracies can fall into this practice, as we saw in France during the Algerian War. Ideocracy wants much more. It strives to suppress—and it must in order to survive—all thinking that is opposed to or outside the official party line, not only in politics and economics, but in every domain: philosophy, arts and literature, even science.

For a totalitarian, philosophy can be Marxism-Leninism, Mao Zedong Thought or the doctrine of *Mein Kampf*. Art is likewise reduced to subservience. For the Nazis, "degenerate art" had to be eliminated and replaced by healthy Nazi art. In parallel fashion, the Communists wanted to strangle "bourgeois art" by means of socialist realism. The most dangerous gamble that ideocracy makes, however—and where its intrinsic irrationality is laid bare—is denying any autonomy to science.

The Lysenko affair in the Soviet Union comes to mind. Lysenko was a charlatan who, between 1935 and 1964, virtually destroyed biological science in the Soviet Union, dismissing the whole enterprise, from Mendel to Morgan, as "fascist deviationism in genetics," or even as "Trotskyist-Bukharinism in genetics." In his eyes, modern science committed the unpardonable sin of contradicting dialectical materialism, of being incompatible with the theory of evolution according to Engels, who, twenty years after the publication of Darwin's *Origin of Species,* had continued to trumpet (in *Anti-Dühring*) his belief in the discredited Lamarckian doctrine of the inheritance of acquired characteristics. Supported by the ruling oligarchy, Lysenko became president of the Academy of Sciences of the USSR, from which he barred authentic biologists when he didn't have them deported or shot. All textbooks, encyclopedias and university courses were purged in favor of Lysenkoism—with catastrophic consequences for Soviet agriculture, already in a terrible state thanks to the Stalinist collectivization. The bureaucracy enforced this pseudoscience on all the "agrobiological" kolkhozes (collective farms), proscribing fertilizers and adopting a primitive strain of wheat going back to ancient Egypt, which succeeded in reducing yields by half. Hybridization was forbidden, since according to Lysenko it was scientifically established that species transform themselves spontaneously into other species without any need for crossbreeding. His mad lucubrations were the coup de grâce to an agriculture that had already been smothered by the nonsense of agrarian socialism. Thus was made irreversible the chronic famines—or "controlled scarcity," in Michael Heller's phrase—that accompanied the Soviet Union until the day of its collapse.

The important lesson of Lysenko's pseudoscience is that ideocracy is compelled, on pain of suicide, to subordinate all intellectual life to politics. Louis Aragon, leaping at any opportunity to discredit himself, defended Lysenko in *Les Lettres françaises,* where he bellowed, "I refuse to politicize chromosomes!" Yet that is exactly what he was doing. The vital, "ontological" fact for the Communist ideocrats, even in the scientific realm, was the class distinction: the famous antithesis between "bourgeois" and "proletarian" science.

The extra-scientific criterion of scientific truth for the Nazis followed from the same mindset, with the difference that they were obsessed with race rather than class. The two *démarches* are intellectually identical, insofar as both deny the specificity of knowledge as such and subsume everything under ideology. Thus Rauschning quotes the German chancellor as saying:

> There is no such thing as Truth, in the moral or in the scientific domain.

> The notion that science can be divorced from all preconceived ideas could only have been imagined in the era of liberalism; it is absurd.

> Science is a social phenomenon . . . .

> The slogan "scientific objectivity" has been concocted by the learned professors so as to escape very necessary supervision by the power of the state.[10]

Here again we see the difference, more phenomenological than ontological, between utopian and direct totalitarianism. The Communists, just as eager as the National Socialists to subjugate knowledge to power, did so in the name of a purportedly true science to which they alone possessed the key. Hitler, on the other hand, decreed without any fancy wrappings that Truth does not exist and therefore it is the prerogative of power to define it, or at least to keep it subordinate. He continued:

> What's called the epistemological crisis quite simply boils down to the fact that these gentlemen are beginning to realize that their "objectivity" and "independence" have led them into a cul-de-sac. The elementary question that must be asked

before undertaking the slightest scientific activity is: *Who desires to know something?* That is, *who* wants to find their bearings in the world? It is self-evident that there can be no science except in relation to a specific human type in a specific era.

There well and truly exist a Nordic science and a National Socialist science, and they must stand opposed to Judeo-liberal science, which moreover no longer works and is in the process of destroying itself.

It will be noticed, *en passant,* that this dismissal of the truth of science by invoking social or geographic origins—this refusal to acknowledge science's distinctively objective character—is precisely echoed by postmodern philosophers at the century's end. Thus Bernard Latour, among others, writes with regard to Einstein, "The theory of relativity is social through and through." And the empirical verification of scientific laws hangs on the gender of the researcher, according to Luce Irigaray in her article asking "Is the Subject of Science Gendered?"[11]

The totalitarian state professes to be the exclusive and unique producer of culture, and its spokesmen therefore constantly inveigh against that dedicated enemy of the state: the individual. In his celebrated lecture of 1819, *De la liberté des Anciens comparée à celle des Modernes,* Benjamin Constant hailed the dawning of the era of private autonomy, defining modern citizenship as the guarantor of individual liberty. At that historical moment, however, humanity was in fact entering a phase of uninterrupted growth in state power, even in the democracies; and as for the totalitarian regimes, whose intellectual foundations were being laid throughout the nineteenth century, their principal obsession would be the complete annihilation of the individual.

As early as 1840, Pierre-Joseph Proudhon, that luminary of "libertarian" socialism, was proclaiming that "to foment individualism is to prepare the dissolution of the community."[12] In his *Qu'est-ce que la propriété?* (What Is Property?), Proudhon stressed the interdependence of private property, liberalism and individualism; in this he was correct, but his program was designed to

wipe them out. A strange kind of libertarian! And Benito Mussolini, who was schooled in socialism during the first part of his
political career—indeed, in the left wing of the Italian Socialist
Party—understood clearly this linkage between liberalism and
individualism. In *Il Fascismo* (1929), he put it plainly:

> The principle according to which society exists solely for the
> well-being and liberty of the individuals composing it does not
> seem to conform to nature's plans. If the nineteenth century
> was the century of the individual (liberalism means individu-
> alism), then the present century may be regarded as that of
> collectivism.

Everyone knows that Karl Marx advocated the suppression of
the state as the way to emancipate the individual—as would his
disciple Lenin in the following century. But it should be obvious
by now that the hallmark of utopian totalitarianism (and what
chiefly distinguishes it from direct totalitarianism) is to effect the
opposite of its vaunted program: namely to impose tyranny in the
name of liberty. If liberal society has been described as "rights
independent of the state,"[13] socialist society is, above all, the state
absent rights. Marx was not being self-contradictory when, in
his essay *On the Jewish Question* (1843), he railed against human
rights: "None of the so-called rights of man therefore go beyond
egoistic man, beyond man as a member of bourgeois society—
that is, as an individual separated from the community, withdrawn
into himself and preoccupied only with his personal interests and
private caprice."

Not surprisingly, we encounter the same philosophical
coherence with Adolf Hitler—toward whom the ingratitude of
today's socialist thinkers is quite scandalous. He confided to
Otto Wagener, "Now that the age of individualism is over, our
task is to find the road that leads from individualism to socialism
without a revolution." Marx and Lenin, added Herr Chancellor,
saw clearly the goal to be attained but chose the wrong road. An
eminent National Socialist, Richard Walther Darré, the Reich
agricultural minister and an intimate of the Führer's, elaborated

on this insight when he insisted that "Jewish political theory" had always been "oriented toward the interests of the individual, whereas the socialism of Adolf Hitler is at the service of the whole of society."[14]

The frenzied association of Jewishness, individualism and capitalism drives Marx's anti-Semitic eructations in the above-quoted essay on "the Jewish question," which is little read but which Hitler evidently paid close attention to. He almost literally plagiarized whole passages where Marx spits out furious invective against the Jews, such as this: "What is the secular basis of Judaism? Practical need, self-interest (*Eigennutz*). What is the worldly religion of the Jew? Huckstering. What is his God? Money." Marx winds up by exhorting his readers to see that Communism, "an organization of society that would abolish the preconditions for huckstering and therefore the possibility of huckstering, would make the Jew impossible." In the rhetoric of incitement to slaughter, it would be harder to find anything more inspiring.

In every totalitarian system, the individual—Jewish or not—must be abolished. The Soviet "new man" must be identical to all other Soviet men: a cog in the vast grinding machinery of socialism. Dear to Stalin's heart, this robotic slave was deserving of a toast, one that the Little Father of the People did not hesitate to offer: "I drink," he perorated, "to those simple, ordinary, modest folk, to those cogs that keep our great machine of state in working order."[15] The reification and standardization of the individual, his reduction to the role of a tool in the hands of the party, must pre-empt his liberty, his thought, his morality. "In our society," intoned Leonid Brezhnev, "morality is whatever serves the interests of Communism."

The abolition of the individual is tantamount to the abolition of the human being, whom no one has ever encountered other than as an individual. Again, on this point the similarity between Communism and Nazism has struck many observers—at least those who were not brainwashed by propaganda or induced by party allegiance into professional lying. In 1936, André Gide visited the Soviet Union, which from a distance he had admired, and he returned disabused. The champion of liberty expressed his disillusion in a book that fell like a ton of bricks on the pate of the French left: "I doubt if in any country today, except perhaps in Hitler's Germany, people feel less free, are more bent down, more fearful, more terrorized [than in the USSR]."[16] Here Gide was being unfair to Hitler, who after all had been in power barely three years, not nearly long enough to accomplish his agenda, while the Communists had had nearly twenty years to enforce theirs, to break the mold of normal humanity and metamorphose it into *Homo sovieticus*.

There is a conception of the state that Lenin and Hitler shared. In a *Pravda* article titled "The Proletarian Revolution and the Renegade Kautsky," Lenin wrote:

> The State is in the hands of the dominant class, a machine destined to crush the resistance of its class enemies. In this respect the dictatorship of the proletariat differs not at all, fundamentally, from the dictatorship of any other class.

Further along in the same article, we find:

> Dictatorship is power directly based upon violence and is constrained by no law. The revolutionary dictatorship of the proletariat is power acquired and kept by means of violence, which the proletariat exercises over the bourgeoisie, power unconstrained by any laws.[17]

Turning, if we are so inclined, to *Mein Kampf*, we find in the chapter dealing with the state that Hitler expressed himself in almost identical terms. True, the "dictatorship of the German people" replaces that of the proletariat; but if we take into account the Führer's numerous anticapitalist diatribes, the concepts are hardly very distant from one another. Totalitarian political systems invariably establish a repressive machinery aiming at the elimination not only of political dissidence but of any differences in individual behavior; they are fully aware of their incompatibility with *variety*.

Hostility toward the individual, on the grounds that the individual is organically linked to liberalism and capitalism, would persist among socialists well after the fall of Soviet Communism and the watering-down of the Chinese version. From the optically challenged perspective of the left, Communism's implosion only confirmed the end of liberalism. Thus, for Miguel Benasayag, an Argentine Marxist and author of the succinctly titled essay *The Myth of the Individual,* the myth in question is associated with another: the Myth of Capitalism. Perhaps laboring under a misinterpretation of René Girard's ideas, Benasayag announces that in a "sacral society" (liberal society?), "the founding principle is never explained. . . . Capitalism does not escape from this rule. And its foundational, indivisible principle will be constituted by that rather paradoxical character, the individual."

Here this philosopher is being too pessimistic. The individual is perfectly divisible. The proof is that the Nazis and the Communists cut up tens of millions of them into countless pieces.

CHAPTER EIGHT
Truncated Memory

The left's vigilant refusal to acknowledge the equivalence of Nazism and Communism or even to make comparisons between them, despite their evident affinity, has a practical rationale: the daily execration of the one serves as a barrier against careful examination of the other.

The incessant drumming on the subject of Nazi atrocities— a sacred ritual devoutly referred to as the *"devoir de mémoire"* (duty of remembrance)—keeps up a constant background noise that discourages vigilance when it comes to remembering Communist atrocities. As Alain Besançon puts it, the "hypernesia of Nazism" turns attention away from the "amnesia of Communism." That is why any analysis or research by the minority of historians inclined to point out the essential similarity of the two systems provokes hurricanes of vengeful rage. The objection will be raised—and with reason—that no reminder of Nazi criminality can be overstated. Remembering Nazi crimes is an obligation, but the insistence on doing so becomes suspect when it is an exercise in postponing indefinitely the acknowledgment of Communist criminality. Of what moral or educational utility is remembering a crime if it serves to conceal other crimes of equal magnitude?

Indicative of how successful this decoy action has been is the meaning that the phrase *devoir de mémoire* has come to assume: usually it is a call to remember Nazi crimes in particular. Other crimes may possibly be added to the list, provided that they have no connection to the great Communist parent companies' field of action and do not reflect badly on the socialist conception of the world.

Censorship of this sort, ensuring that references to the left's crimes are few and far between, has been countersigned by the right, which with customary eagerness was quick to internalize the cultural commands of its adversaries. Thus in July 1999, Jacques Chirac went to Oradour-sur-Glane to inaugurate a "Remembrance Center." It was in this village on June 10, 1944, that SS troops of the Das Reich Division massacred 642 people, including 246 women and 207 children, by burning them alive in the church. Chirac's visit was a noble and pious reminder from our head of state. In his speech at the ceremony, the president condemned, over and above the holocaust (in the literal sense) of Oradour, "all" the massacres and genocides of history, "and first of all, of course, the Shoah." He went on to mention the Saint Bartholomew's Day Massacre and those in "the villages of the Vendée during the Terror." (The president was being courageous here, given the taboo of Jacobin origin that has long denied the memory of this French genocide, which remains quite memorable nevertheless.) Guernica was on the list, as were the Sabra and Chatila killings—that stone in the garden of Israel. Then came the intertribal genocide of Rwanda in 1994 and the thousands of Bosnians killed in the name of "ethnic cleansing" between 1992 and 1995, and finally the more recent carnage in Kosovo. In all these exterminations, as in Oradour, "the executioners made no distinction between men, women and children," said Chirac in his forceful and indignant conclusion.

It will be noticed—or rather, *no one* noticed—that in this sweeping panorama of "all" the crimes from "every" time and "every" place, not a single Communist massacre is mentioned.

Katyn never happened. Under the direction of a Gaullist head of state, Lenin, Mao, Pol Pot, Mengistu and Kim Il Sung are made to tiptoe off the stage of historical memory. Let's make a blank slate of the left's past! And the Communist despotisms of today, ever active and ingenious in the art of filling progressive cemeteries and re-education camps, are passed over in silence: China, where every day, with impunity, tortures are perpetrated that equal those of Pinochet, for which he was duly prosecuted; and likewise Vietnam and North Korea, and of course Fidel Castro, whose angelic sweetness shines so brightly that he has become Our Lady of Lourdes for legions of political and ecclesiastical pilgrims.

In French, the word *mémoire* means "the faculty of retaining and recalling past experience," but for several years now it has been used as a synonym for *souvenir* in its secondary sense of "act of recollection" or "remembrance." Thus the expression *devoir de mémoire* has come to acquire the exclusive connotation of a "duty to observe remembrances" of Nazi crimes, and of the Holocaust in particular. *Mémoire* and Nazi crimes are henceforth interchangeable terms. It turns out that the duty to remember, in this sense, entails the duty to forget everything else.

On the day after Chirac's remarks at Oradour, the regional newspaper *Ouest-France* carried the headline "UNE MÉMOIRE CONTRE LA BARBARIE" ("One Memory Against Barbarism"). Are they suggesting that one solitary memory, one individual's alone, remembers that barbarism? That would be a sad outcome indeed! But let's not overlook the subtext: The constantly reiterated reminders of Nazi barbarism must teach up-and-coming generations about their duty to eradicate future barbarism; but Communist regimes, having never manifested the slightest barbarism, are beyond the scope of the "duty of remembrance." And the Communist regimes, which busily go about their work of torturing and persecuting even today, are not the subjects of a "duty of vigilance."

Resistance to Nazism becomes ever more ferocious as Nazism recedes further into the past. The French Ministry for Veterans' Affairs, with less and less on its plate as there are fewer and fewer veterans, dreams of changing its job description to "Ministry for

Remembrance" and even setting up a "remembrance tourism."[1] It's a sure bet that the organizers of ethical travel itineraries will never distribute tickets for such "remembrance sites" as the Lubyanka prison in Moscow, the now abandoned gulag camps, or the fully functioning labor camps of today's Chinese Laogaï. Our vigilance with regard to the Third Reich's crimes continues to grow, and this in itself is a healthy fruit of historical consciousness. But when this vigilance increases tenfold after the facts about the Communist systems have become better known, or at least more difficult to evade, we are left to wonder about the motives for this exclusive preoccupation with Nazi crimes.

On the same day as Chirac's Oradour speech, Prime Minister Lionel Jospin, not to be outdone in the hemiplegic ethics race, was also doing some "remembrance tourism," to Auschwitz. He was accompanied by his wife, herself of Polish origin. And for this, who could not be grateful? The "uniqueness of the Shoa," to use Alain Besançon's words, can never be recalled too often.[2] We may regret nonetheless that our two "remembrance tourists," while they were in Poland, didn't feel duty bound to extend their trip as far as Katyn. The duty to remember is either universal or it is partisan pharisaism. And you insult the memory of the Nazis' victims if you exploit them in order to bury the Communists' victims in forgetfulness.

I have often noticed that the place name "Katyn" means nothing to most young people, for the reason that their teachers and the media are careful not to mention it. So here is a brief summary of the facts: In September 1939, after the defeat of Poland— which had been invaded simultaneously by the Nazis from the west and by the Red armies from the east—an occupation zone of 200,000 square kilometers was tossed by Hitler as a bone to his Soviet friends, along with other territories in the Baltic region, to reward them for their invaluable help. Stalin immediately set out to purge the Polish officer corps of undesirable elements, and on his express written orders, many thousands of prisoners were murdered, including over four thousand at Katyn, a village near Smolensk and location of the best-known mass grave, and about twenty-one thousand at various other places. To these must be added some fifteen thousand enlisted troops who were probably drowned in the White Sea. Carried out over a few days according to a pre-established plan, these mass murders of defeated Poles, exterminated for the sole reason that they were Poles, indisputably were crimes against humanity and not simply war crimes, since the war was over as far as Poland was concerned. According to the Geneva Conventions, to execute prisoners from a regular army who have fought in uniform constitutes a crime against humanity, especially if the conflict in question has been terminated. The orders from Moscow were to eliminate all Polish elites in the Soviet-occupied zone: students, judges, landowners, state officials, engineers, professors, lawyers, and of course military officers.

When the mass graves were discovered, the Kremlin blamed the killings on the Nazis. The Western left, naturally, rushed to obey its master's voice. Here I am not alleging that *all* the non-Communist left was servile, but those who did have doubts remained very discreet—plaintively perplexed rather than categorically accusing. For forty-five years, to say out loud that Soviet guilt was highly likely, if only for the simple reason that the crimes were committed in the Soviet-controlled zone and not the German-controlled area, was to get yourself instantly classified as one of those obsessive "viscerals" of "simplistic" anticommunist prejudice.

Then lo and behold, thanks to Gorbachev and glasnost, the Kremlin in 1990 acknowledged, in a formal TASS communiqué and without attenuating evasions, that "Katyn was a grave crime of the Stalinist era." And in 1992, after a preliminary inventory of Moscow's archives, a secret 1959 report made for the KGB chief Alexander Shelepin was released for international inspection. It recorded "21,857 Poles of the privileged classes, shot in 1939 on Stalin's orders."

The matter thus resolved by the Soviets themselves, one might have hoped that Western revisionists—who for decades had been wheeling out the "fascist" epithet for anyone who believed in the Soviets' culpability—would now make honorable amends. But that is not to know them. Likewise, it would have been nice if the

French prime minister had made a small "touristic" gesture of remembrance by visiting the Katyn graves, to show that leftists had recovered their memories and had finally stopped being moral and intellectual self-amputees.

This persistent discrimination stems from the no less tenacious aberration that holds fascism to be the antithesis of Communism, and hence the victims of the latter, in their tens of millions, to be somehow less victimized than those of the former. One would like to challenge the deniers and demand of them, "On what grounds do you remain silent?" It isn't fascism that is Communism's foe; it is democracy, that eternal enemy of freedom's assassins.

A voluntarily truncated memory is not equitable; it is really not memory at all. Memory will continue to be absent as long as the left and the right alike continue to apply a double standard, treating the conquering criminals differently from the vanquished criminals.

One reason for the veil cast over Communist crimes is cowardice, because it is easier by far to be angry with dead totalitarians than with the living varieties. You need only note how respectfully even the weak Communist regimes of today are treated to get a better appreciation of the colossal servility that was displayed toward the powerful USSR between its victory in 1945 and its disappearance in 1991. Obligatory among partisans and sympathizers in the West, this slavishness was surprisingly on wide display even among those resistant to its ideology. In the context of the Cold War, this attitude could be explained away as motivated by considerations of *Realpolitik*, but it survives today among people who don't always have the courage to stand up to those on the hard left, who are still in denial vis-à-vis the all-encompassing failure and criminality of real socialism.

On the one hand, the Third Reich has been wiped off the face of the earth as a political entity for more than half a century now, whereas Communism endures, albeit diminished in extent; and

Nazi ideology has disappeared as a cultural force, except among some marginal groups whose influence is small but whose importance is carefully inflated so as to keep alive the myth of an eternally reincarnating "fascist danger." Conversely, Marxist-Leninist ideology, however discredited, continues to permeate our interpretive schemas and cultural activities. Stalinist-Leninist methods remain in everyday use: calumny, lies, disinformation, misrepresentation, slander, trumped-up charges, abuse, exile to the fascist, Vichy, anti-Semitic camp—affronts as unmerited as they are insidious—are standard practices in our political and even artistic and literary life. The most venial anathema consists in treating anyone who happens to disapprove of your sect as a Nazi, even if the point of disagreement has nothing to do with politics. It is revealing, by the way, that the French law that since 1990 has criminalized denial of Nazi crimes—but by its silence on the subject, effectively authorizes doubts about Communist crimes—originated with a Communist! I don't mind in the least being told to heap daily execrations on Himmler's former admirers, provided that it is not former admirers of Beria who are admonishing me to do so.

May the left refrain from calling me a fascist because I have been suggesting a parallel between the SS and the Cheka! I cannot claim originality on this point; the likeness was established by Stalin. It was he who dubbed Beria "our Himmler," and it was in these terms that he introduced the head of the Soviet secret police to Franklin Roosevelt. The American president was taken aback by such a display of cynicism.[3]

The periodic fits of amnesia experienced by Communism's erstwhile allies go hand in hand with indulgence toward the surviving Communist regimes. Such blind spots, which in the past worked to the benefit of the Soviet Union and are hardly surprising among the left, are also found on the right. It's an old tradition: Wasn't it, after all, a politician whom we would nowadays call a "centrist," the Radical-Socialist Édouard Herriot, who, after promenading (or being promenaded) about Ukraine in the early 1930s, declared that he had seen nothing but prosperous, happy and well-nourished people? While this pompous imbecile was conveying his awestruck impressions to the French public, fifteen million Ukrainian peasants, expelled from their farms, were being deported to Siberia; a million were being executed on the spot; and six million were starving to death as the result of a deliberately engineered famine. Thirty years later, despite such unfortunate antecedents, package tour pilgrims to China were afflicted by similar attacks of blindness when they failed to discern the carnage of the so-called "Cultural Revolution." This was nothing but a sadistic, blood-soaked purge unleashed by the Great Helmsman himself. The Red Guards lynched and tortured millions of their compatriots. A bestial dementia had been released in the land, which Zhou Enlai was later to characterize as the greatest catastrophe that China has ever endured.

Already by 1961, the Great Leap Forward had been, according to its most recent historian, Jean-Louis Margolin, "the greatest famine in history"—a famine that Mao Zedong had planned for his people in accordance with that special blend of economic idiocy, agronomic incompetence and cruelty that distinguishes Communism.[4] It was "a political famine, in essence," adds Margolin. It raised the mortality rate from fifteen in a thousand during normal times to sixty-eight in a thousand. In 1994, documents from Chinese CP internal archives that filtered out to the West proved that the total number of deaths owing to the Great Leap Forward and the Cultural Revolution had to be revised upward by several tens of millions.[5] Between 1959 and 1961—when Western parrots were mechanically squawking the line that "Maybe Mao has suppressed freedoms, but at least thanks to him the Chinese people can eat their fill"—deaths caused by food shortages were close to *forty million*. Yet not only did visitors and the Western press pass over this collective assassination in silence, but when Margolin published his findings in 1997, the European left responded with indignant shouts.

During the last two decades of the century, Western political leaders and businessmen competed for laurels in obsequiousness as they went on the China or Vietnam circuit. The sorry state of human rights—or rather, the absence of human rights—in late twentieth-century China is well documented, as is the strong resolve of China's one-party oligarchy to maintain hegemony in the political if not in the economic domain. Ten years after ratifying an international ban on torture, China continues to practice torture in all its prisons, and particularly those in Tibet. In 1998 and 1999, the incarceration of dissidents and ideological repression redoubled in intensity, dashing the hopes of some commentators who were forecasting that the relative liberalization of the economy would gradually bring about political and cultural liberalization. In the last month of 1998, a new set of rules (you can hardly call them laws) further restricted freedom of expression, if that was possible, in newspapers, books, films, television, videocassettes, the Internet and software. Any infractions of this intensified censorship will be considered "an attempt to subvert the state" and punished with life imprisonment.[6] I have already mentioned the Chinese network of concentration camps, the Laogaï, of which there are several thousand throughout the land; exact figures can be found in *The Laogaï Handbook,* published in California and periodically brought up to date by the Laogaï Research Foundation.[7] The death penalty is summarily applied even for minor offenses; every year there are several thousand executions.

In view of these facts, giving a negative or ambiguous answer to the question of whether or not Communism is intrinsically criminogenic, in China as in the Soviet Union, can only be a symptom of ideological obsession divorced from reality. The mystery is not the issue of Communist criminality; the mystery is that in 2000 we still must debate it.

The leadership of the Chinese CP has no intention of relaxing its totalitarian grip on the nation. On the contrary, Jiang Zemin, head of state and party boss, ruled out Western-style democracy "forever," as he firmly put it in December 1998, announcing that "the fundamental Communist Party line" would remain unchanged "for a hundred years to come." Here is a man of conviction, a quality that Western politicians prize above everything else. Twenty years earlier Deng Xiaoping had cried, "Liberate

117

thought!" Now Jiang was decreeing, "Subversive and separatist activities must be nipped in the bud." (The second adjective evidently alludes to Tibet.)[8]

Summary executions, arbitrary arrests, massacres, torture, labor camps, deportation of populations, annexation and persecution of defenseless nations, show trials—clearly these are humanitarian acts in the eyes of our Western democrats, as long as it is Communists who commit them. They constitute crimes only when perpetrated by Hitler or Pinochet, although the latter's efforts make him but a modest journeyman in comparison with the industrial efficiency of Stalin or Mao. There is nothing new here. But the benevolent pardon we extend to China is all the more imprudent in that this power remains a strategic threat. China's nuclear arsenal is steadily growing. Thanks especially to skills in espionage and theft, the technical know-how stolen from American labs has enabled the Chinese to build the most advanced type of nuclear warhead.[9] And Beijing's intransigence toward Taiwan will continue to threaten regional stability.

The capitalist democracies are willing to swallow all this under the pretext of economic realism. China is potentially the world's largest market and we cannot disregard it, goes the usual line. Maybe. But China, like the late lamented Soviet Union and today's Russia, buys our products with money largely borrowed from us, which for the most part it doesn't repay. Chinese debts either are not repaid—in January 1999 there were yet another four billion dollars' worth of bankruptcies—or are "rescheduled," which is euphemistic jargon for repayment in never-never land. Every year the United States alone disburses sixty billion dollars in risky loans to the Chinese regime.

Moreover, the credulous West is falling into the trap of accepting the outrageously falsified statistics that exaggerate the extent of China's economic boom and hence its purchasing power. Jean-Claude Chesnais, director of research at the Institut National d'Études Démographiques, has dissected the reasons why the glamorous Chinese statistics are so unreliable.[10] Unlike India, China has no tradition of modern data collection and analysis; its first central office of statistics wasn't set up until 1952 and was shut down twelve years later during the Cultural Revolution, the authorities wanting at all costs to avoid exposure of the economic and demographic damage inflicted by this collective insanity and the ravages of the Great Leap Forward that preceded it. Reopened in 1978 during the policy shift toward liberalization, the statistics bureau lacks competent specialists and does not meet international standards. Its publications are shoddy, always at the mercy of political upheavals and propaganda directives. In the areas of life expectancy, mortality rates and population growth, they pile up a mass of incoherent and contradictory estimates. Although China's economic expansion since the beginning of the 1980s is undeniable, spurious statistics have been used to inflate its dimensions. The main concern has been to spread the fable that China's per capita standard of living is superior to India's. The opposite is true.

Unfortunately the international experts, unperceptive or politically conniving, too often ratify Chinese lies and hence effectively collude in misleading Western business representatives. The 1998 issue of the *World Bank Atlas* attributed to China an annual per capita income growth rate of 11 percent between 1990 and 1996. To this, Jean-Claude Chesnais objects, "Such an order of magnitude is without precedent. Therefore there is good reason to think that it is wildly inaccurate, an invention cooked up by the Chinese authorities."

We have learned nothing. The cocktail served up by the democracies for seventy-five years to regale the USSR is offered anew to China: a mix of one-third indulgence toward violations of human rights, one-third apathy in the face of strategic intimidation, and one-third economic obligingness as we shower credits on the sterile lands of collectivism with a prodigality verging on simpleminded folly.

The left's refusal to examine history—its self-amputation of memory—determines the angry response every time another book comes out bearing witness to Communism's economic ineptitude and its manifold crimes against humanity. Voluntary blindness of this sort, a flight from anything that might disturb equanimity, is coupled logically enough, on both sides of the political spectrum, with an incapacity to learn lessons from history that might help us with the policy decisions that confront us today. As the Russian dissident Vladimir Bukovsky and the Chinese dissident Wei Jingsheng write, "History has abundantly proved that the strategies of détente were bad. Yet once again we are assured, as we were twenty-five years ago [with regard to the Soviet Union], that—in the case of China this time—trade with the West and some smiles along the way will be all that is necessary to transform a totalitarian society into a democratic one."[11]

Communist regimes, never strong except in relation to the West's chronic weaknesses, have no trouble taking advantage of us. China ventures to impose censorship not only at home—par for the course in dictatorships—but also abroad, as it attempts to interfere with sources of information about its crimes. Films are targeted, especially those dealing with Tibet or Tibetan Buddhism. And the oligarchy's capricious demands are not infrequently catered to.

In 1996, the international media magnate Rupert Murdoch, complying with China's regulations, withdrew the BBC's World Service rights to relay the Asia-based Star TV, which he controls. The reason? Because the BBC had aired three broadcasts that Beijing deemed "anti-Chinese" (i.e., that told the truth). The first BBC production exposed the death camps for orphans that exist in contemporary China; the second looked at factories whose workforce consists of prisoner-slaves; and the third dealt with the reminiscences of Mao Zedong's personal physician, Dr. Li Zhisui, retired now in the United States. Dr. Li's portrait revealed Mao as a pitiless tyrant, a paranoiac and a dissolute sex maniac.[12] And the Helmsman emerged also as an individual of staggering intellectual poverty, something that should have been apparent all along simply from his writings.*

In 1998, Murdoch went a step further in Sinophile servility by forbidding one of his publishing houses, HarperCollins, to bring

---

* See Appendix C for an article that I wrote in 1968 for *L'Express* on the strange misapprehension about Mao's intellectual level.

out a book by Christopher Patten, former governor of the British Crown Colony of Hong Kong. It was a cowardly gesture and a foolish one, for Patten's book, snapped up by another publisher, enjoyed large sales thanks to the publicity garnered by this flagrant breach of contract.[13] Patten shows that the West's frenetic bowing and scraping does not comport with what ought to be a realistic economic relationship with China. The West enjoys economic superiority, but obsequiousness prevails because of the obsession with China's market, though a market so insolvent hardly merits such levels of awe. Every year since the Tiananmen Square massacre in 1989, a timid resolution is presented to the United Nations ad hoc committee by one democratic country or another condemning violations of human rights in China; and every year it is tossed out.

In the flagship Communist countries—those that were the prototypes for the satellites and faithful franchises—we find a convergence of features that cumulatively result in the annihilation of entire populations. First, there is what might be called direct destruction: periodic purges and mass executions. Then there is indirect or deferred destruction: deportation of populations, deliberately inflicted privations and mistreatments, internments in labor and re-education camps—all conducive to high death rates. Another element is the strange genius exhibited by all Communist regimes for sweeping economic transformations, particularly in the domain of agriculture, prosecuted with implacable determination and a stupidity so inventive that it cannot be entirely involuntary. The productivity of the most fertile land is made to drop by anything from 50 to 80 percent, creating famines that can cost millions of lives. Finally there is the zeal to wipe out culture and anything that deviates from Marxist-Leninist dogma. An example is Tibet, where the Chinese, who numbered around 1.3 billion at the turn of the century, are not satisfied with merely conquering a small nation of six million, reducing them to slavery and despoiling their land of its meager resources (mainly forest products); they are pathologically obsessed with the idea of abolishing Tibetan civilization and culture as well.[14]

While none of these totalitarian specialties is ever entirely neglected, some Communist societies do better in one area than in the others; some shine now in one, now in another; but at their peak, the very best perform brilliantly in all four, all the time. It seems likely, then, that in the combination of these basic ingredients lies the structural and functional foundation of every Communist power, in every latitude and in all historical contexts.

Is the word "genocide" appropriate for the overall results of the system?* Given the sheer quantity of human lives destroyed and the scope of the cultural ravages inflicted, the question seems rather specious. Whether to use the term is made to revolve around entirely qualitative considerations. But whatever side of the issue one comes down on, theorizing does not alter the fate of the victims one jot. Will those whose deaths we have determined were not by genocide be resuscitated on that account? Will the mass graves where so many millions of corpses lie be miraculously transformed into nurseries?

Although aspects of Communist totalitarianism were closely paralleled in the Nazi state, you don't find the Nazis deliberately instigating economic failure. They were perfectly willing to starve the populations of conquered nations in order to feed their armies, but they never set out to starve the German people, slaughter the German peasantry or devastate German agriculture in peacetime by enforcing deranged edicts. In Nazi Germany, penury was a consequence of prolonged warfare, not of policy.

Between 1994 and 1999, according to a report drawn up by the Buddhist organization Good Friends, three million North Koreans perished, victims of a famine that the rulers blamed on the floods that afflicted North Korea in 1994, but which cannot be rationally explained other than as an effect of their own policies. This subterfuge of blaming disasters on nature's intemperance is as old as Communism itself; Mengistu made skillful use of it during his

---

* For the French Criminal Code's definition of what constitutes "genocide," see Appendix D.

ten years as Ethiopia's guiding light. The North Korean famine did not prevent Pyongyang from finding the necessary cash to build nuclear weapons facilities on the pretext that they wanted to develop a peaceful uranium-dependent energy industry. In conformity with the democratic habit of backing down before such threats, the United States, missing an opportunity to exploit North Korea's weak position, immediately proposed a deal, offering food assistance and free gasoline in addition to civil nuclear power plants, in exchange for Pyongyang giving up its nuclear weapons ambitions.

In conformity with Communist habits, Pyongyang pocketed the donations, which in classic fashion went to the elite for their comforts and not to the people in need. And secretly, in underground facilities, work continued apace on atomic bombs. Inspection teams were denied access—unless they came bearing gifts. Ever more fired up as the people became more famished, the bosses even threatened to wreak destruction on the United States and wipe it off the map "once and for all."[15] In the promised land of dynastic Communism, the "well-loved leader" Kim Jong Il, like his father, Kim Il Sung, shows himself to be a faithful disciple of Stalin and Mao. What is distressing in all this is that the democracies seem incapable of recognizing the past when it returns disguised as the present.

Once again we see how failure to take stock of past Communisms, or the past of present-day Communisms, is the basis of the indulgence we accord to the contemporary regimes. The two cosmetic exercises are complementary—hence the efforts to avoid acquiring too much knowledge of the historical record and of today's actuality alike. Given that today we are so deferential to the philosophy of human rights, an impartial acknowledgment of the facts would leave us with no option but to harmonize our political criteria with our moral principles. It would compel equal condemnation of equal crimes, regardless of who commits them. But this outcome is what we are determined to avoid.

When the left reacts with unvaried "amazement" each and every time a new book comes out telling them that Lenin was just as criminal as Stalin, and perhaps even worse, it can only be because the left has repressed the memory of a similar book that preceded it. The accredited thinkers were dumbfounded when Hélène Carrère d'Encausse's *Lénine* came out in 1998.[16] Had they totally forgotten, in the space of a few short months, the shock inflicted on them the previous year when *The Black Book of Communism* hit the shelves? Did they retain no memory traces of being equally stupefied in 1982 by Dominique Colas's *Le Léninisme?*[17] Did no psychic stigmata remain from the terrible emotional trauma they had endured when Jacques Baynac's *La Terreur sous Lénine* was published in 1975?[18]

In the last-mentioned work, the author estimates the number of victims under Lenin's benevolent rule between 1918 and 1920 to be around two and a half million. But the original trauma suffered by the "progressive" intellectuals was having to live through these crimes when they were being perpetrated, for as Christian Jelen has amply documented in his book *L'Aveuglement*,[19] already by 1918 and in Paris the Human Rights League had to be fully aware of what was happening. This was a blow from which the left swiftly recovered; yet it manages nevertheless to go from surprise to surprise without ever losing its ability to be utterly taken aback at each new revelation of already well-known facts. For these people, memory apparently is nothing but a sieve. The tireless flight from history serves a double purpose: on the one hand, to deny or attenuate the guilt borne by Communism's partisans or accomplices of yesteryear; and on the other, to reinforce the image of the Nazis as the only ideologues who could be intrinsically criminal.

Thus in 1990, on Ho Chi Minh's birth centenary, Unesco organized a celebration in the dictator's "memory." The commemoration's themes were all uncritical reruns of the mendacious pro-Hanoi propaganda of the Sixties and the mythic Ho Chi Minh manufactured out of whole cloth by the Communist organs. The acronym "Unesco" stands for "United Nations Educational, Scientific, and Cultural Organization"; but were it genuinely scientific, it would have brought together authentic historians who would have been quick to demolish the Ho Chi Minh transfiguration; and if educational, it would never have placed its resources in the service of an exercise in brainwashing; and if it had ever truly served culture instead of censorship, it would not have rigged the colloquium so as to banish false notes of "visceral anticommunism." Unimpressed by Unesco's propaganda, Olivier Todd, an expert on Vietnam who had served there for a long time as a special correspondent and was even briefly held captive by the Vietcong, published a study in which he castigated the "Ho Chi Minh myth" in forceful terms. Todd deplored:

> the extraordinary sycophantic naïveté of so many journalists and diplomats, proof of political manipulations within Unesco. This international organization, an offshoot of the United Nations, is getting ready to celebrate Ho Chi Minh as a great "statesman," a "man of culture" and "renowned liberator" of his people. The international community is invited to subsidize this labor of hagiography, this mythologizing of the Communist "Uncle"—in the year after world Communism was dumped into the trash cans of history.[20]

The whole affair was all the more risible in that the regime issuing from Ho Chi Minh Thought—first in North Vietnam and then, after the fall of Saigon in 1975, throughout the whole country—had had ample time to manifest its fundamental traits, which scarcely differed from those of the most repressive Stalinism. This family resemblance had not escaped the notice of an admirer of Ho Chi Minh's, the author and journalist Jean Lacouture. Interviewed by the journal *L'Histoire*,[21] he was asked, "Was it through unawareness of the facts that you were mistaken about North Vietnam?" He replied, "No, I knew what was going on. Where my articles fell short was that they failed constantly to remind the reader of the Stalinist character of the regime." It is hard to see what other "character" the regime could possibly have had, since its founder, stepping onto the stage of history in 1945 under the name "Ho Chi Minh," had been a Comintern agent under the name "Nguyen Ai Quoc" for thirty years already. We know much more about his career in the shadows and his real mission in Indochina since the opening of the Soviet archives.[22] But Unesco is indifferent to these documents, which have shed light on many previously murky areas. Devoted to *la science* in its highly original manner, the organization seemed unaware that since 1975 the Vietnamese regime had faithfully fulfilled all the predictions made for it by Aleksandr Solzhenitsyn in a memorable television broadcast.[23] His lucid comments had elicited only a sarcastic response from the left.

In 1990, did Unesco have the moral right to celebrate such a blindly laudatory mass in the dictator's memory? In fifteen years, the regime inspired by Ho Chi Minh's doctrine had relentlessly recited the dismal rosary of the "philanthropic ogre," to use Octavio Paz's phrase: police terror, executions without due process, ideological brainwashing, concentration camps where mortality rates were more or less high according to geographical location and the severity of re-education, as well as torture, contrived shortages, population flight—this time by sea, where the boat people died in large numbers, drowned or murdered by pirates. A conservative estimate yields a figure of *more than a million* deaths directly or indirectly caused by Hanoi since 1975. While this cult-movie scenario was playing out, Western politicians were falling all over themselves in their rush to Hanoi. At the front of the pack were the French, bubbling with eagerness to disburse the alms of the capitalists to the nomenklatura, who—and this is another characteristic of all Communisms without exception—were shamelessly wallowing in the most dissolute corruption. Our statesmen pushed cynicism so far as to label as "reactionaries" the French citizens of Vietnamese extraction who were scandalized by the extravagant servility that was being shown toward this throne of Asiatic despotism.

With ideological conformity goes behavior that toes the line. Jacques Toubon, in his capacity as minister of culture for a right-leaning government, had occasion to present an award to the writer Duong Thu Huong. He said:

Since early childhood you experienced the Japanese invader and the French colonialist. But it was American imperialism that drove you, at the age of twenty, to commit yourself to the struggle for the independence and reunification of your country.... It is entirely natural for our two countries, who work together on the international scene and are important partners in the French-speaking world, to develop a special relationship as regards literature.* It is a pleasure for me to present you with the insignia of Chevalier des Arts et des Lettres.

Let me point out to younger readers that although Toubon, in this noteworthy discourse, adopted the Communist fables about the evolution of Southeast Asia since 1945, the minister of culture has never belonged to the International. He therefore acted out of conformism rather than conviction. It turned out that his subservience was not sufficient to get him off the hook as far as Hanoi was concerned. On the contrary, Hanoi was unsparing in its denunciations, for Duong Thu Huong, although at one time a member of the Vietnamese CP, was less docile than the French authorities who decorated him. In his acceptance speech he dared to say, "Ho Chi Minh is the idol of the Vietnamese people, but he is not my idol." The Hanoi oligarchy practically accused Toubon of plotting to destabilize the Vietnamese state—a fair recompense for the billion francs received in French aid.

Since nothing of what we have learned about Communism during the past twenty years has penetrated the minds of Unesco and the Western political elites, how could the mass media be better informed or more honest? Their critical role, such as they conceive it, most often consists in reproducing unaltered the critiques that passed as nonconformist during the Sixties. This is what they call "having a sense of history."

Thus in February 1995 the Franco-German network ARTE broadcast a "major documentary," more than an hour long, titled

* In 1997, Hanoi would offer to host a summit of countries that share French as a linguistic inheritance.

Le Vietnam après l'enfer (Vietnam after Hell). This was a crude, incompetent propaganda film that might have been cooked up by some sclerotic agency of the Hanoi bureaucracy. It is legitimate to criticize French policies in Indochina up to the Geneva Accords of 1954, and likewise America's actions after their intervention following upon North Vietnam's breaking of these accords. But the question that needed to be asked in 1995—the question that has a bearing on the present—is this: After the Western defeat, were the regimes that took power in Vietnam, Cambodia and Laos actually liberating regimes? Or were they regimes bringing subjugation and servitude and, most glaringly in the case of Cambodia, genocide? Can you understand what happened politically and historically in the period between 1945 and 1975 if you disregard what happened afterward?

Apparently you can, for that was precisely the tack of ARTE's "documentary." It was an exercise in selective memory, equivalent to assessing the Nazi record without reference to the Kristallnacht pogrom, or Bergen-Belsen or Auschwitz. No serious historians of Communist genocides attempt to cover up those perpetrated by the Nazis; that remains a specialty of those gifts to the left, Le Pen and Faurisson, who represent only a few and are condemned by many. Yet again we see the surreptitious reintroduction of the postulate: The crimes of "the left" are not crimes; only those of the Nazis and Pinochet deserve to be so called. It was a postulate officially endorsed by French justice in the Boudarel affair.

Briefly, Georges Boudarel was a militant Communist who between 1952 and 1954, during the Indochina War, served in a Viet Minh camp as a "re-educator" for his fellow countrymen, the French prisoners.[24] The Geneva Accords led to staffing cutbacks in this line of work, and Boudarel found himself without a job. Switching careers, he went into teaching, ending up as a history professor at the University of Paris VIII, where, as colleagues of his had the effrontery to say in his defense, he was "highly esteemed as a specialist . . . in Vietnamese issues." Years later, at a public colloquium, he happened to be recognized by former prisoners of Camp 113, where he had exercised his talents and where 70 percent of the inmates died. These men pressed charges against Boudarel for crimes against humanity, formally lodged on April 3, 1991.

The left immediately began to mobilize. Articles and petitions were fired off from every side in Boudarel's behalf. The French legal system—independent from the state but not from ideological pressure—did not remain deaf to this campaign, which after all was inspired by such a lofty conception of human rights. And on April 1, 1993, the Court of Appeal rejected the suit brought by the former prisoners of Camp 113, declaring that the lower court had been in error when it maintained that the actions of which Georges Boudarel stood accused constituted crimes against humanity, for "crimes against humanity are crimes committed during the Second World War by the Axis powers."[25]

The above definition is not only a falsification of history, but a license for murder. If crimes against humanity committed *after* the Second World War and by states other than the Axis powers are not punishable, all is allowed, and impunity is granted to murderers forever after. Why then do we pursue Pinochet and Milosevic?

It was the national minister of education, Lionel Jospin, who came to save the honor of the left. When asked to come to the rescue of the debonair torturer—who for many people was the true martyr—and in response to the extraordinary performance of the prudent monkeys who saw, heard and spoke no evil, Jospin said, "I think that to be opposed to colonialism was a justifiable stance. But to come down on the side of those who were, after all, our country's enemies—whatever position you have regarding the necessary evolution of France's colonial empire—that's a step I am not willing to take. Even anticolonialists are not obliged to take that step." And in words that encouraged me to hope that one day a French left will be reborn such as I will be able to join once again, Jospin added, "But above all, in my view, nothing can justify an intellectual, a professor, becoming a *kapo* in a prison camp, a concentration camp in which men from his own country were dying. In my opinion, such a man does not deserve a support committee." By his use of the word *kapo*, the minister showed a willingness to break the taboo that ordinarily forbids the comparison.

Had the magistrates on the Court of Appeal read this profession of faith when they drew up their summary? To appreciate the level of disingenuousness—or in the most generous interpretation, incompetence—revealed by the decision, a rereading of the founding text of the Nuremberg Tribunal should suffice. Here, "crimes against humanity" are defined as: "Murder, extermination, enslavement, deportation and other inhuman acts committed against any civilian population before or during time of war, or persecutions on political, racial or religious grounds." Crimes perpetrated against prisoners of war fall under the same definition. Commenting on the text, Michel Moracchini, who was assistant to Casmayor, a French member of the tribunal, remembered that "Professor Donnedieu de Vabres [also a French representative], in his commentaries, never failed to stress the universal character—independent of time and place—of the concept of 'crimes against humanity.' Everyone who wrote about or worked in this area, including the International Law Commission, was in agreement with him and inspired by his views."[26]

So to restrict the definition to the war years, and only to the actions of Germany, Italy and Japan, flies against the entire development of legal principles since Nuremberg, which resulted in the establishment of the International Criminal Court. Logically, this is about as nonsensical as would be a ruling in common law to restrict the definition of "premeditated murder" to killings committed (let's say) between January 1, 1930, and December 31, 1935, and to *département* zones (let's say) between 1 and 30 exclusively. An absurdity like this, coming from such eminent jurists as those on the Court of Appeal, can be explained only as emanating from the postulate—implicit, mandatory, omnipresent—that Communist crimes can never in any circumstances be classed as crimes against humanity, and perhaps not even as crimes at all.

Further confirmation of this postulate followed the Spanish judge's call for Pinochet's extradition. Inspired by this precedent, members of the Vietnamese diaspora in the closing months of 1998 thought of bringing legal action on behalf of their parents against some of the Hanoi chieftains. Their plaint was declared inadmissible on grounds of the statute of limitations that applies to actions going back more than ten years, even in cases of murder, torture or false imprisonment. But the crimes that Pinochet stood accused of also went back more than a decade. We must conclude that similar or identical crimes against humanity cannot be annulled when they are the deeds of a dictator classified as "fascist," but are easily dismissed when they are the work of Communists. The doctrine of "Communist exceptionalism" is very clear, even though it violates both existing international law and France's new Criminal Code.

The ambivalent attitude of the democracies' leadership and media toward totalitarianism reaches the limits of cynicism and absurdity in their dealings with Fidel Castro. Everyone knows about the caudillo of Havana's violations of human rights. The press, even at the left of the spectrum (apart from the explicitly Communist pamphlets and *Le Monde diplomatique*), no longer bothers to conceal the ferociously repressive character of Cuba's police state; yet Castro continues to be invited everywhere and received with accolades. Prime ministers and bishops—even the Holy Father himself—queue up for the honor of being invited to Cuba by the sanguinary Bearded One. The murderous clown deceives the useful idiots with the empty promises they are avid to hear; and when they leave, his dupes eagerly grant press conferences in which they congratulate themselves for the dictator's honorable intentions. But barely have they boarded their plane for the flight home when the Cuban police crack down all the harder, exposing their pathetic credulity for what it is.

This is what I like to call the "Cuban paradox": the left protects Castro yet harbors no illusions about him, as the title of an excellent article by Alain Abellard in *Le Monde diplomatique* makes plain: "Cuba: The End of an Illusion." You might think that waiting until 1999 to be disillusioned in this regard hardly speaks to exceptional perspicuity. But we are so accustomed to the taboo against telling the truth about Marxist dictators past and present that it's good to see the taboo being cast aside from time to time. Abellard informs us that repression of the island's people is increasing—a trend exactly the opposite to what Cuba's apologists have been predicting for forty years. "Even moderate demonstrations are no longer tolerated," and a new law punishes with twenty years in prison any "collaboration with foreign media, directly or by means of a third party."[27]

There was a reason for this decree. Some media have broken free from the rule of silence forbidding the slightest mention of Cuban tortures and executions. On January 8, 1999, the ARTE television channel aired—late in the evening and ten years after the event—a documentary about the show trials of 1989 whereby Castro put to death four of his generals on the pretext of drug trafficking. There had been trafficking, and on a large scale, but the dictator himself was its kingpin and principal beneficiary. *Forbes* magazine, in its annual list of the world's greatest amassments of wealth, estimated Castro's to be in the two-billion-dollar range. The real reason for the executions was the generals' forthrightness in questioning the large sacrifice of young people's lives in the military interventions that Cuba, under Soviet orders, had made in Ethiopia and Angola. The Caribbean Stalinoid organized a trial in Havana, a replay of its bloody predecessors in Moscow, Budapest and Prague—a tropical *L'Aveu.*[*] After promising that General Arnaldo Ochoa and his comrades would be acquitted if they "confessed," which they proceeded with naïve confidence to do, he had them shot. A keen aficionado, Castro watched the dawn executions of the "traitors" over closed-circuit television.

This time around, the macabre show fell flat. Unlike the judicial murders in the USSR, Czechoslovakia, Bulgaria and Hungary, which had been greeted with acclamation by the Human Rights League and perspicacious approval from a whole raft of celebrated Western intellectuals, the Cuban rerun did not meet with the *succès d'estime* nor even the discreet connivance that Castro was expecting. The most left-wing of the French television weeklies, *Télérama,* in a preview of the documentary, published a

---

* *Translator's note: L'Aveu* is a 1970 Costa-Gavras film about an Eastern European show trial, starring Yves Montand and Simone Signoret.

long interview with the daughter of General Antonio de la Guardia, also one of the victims.[28] Citing the precedent of the Pinochet suit, which the media were widely publicizing at the time, Ileana de la Guardia stated her intent to bring legal action against Castro for her father's murder and for the arbitrary imprisonment of her brother for the crime of failing to denounce him. (The obligation to denounce members of one's own family is, by the way, yet one more shared feature of the Nazi and Communist systems.)

When she invoked the legal proceedings against Pinochet, Ileana de la Guardia showed that she did not understand the moral and mental universe of the international left—nor of the terrorized right, which typically confines itself to obedient emulation of the left's positions. Castro can no more be indicted than Boudarel, and for the same reasons. An impressive display of the legal iron curtain separating the political crimes of the left from those of the right was provided when two sets of events happened to coincide: while the elderly Pinochet was being served with an arrest warrant as he visited a clinic in London, Castro was being treated very differently at the annual Iberian-American summit in Oporto. He strutted before the gathered Spanish and Portuguese grandees, acknowledging their ovations and emotion-filled gazes. How deplorable to witness the king of Spain, an honorable man and champion of democracy, embrace one of its worst enemies! And on another occasion, how nauseating it was to see the president of the French National Assembly lavish similar tokens of amity on the tyrant! The Spanish judge responsible for issuing the warrant for Pinochet's arrest would never for an instant have contemplated taking advantage of Castro's fortuitous presence in Europe to do likewise against him. Such restraint instantly transformed the action against Pinochet into an imposture, demonstrating once again that the level of criminality that may be ascribed to the actions of political figures is measured not by the yardstick of crimes against humanity they may actually have committed, but by their political coloration.

Contrary to the glossy postcard image eagerly bought by political tourists, the Cuban regime is not at all a friendly dictatorship tempered by a dulcet tropical clime, but rather a faithful replica of the Stalinist paradigm whose steel grip has never slackened. Since 1959, fifteen to seventeen thousand political prisoners have been shot on the island. During the summer of 1994 alone, seven thousand Cuban escapees perished at sea—the *balseros,* as they are called, who "vote with their oars" and whose frail boats and rafts are machine-gunned by Castro's helicopters. By way of comparison, the number of executions attributable to DINA, the Chilean secret police, during Pinochet's entire dictatorship is put at 3,197. Of course, statistics by themselves do not constitute a moral criterion: a single killing may add up to a crime against humanity. Nevertheless, statistics do enable us to measure the extent of the terror inflicted by a dictatorship and should therefore not be overlooked by those whose job it is to keep us informed.

Recall that the seventeen thousand or so people shot by Castro's regime were living on an island whose population was approximately ten million, whereas Pinochet's repression cost the lives of 3,197 in a population of fifteen million. In Cuba we find every sort of prison; in the most dreadful of them, torture is used on a daily basis as a means of keeping order. We find the whole gamut of concentration, re-education and "strict regime" labor camps, faithful copies of the Soviet models of the *grande époque.*[29] We find, as in Nazi Germany, camps reserved for homosexuals, others for AIDS sufferers. (In 1987, Le Pen recommended the latter institution for France, to the great indignation of the left.) But I won't continue here with this lugubrious inventory; the interested reader can find the details in *The Black Book of Communism.*[30] Rather, let me point out the singularity of foreign reactions to the Cuban phenomenon. With regard to the other Communisms, the left's strategy has been to deny evidence and conceal testimony. But in the case of Cuba, with a few marginal exceptions the left no longer makes any effort to do so. The facts are openly acknowledged. Cuba, less formidable than China or just unluckier, could not even escape condemnation by the UN Human Rights Commission, which in 1998 ruled against her by a vote of 21 to 20, with 12 abstentions. A not insignificant indicator: the resolution was proposed by Poland and the Czech Republic.

Nevertheless, the French left persists in its protective attitude toward Cuban Stalinism, carefully watching over the immunity that Castro enjoys. I am almost tempted to say: In the old days, *at least* they were lying! Today, fully conceding that the regime depends entirely on the most extreme violations of human rights, they still refrain from withdrawing their solidarity—which may be worse. Not everyone on the left subscribes to Mme Danielle Mitterrand's words: "Cuba represents the apex of what socialism can achieve," a statement that amounts to the most crushing condemnation of socialism ever enunciated. But everyone, even "on the right," works all the harder to claim allegiance (already tested to the hilt in the case of the Khmer Rouge and that of Erich Honecker) to the basic principle: Even when we know all about the crimes of a totalitarian mass murderer "of the left," he must remain exempt from the blame or punishment that—as a duty of remembrance—should be inflicted upon the assassins of the right.

The paradox of the Cuban exception lies in this: the Caudillo's friends feel no necessity to refute the indictment brought against him; on the contrary, they freely endorse it. "We are fully aware that Fidel is a murderer. So what? He's one of us. Don't go after our guy!" Avowals of this sort, however, do not extend to one area about which the left (here again followed religiously by the right) is in angry denial: the Cuban economy. For socialists, poverty cannot have—*must not have*—any other cause but capitalism and the free market.

In the same vein, when leftists harp on poverty in Morocco, a nation where poverty certainly exists but basic necessities are not lacking, they conveniently skate over the chronic penury of Morocco's neighbor, Algeria. Potentially a far richer land, Algeria has been pauperized by socialism over the last three decades. The ideologues, in their attempts to exorcise the permanent nightmare of actually existing command economies, have always resorted to inept cosmetic operations or fanciful narratives.

But the laurels for beautification go to the mystical visions of the East German economy that were circulating before the demolition of the Berlin Wall. In an extended essay in *Le Monde diplomatique*, Manuel Lucbert informed us in 1976 that East Germany "represents the most perfectly realized form of a socialism that is authoritarian, of course, yet developed," where the "velvet glove of consumption" makes the political "glove of iron" acceptable.[31]

Well, anyone who traveled around in the GDR during the last fifteen years of its existence could not fail to be enlightened by the country's state of dilapidation: buildings so rickety that ropes were strung along the sidewalks as a warning to pedestrians who might otherwise be flattened by falling masonry; a lamentable infrastructure; uncompetitive industries that were using machinery dating from the 1920s and were belching out greasy black smoke from ancient chimneys. Yet no sooner had the German reunification been accomplished than the left blamed this socialist cataclysm on the irruption of the market economy! Let's not forget that between 1990 and 1998, in addition to private investments, public funds to the tune of 1,370 billion marks—equivalent to a third of France's annual budget—were transferred to the East. By 1999, after these huge infusions of capital, the former East Germany had made considerable progress but was far from reaching the living standard of its cousins in the West, so difficult is it to recover from the illness of socialism.

It is difficult also for socialism's devotees. Michel Tournier, parroting a book by Lothar de Maizière, the GDR's last prime minister, calmly states that East Germany was a "zone of prosperity" and that Konrad Adenauer, having "launched the Federal Republic into everything-goes Americanization, will be reckoned one of the century's most disastrous political leaders."[32] East Germany's legendary "prosperity" had inspired M. Lucbert to wind up his article thus: "Facing a West Germany blighted with unemployment and violence, East Germany's counter-model has gained in credibility." But in that year, 1976, unemployment in the Federal Republic stood at less than 5 percent; and with regard to violence, Lucbert was doubtless thinking about the Baader-Meinhof Gang, also known as the Red Army Faction, dear to Jean

Genet, Jean-Paul Sartre and a large number of the Parisian intelligentsia. We know today, thanks to the opened archives of East Germany's Stasi secret police, that the gang was created by them and received orders directly from Erich Honecker himself.

In the case of Cuba, cosmetic embellishment is inadvisable; too many tourists visit the island and witness the prevailing shortages. So the left resorts to the parrying tactic of attributing the poverty to an imaginary cause. For other actually existing socialisms, the excuse is usually of a meteorological sort: thus when ten thousand North Korean children starved to death in a single year, 1997, Pyongyang adduced as cause a disconcerting confluence of torrential rain and drought. But it would be hard to put Cuba's climate in the dock, and therefore guilt had to reside somewhere in human deeds. Not to worry: these have nothing to do with socialism! No socialist failure can ever be imputed to socialism, so the blame must be located elsewhere.

Deprived of a convenient climatic scapegoat for Cuba's stagnation, the left seized on a sacred word: "blockade." Even in a highly critical piece on Cuba by François Maspero, "Le Bel Hier et les ombres d'aujourd'hui" (The Beauties of Yesterday and the Shadows of Today), we are met with the subtitle: "Thirty years ago, François Maspero believed he had found another way we could live. Today, the blockade is still in place, and Castro also."

My intention is not to rehearse the history of Cuba and the other Communist countries once again. The facts are well known to the point of banality. Rather, my aim is to sketch out the psychological mechanisms that induce so many lucid thinkers to excuse famines, torture and criminality on one condition: that they were Communist-caused. It's an investigation that condemns me to the unhappy duty of returning again and again to the same old truisms. For this I apologize to my readers, but I am not responsible for these depressing realities; I am merely describing them.

To get Castro off the hook, the trick is to play on a confusion between "blockade" and "embargo." Apologists would have us believe that Cuba—which in 1959 had the third-highest standard if living in Latin America, just after Uruguay and Chile, with the highest literacy rate and the largest number of physicians per capita—has been ruined not by socialism but by America's "blockade." Turning to *Le Petit Larousse,* we find that the word is defined as: "The blocking of a harbor, surrounding of a town or an entire country so as to prevent resupply and communication with the outside. Economic blockade: The totality of measures taken against a country so as to deprive it of all commerce." It is obvious that Cuba has never been the target of the slightest blockade. It *has* been subject to an embargo relating exclusively to commerce with the United States. An embargo is the "suspension of trade in one or more products, as a sanction or as a means of applying pressure on a country." The United States decided not to buy anything from or sell anything to Cuba, but has not surrounded the island with her navy so as to cut it off from the rest of the world. A nation is free to choose its clients and suppliers, as is an individual person. Why then does this nonsense of "blockade" keep on reappearing, even in highbrow journals?

Besides being generously supported by the Soviet Union, which bought its sugar crop at above world market prices and sold it in exchange for petroleum at well below, Cuba has always been free to trade with Latin America, Canada and Europe—especially Spain. When payment for supplies comes due and is delayed or forgotten altogether, the catering nations have typically shown an indulgence verging on economic aid. And there have been numerous investors from abroad. In 1988, inaugurating the Sixteenth International Havana Fair, Castro boasted that more than 1,400 foreign firms were represented—a sign, he said, that the "American blockade" had been defeated.[33] In addition, Cuba receives foreign aid amounting to several billion dollars annually from the United Nations and diverse NGOs; and Cuban exiles remit roughly one billion dollars annually to their families remaining on the island, contributions that help keep the standard of living from sinking even lower. In all, the subsidies make Cuba, whose population numbers barely over ten million, one of the most aided nations in the world; so if its economy has been mired in stagnation for forty years, the cause is systemic and has nothing to do with a blockade that can be demonized all the more readily insofar as it doesn't exist.

But it's a sure bet that when the regime finally collapses and Cuba is forced to return to a market economy, the slowness of recovery and persisting socialist infirmities will be blamed on "excessive liberalism."

Visiting Warsaw in 1999, Lionel Jospin warned Poles to "be on guard against ideology." Coming from Jospin, this can only mean liberal "ideology." A socialist once again reveals a chronic incapacity to grasp that liberalism is not an ideology. For a Marxist, or ex-Marxist, to lecture a people who had been subjected to *real* ideology was ludicrous as well as inappropriate, since of all the nations recovering from sovietization, the Poles have been the most successful in adapting to market disciplines. Given the context, the "pragmatism" that Jospin exhorted the Poles to observe could mean nothing else than a return to statism. The gravest sin is still making profit. The commentator on the French radio station where I learned about the prime minister's recommendations was in full agreement with them: he denounced the "utilitarianism" and "materialism" of today's Poland. Which implies that the potentates who in the good old days eradicated the free market, the Gomulkas and the Giereks, were models of disinterestedness: mystics aglow with the loftiest spirituality.

It goes without saying that the new Polish economy has experienced crises on its path to recovery and will experience more in the future—and inevitably the socialists will emit shrill cries condemning the failure of "savage" liberalism, as they did during the Asian economic crisis. Of course, liberal economies don't always work. But what better alternative is there? The choice is between something that is not always functional and something that is *never* functional.

Socialist memory blocks are not confined to the domain of totalitarian criminality; they extend also to economics. The affliction is on full display in the French ultra-left movement that calls itself "Droits devant" (Focus on Rights), which sees in the free circulation of investment capital inherent to the globalization process an example of "liberal barbarism and a world ruled by the tyranny of the market."[34] Apparently, for the author of this phrase, collectivist states were refined civilizations where authoritarian distribution of resources created regimes of political liberty. Amnesia on this scale borders on provocation. For the enemies of political liberty are forgetting that their model has already been tested, and that in a handful of fossilized polities it is still being tried out. Are they unaware of the consequences? That is difficult to believe. And don't they know that the chronic penury of numerous underdeveloped countries is caused not by the inequities of capitalism, but only too often by their rulers' enforcement of the *dirigiste* and collectivist model, even when they have not officially labeled themselves Communists?

As for the "tyranny" of the market, this phrase is at best a metaphor, whereas the tyranny of totalitarianism in societies that have suppressed the market is a concrete and abundantly docu-mented reality, which goes far beyond simple political despotism. For another bizarre omission is the habitual failure to mention that Communist societies have been the only contemporary soci-eties to have restored slavery as an institution. More precisely: to have practiced slavery with their own people.

The Nazis also reintroduced slavery, but in time of war and with slaves who were deportees from conquered lands. The Com-munists do better: they systematically enslave large numbers of their own populations in time of peace and in the service of—dare I say it?—their normal economies. This frequently forgotten aspect of socialist economies goes to show that, however unpro-ductive they actually are, they would be even less productive if they did not typically resort to forced labor—a factor stressed in Yuri Orlov's samizdat discussion of the "slave-state socialism of the Stalinist era, when prisoner-slaves constituted about one-quarter of the Soviet Union's workforce."[35] It is a distinguishing trait of nearly all Communist societies, or at least the most representative ones, to require the services of a large unpaid workforce just to survive.

This compelling thesis is given support by Jacques Rossi, a man who lived nineteen years in the heart of the Soviet paradise. His vivid account helps us understand how the gulag—and its emulators in China, Cuba, Vietnam and North Korea—far from being a perversion of Communism, is an indispensable part of it, even its quintessential paradigm. In Rossi's words, "The gulag was not an aberration or a deviation, it was the very essence of the system."[36] Also: "Marxism, being a utopia, can be realized only through violence and terror."[37]

Many thinkers had been able to foresee the consequences of Utopia before it came into being and confirmed their predictions. Their writings include Alfred Sudre's *Histoire du communisme* (Paris, 1849); Adolphe Franck's *Le Communisme jugé par l'histoire* (Paris, 1871); and Eugen Richter's *Sozialdemokratische Zukunfts-bilder,* the French translation of which came out in 1895 under the title *Où mène le socialisme?* with a preface by Paul Leroy-Beaulieu.[38] Karl Jaspers, in his essay on Max Weber, records the following conversation between Weber and Joseph Schumpeter:

> The two men met in a Vienna café, with Ludo Moritz Hartmann and Felix Somary also present. Schumpeter indicated how gratified he was by the socialist revolution in Russia. Hence-forth socialism would not be just a program on paper—it would have to prove its viability.
>
> To which Weber, showing every sign of deep dismay, replied that Communism at this stage of development in Russia virtually amounted to a crime, and that to take this path would lead to human misery without equal and to a ter-rible catastrophe.
>
> "That's exactly what will happen," agreed Schumpeter, "but what a perfect laboratory experiment."
>
> "A laboratory in which mountains of corpses will be heaped!" retorted Weber in feverish tones.
>
> "You could say the same thing about any dissection room," said Schumpeter.

This exchange must have occurred at the beginning of the Bol-shevik regime, since Max Weber died in 1920. Thus one of the twentieth century's greatest sociologists and one of its greatest economists were in substantial agreement about Communism: they had no illusions about it and were fully aware of its crimino-genic tendencies. On one issue, though, they differed. Schumpeter was still in thrall to a belief that Weber did not share, namely the illusion that the failures and crimes of Communism would serve as a lesson to humanity. Exasperated, poor Weber could no longer contain himself. Jaspers continues:

> Every attempt to deflect their conversation to other topics failed. Weber spoke ever more loudly and vehemently. Schumpeter remained guarded and quietly sarcastic. The others present listened with curiosity, waiting to see what would happen.
> "I can't take any more of this!" Weber finally exclaimed, abruptly rising from his seat. He walked out, followed by Hartmann, bearing Weber's hat. Schumpeter remained calmly seated, commenting with amusement: "How could someone shout like that in a café?"[39]

As an economist, Schumpeter believed that economic failure amounted to refutation. But the sociologist knew that Utopia is never refuted. Were he alive today, Max Weber would no doubt be gratified to see how his pessimism became justified, barely eight years after the fall of the Berlin Wall, when perceptive thinkers thought they saw a Return to Marx in the offing—when, for example, a *Télérama* cover in 1997 boasted a big portrait of Karl Marx with his immense white beard alongside the aggressive question: "MARX: THE RETURN?" The return had become necessary because of the "ravages of capitalism," a diagnosis that shouldn't surprise us in the least, coming as it did from a magazine that makes no secret of its ideological slant.

But how are we to react when a politician as prominent as Francesco Cossiga, former president of the Republic of Italy and former leading light of the Italian Christian Democratic Party, in a television debate with Silvio Berlusconi, heaps praise on *The Communist Manifesto*? In his capacities as head of state and head of government, M. Cossiga has come across as someone of intermittent mental equilibrium, routinely trotting out worrisome verbal initiatives. But when we hear a Christian Democrat— heir to the doctrine of Alcide De Gasperi, Robert Schuman and Konrad Adenauer—proclaim that *The Communist Manifesto* offers effective remedies for unemployment and other scourges of capitalism, we are led to wonder if it might not be better to do away entirely with the teaching of history in our schools. Isn't it in fact, as Tolstoy and Valéry feared, the most useless of all branches of knowledge? When it comes to the history of Communism, at least, its uselessness would seem to have been definitively established.

CHAPTER NINE

The "Most Favored Totalitarian State" Clause

As the century turns, one might think that the Great Evasion (*l'opération "grande parade"*) practiced by the left has succeeded.* Despite the publication of numerous important and widely read books on the Communist cataclysm, there has been considerable resistance from the academic, political and media establishment, who look for ways to refute or attenuate the message of these works. Admittedly, some dikes have been breached and ideological fortifications have crumbled here and there, but the core principle—that the totalitarianisms of the so-called left and the so-called right must be treated differently—holds firm. The 1980s will be recognized as the decade of the collapse of the Communist regimes and the relative failure of social-democratic policies, and the 1990s as the decade when efforts to erase the lessons of that history were largely successful. The laurels went not to those who

---

* *Translator's note:* Revel is invoking the original title of this book, *La Grande Parade*. See the Introduction for the punning implication of the French word *parade*.

"dared to say no" to Communism when it reigned supreme over so many peoples in the world and bewitched so many minds, but to those who had rushed to serve under its banners, with enthusiastic applause.

To have been a servant of Communism, even at the moment of its greatest crimes, no longer discredits anyone. But to have fought against Communism, or merely to have criticized it, still today relegates you to the ranks of accomplices to fascism or nostalgists for Vichy, if not to the ranks of those who actually perpetrated the Holocaust. So the work of a great writer like Emil Cioran, who in his youth was derailed by fascist ideas, is branded with infamy, although in reality his writing amounts to a sublime and monumental abjuration of his early sins. On the other hand, the posthumous glory of a Louis Aragon is not diminished in the least, although he devoted his entire life into old age to actively supporting a murderous regime that perpetrated fresh crimes daily, not only approving of the routine killings but hoping for them. You could even say that his ignominy, being on the correct side, adds to his glory. The real risk, in fact, was that *no one* would clumsily politicize a critique of his meager literary merits with a mean-spirited reference to his Stalinist career.

Reacting to the shamanic trances we saw displayed on Aragon's birth centenary in 1998, David Bosc wrote, "We see how crimes, with their lurid glow, can enhance an uncertain, flickering talent."[1] But it has to be Communist crimes, I would add: these alone possess the power of purification. This point aside, I share Bosc's conviction that the aesthetic value of Aragon's post-surrealist work—trashy verse and mannered novels, pastiches akin to the reproduction furniture you can buy in the Faubourg Saint-Antoine—would have been applauded with less frenzy if his devotees, especially those on the right, had not been haunted by the fear that Aragon was insufficiently appreciated as a writer because he happened to have sunk so low as a man.

In contrast, because he has distanced himself from Marxism, Mario Vargas Llosa's literary renown is fatally compromised. For example, in 1995 he was invited to take part in the radio show

Pentimento, hosted by Mme Paula Jacques, and the following exchange took place:

> *Paula Jacques:* How is it that a young man enamored of revolution could years later turn into a presidential candidate running against the left, or at least on a right-wing platform?
>
> *Mario Vargas Llosa:* Well, the left, when I entered university, rightly stood for resistance to the military dictatorship— for generosity, for concern over the lot of the poor and for a moral stance against injustice. Twenty years later, the Peruvian left stood for Stalinism, for solidarity with horrifyingly cruel regimes, gulag regimes, where millions of people were sacrificed with arbitrary brutality. The European left had already distanced itself from authoritarian socialism, but in South America this process was only just beginning. There was already a very deep change that I identified with.
>
> *Paula Jacques:* Wouldn't you say that one tends to become more pragmatic with age, that one wants to keep what one has, as far as you are concerned?
>
> *Mario Vargas Llosa:* No, the battle I fought in Peru was a risky battle. In 1987 we had the Shining Path, which killed more than thirty thousand people in Peru alone! I tell in my book *Fish in the Water* how, during the electoral campaign, almost fifty of my colleagues were assassinated by terrorists.[2] So when you're defending liberalism and democratic reforms, it's not just a question of being pragmatic. It took a lot of guts, you know.

Vargas Llosa's skeptical interviewer remained unimpressed by his testimony. According to her, terrorism and Stalinism, however blameworthy, are not reason enough for someone to "betray" the left. And since this is what he was guilty of, he could not conceivably have acted in good faith, with intellectual honesty and rigor. No, wasn't it rather because Vargas Llosa, a world-renowned man of letters, had made money and had joined the bourgeois "ownership class," with the advantages this entails? We can at least wonder.[3]

Contrariwise, not the slightest suspicion of doubt can besmirch the memory of an old companion of the Communist International, the veteran Australian journalist Wilfred Burchett. This man's name probably means nothing to 90 percent of readers today. Burchett was the journalist who invented the lie of American bacteriological warfare during the Korean War, a calculated piece of disinformation orchestrated by the world Communist press, with the French press in the forefront. In his memoirs, Pierre Daix—in those days the editor of the Communist *Ce soir,* an evening daily paper as leftist as *L'Humanité* in its positions, but long since disappeared—came around to confessing, "I gave Burchett's cables the full treatment . . . . False information, incitement to hatred—the whole panoply of journalistic dishonor is on display in them."[4] Burchett alternated between living in Bulgaria and Hungary in 1949, the year that Traicho Kostov was hanged in Bulgaria and Lészló Rajik was hanged in Hungary. In his articles for the Western press, Burchett sought to justify the executions of these "traitors." That's what he was paid for. And during the Sixties, he promenaded around the world with passports from Cuba and North Vietnam. But enough said—it has been exhaustively proved that Wilfred Burchett was the quintessential hostile agent in the service of enemy powers.

I slipped a reference to this indefatigable salesman for Stalinism into *The Totalitarian Temptation.* For my sin I was reprimanded by the left-wing press, especially in *Le Monde diplomatique,* where Claude Bourdet accused me of being inspired by anti-Burchett slanders emanating from "the Australian extreme right." I must confess my complete ignorance, then and now, of what the Australian extreme right may have vented against the man. But supposing that Claude Bourdet was not making things up, classifying the liberal right as the *extreme* right—in accordance with the fine-tuned taxonomy of the sectarian left—I had no need of Australian prompting to make me wonder about a disturbing oddity: How was it that Burchett, an eminent, notorious collaborator with the Soviet secret agencies, could also be one of the regularly published commentators on international politics during the 1970s in the weekly publication of the French Socialist Party, *L'Unité*? Were the publishers merely incompetent, or were they conniving?

The protection enjoyed by this wretched scribbler and, when all is said and done, dispensable lackey—in the very democracies that he was intent on destroying—is easy to understand, however. In the 1970s, the sacred union of the left entailed obligations, and anticommunism was rigorously prohibited. If the taboo had been removed twenty years later, it was in theory and not in practice, and defensive lying in behalf of Communism continued to be permitted and even recommended. Thus in 1995 the French cable network Planète offered what was supposed to be a "documentary" but was actually a piece of dithyrambic puffery in honor of the obscure (for the viewers at least) Burchett. Consider the lyrical terminology in the announcement of the broadcast in the television supplement to *Le Nouvel Observateur,* beginning with the title: "For Having Told the Truth, This Australian Would Be Banished."[5] What banishment? None was ever reported, since Burchett abandoned his Australian nationality in favor of Cuban, Bulgarian and North Vietnamese identities. Then, to claim that Burchett told the truth is to claim that the Americans really did wage bacteriological warfare in Korea and that Rajk and Kostov really were traitors, as Stalin wanted the world to believe, and thus deserving of death. Today, no Communist party, in the former Soviet Union or elsewhere, still maintains these propositions, and you have to go to Planète or *Le Nouvel Observateur* to see them espoused.

It was only natural that Burchett's unyielding fidelity in the service of truth would be rewarded. He received the Stalin Prize in 1951. The Little Father of the People knew how to reward his hired help.

Yet decades later, *Le Nouvel Observateur* was lamenting, "Unfortunately, integrity very often doesn't pay. That was the misfortune of Wilfred Burchett, a privileged witness to forty years of contemporary history." He was "privileged" because:

> Invariably, Burchett found himself right in the center of the world's hotspots. Yet in an era when capitalism and communism, imperialism and nationalism were in confrontation, it was not always advisable to tell the truth and he came to be banished from his own country. The film, pieced together from hitherto unreleased archives, tells the life story of this great Australian journalist. An unflinching political documentary, it is above all the very opposite of politically correct.[6]

It is not hard to understand why the Soviet propaganda machine, aided by its Western henchmen, did everything possible to pass off this minor player as an independent and scrupulous journalist, for at that time the game was still being played for concrete political stakes. The world was divided into two camps, and the friends of the Soviets went all out to promote their side. But by 1995 the Burchett question, if it ever really was an issue, had turned into *a purely historical issue.* So how can you maintain—on television and in a social-democratic weekly magazine of incontestably high intellectual standards—that a professional falsifier was really a "great journalist," simply because he was not only Communist but working in the service of the International's organs? I daresay no school of journalism, with the exception of Gabriel García Marquez's in Bogotá, would propose this very special colleague as a model for students. Media treatments like Planète's speak volumes about the triumphal rehabilitation of Marxist totalitarianism.

As a thought experiment, imagine the response if a propaganda piece were aired oozing admiration for a journalist who collaborated with the Nazis at a time when they were all-powerful, setting him on a pedestal as a professional ideal. It would be a nauseating thing to do, of course, and the outcry would justifiably be immense. But you get to be honored as an ornament to journalism if it is Stalin's, Mao's or Castro's bloodlettings that you celebrate. For Communism retains its aura of moral superiority.

Symptoms of the double standard can be almost puerile. When Hergé's first Tintin adventure, *Tintin au pays des Soviets* (*Tintin in the Land of the Soviets*), was reissued in 1999 after being unobtainable for seventy years, it was criticized in several places as an exaggerated caricature. But Hergé's depiction of the USSR, on the contrary, is astonishingly accurate; already in 1929 the young author was able to capture its essence, displaying what Emmanuel Le Roy Ladurie, replying to a questionnaire sent out by *Le Figaro*, called "a prodigious intuition."[7] But *Le Figaro* could not bring itself to agree with the historian, finding that Hergé's vision "inevitably suffers, with the passing of time, from its Manichaeism." You read it correctly: *with the passing of time*. Which means: What we have learned since 1929 and particularly since 1989 about Communism as it really was gives us reason to assess it more positively than we might have done at the beginning, when illusions were pardonable; after all, we were carefully kept in ignorance. *Le Figaro*'s point seems to be that as information about Communism becomes more readily available, it must increasingly appear in a better light.

In a commentary on the new edition, the radio station France-Info assured us that *Tintin au pays des Soviets* was "an ideological cartoon with a musty odor about it." The inescapable conclusion: It wasn't adulation of Communism that was ideological, but rebellion against it. Above all, the events that have transpired since the Great Terror of the 1930s up to the invasion of Afghanistan— among which were the anti-Semitic Doctors' Plot, the squashing of the Budapest and Prague uprisings, the Great Leap Forward, the Cultural Revolution, the reign of the Khmer Rouge—clearly invite us to discard an overly severe view of Communism.

Many commentators did not fail to insinuate that Hergé had little authority to speak about these matters because he had "conducted himself badly" during the Occupation. Would it follow, likewise, that a condemnation of Nazism exudes a "musty odor" when it comes from an ex-Stalinist? No, because the fundamental question does not pertain to the political career of the accuser; it is rather a matter of knowing whether or not Nazism per se was monstrous. A Stalinist who asserts that it *was* monstrous is entirely justified on this point, Stalinist though he is. So why is the converse assertion out of bounds? Precisely because Communism has managed to maintain its condescending air of moral superiority. Or, more exactly, because of the unremitting efforts, at the cost of a thousand lies and dissimulations, to perpetuate the hoax of superiority.

When history is written upside-down in this manner, we have to forgive journalists who are lured down the slippery slope. They are likely to have been misinformed by dishonest historians, too many of whom persist in defending the Communist fortress with unshakable vigilance. One example is a recent volume in the *Que sais-je?* series.[8] Simply titled *Le Goulag*, it manages to spare Lenin, whose heritage Stalin is purported to have "betrayed." This is an old figment, a deceiving mirage that has been refuted a thousand times; the revelations of the last few years have made it vanish into thin air. Nonetheless, we are informed that Stalin, the joker in the pack, was the heir not to Lenin, but to the tsars!

It has been firmly established that the Soviet labor camps originated with Lenin. And however repressive the imperial regime, the tsars' political prisoners never amounted to more than a minute fraction of the vast numbers of inmates within the Soviet archipelago. Falling over backward in his attempts to hold Stalin solely responsible, the author of this volume spews forth his bile on Solzhenitsyn, on Jacques Rossi (to whom we owe *The Gulag Handbook*) and on Nicolas Werth (author of *The Black Book's* section on the USSR). He impugns the testimony of the first two and contests the capabilities of Werth as a historian.

The venerable *Que sais-je?* library is an established line of the Presses Universitaires de France (PUF). These short texts, in principle, are scrupulous summaries of our current understanding. Often they amount to the only source of information on a vast range of topics for a huge readership, and above all for students. So the slim volume dealing with the gulag presents what many people over the next decade will read about this subject.

So the question arises: Is there a pilot in PUF's cockpit? That is, a competent series editor who respects the ethical code that should guide his profession? After all, the *Que sais-je?* library is promoted as being impartial, not a series of tendentious pamphlets with blatant *partis pris*. So here we have an abuse of intellectual trust and fraudulent sales practice.

In this example of revisionism, the publication date is instructive: 1999. Twenty-five years earlier, the left had launched its battalions in an all-out effort to defame Aleksandr Solzhenitsyn, twisting the slightest of his words so as to make it seem that he harbored sympathy for Nazism or for Pinochet. By dragging his name in the mud, their intention was to discredit the fatal inventory drawn up in *The Gulag Archipelago*. In 1975, the Association France-USSR even published in its magazine a "report" on the Soviet concentration camps from which it emerged that, in comparison with their luxurious levels of comfort, the Mediterranean Club was virtually a penitentiary.[9] Going back a few years earlier, the incomparable Wilfred Burchett, battling as always with his trademark courage against the "politically correct," likened the prison camps of North Korea (a preferred country of his, by the way, from which he was never "banished") to "holiday resorts in Switzerland."

I offer the above as souvenirs of the times. Such calumnies and tall tales range from the comical to the odious. They are inexcusable, but in France they can be explained in terms of the aberrant requirements of the left's sacred union, and the fear in the hearts of socialists that they might displease the Communists. Even in countries where Communist parties were weak or nonexistent—Great Britain, Scandinavia, West Germany, the United States—the democratic left during the Cold War adopted an ambiguous attitude that caused it to avoid any overly acerbic critique of the Soviet system. Such abject intellectual servitude and moral nihilism stemmed from a political error, certainly, but the error was a response—albeit an idiotic one—to actual facts on the ground. Today, that historical situation is no more. Diehard defenses of Communism are therefore not dictated by any project in the realm of action, and must therefore stem from a psychological need to rehabilitate it, and above all to ward off any comparisons to National Socialism. Another thought experiment: What publishing house would have dared to issue, and what reception would have greeted, a little treatise with academic pretensions that developed an edifying apologia with regard to the Nazi camps?

Apparently, pro-Communist revisionism has been a successful undertaking. The goal of the left's Great Parrying Maneuver (*l'opération "grande parade"*), begun in 1991, has been substantially achieved: to reconstruct, by propaganda and intimidation, the twin fictions of Communism's moral and practical superiority. Little by little, international sensibility has been conditioned to accept an ever-widening abyss between our judgments of crimes committed by despotisms of the so-called right and those of the so-called left. I must insist again on those "so-calleds." The distinction drawn between "right-wing" and "left-wing" totalitarianism is in itself meaningless, because the notions of right and left presuppose democracy, with its pluralism of freely constituted parties and diversity of opinions, freely expressed. One-party totalitarian states with enforced conformity of thought render this political taxonomy null and void. In straitjacketed societies, the lived reality never varies. Right versus left becomes mere rhetorical whitewash, an ideologue's phantasmagoria, a cruel and vacuous sophism. Alas, this empty fallacy, by means of tactical maneuvers as unrelenting as they are hypocritical, has become so ingrained that it even corrupts the democracies' understanding of their own history. The moral double standard has mutated into a rule of decorum—which amounts to saying that moral standards have gone by the wayside.

For example, during the Pinochet affair, a wave of indignation swept across Europe when, on August 6, 1999, a Spanish public prosecutor ordered the quashing—on "technical grounds"—of a warrant that had been issued against the aged dictator the year before, after which he had been under house arrest in London and under threat of extradition to Spain. The Iberian press, from every shade of the political spectrum, vented their anger on the prosecutor, with the left-wing daily *El País* gratuitously labeling him "fascistic." One had to think, "My goodness, what a joy to see such masters of the journalistic craft at work, such imagination in their choice of epithets!" True, their indignation was legitimate, and I shared it too—but I would have shared it more wholeheartedly if the image of that lofty personage, Mengistu Haile Mariam, had not crossed my mind.

Mengistu, dubbed the "Red Negus," was a Communist who ruled Ethiopia from 1974 to 1997. He was an executioner on a scale that utterly dwarfed Pinochet. Mengistu's regime answered to all the criteria of the purest, most classical Communism— and may the sworn Tartuffes dispense with their usual dodge of complaining that we aren't dealing with "real" Communism. The Ethiopian "revolution" begot a certified copy of the Soviet Marxist-Leninist prototype. The Russians granted their African acolytes full rights of franchise, financial credits, and protection in the form of Cuban troops and agents from the East German secret police, the peerless Stasi. The "Derg," or junta of Ethiopian chieftains, immediately proclaimed themselves heirs to "the great October Revolution" and set out to establish their credentials by shooting all the elites who declined to join them or hesitated to obey their orders—although, as in all "revolutions," even total servility was not enough to guarantee survival. There followed the standard clutch of measures: collectivization of farms—in a country where 87 percent of the population worked the land—along with nationalization of industry, banking and insurance.

The results were inevitable and foreseeable: agricultural yields far below the normal, bringing famines aggravated by that other specialty of the house, forced population displacements. As failure upon failure cascaded down, the regime was compelled to invent guilty parties, traitors and saboteurs; after all, it is inconceivable that socialism could be a bad idea per se or that those in power could ever be fallible. And as per custom, the rulers discovered the hooligans responsible for the disaster among the starving, not among those who were starving them. There is a depressing monotony in this constantly repeated scenario, which socialism's advocates, at each repetition, strive to explain away as an "exception." In 1978, there were ten thousand political murders in the capital alone; in 1979, there was a massacre of the Ethiopian Jews—the Falashas. There could be no anti-Semitism involved here, of course; the Derg were men of the left.

In a 1977 report, the Swedish secretary-general of the Save the Children Fund told of how he had seen on the sidewalks of Addis Ababa the publicly exhibited corpses of children showing signs of torture: "A thousand children have been massacred in Addis Ababa, and their bodies, lying in the streets, are being preyed upon by hyenas. You can see their corpses piled up on the verges of the road leading out of the city. Most of the children were between eleven and thirteen years old."[10] Reading this description, I am reminded of a remark by Jean Daniel: "A young man who leans toward Communism at least is haunted by a need for communion. Fascists are only fascinated by domination. That makes an essential difference."[11] I hope Daniel won't hold it against me if I confess that I find his argument less than convincing. How can we still take seriously that old refrain: mass murder sanctified by good intentions? What executioner could be more repugnant than one who presumes to kill his victims for the sake of "communion" with them? If the atrocities of Communist regimes past and present can never tarnish the uncorrupted purity of the ideal, why does the left—including the non-Communist left—so fervently deny, minimize, excuse, forget or ignore these atrocities? The left does so because it knows full well that the omnipresent criminality of Communism and its capacity to destroy economies and cultures calls into question the very heart of socialism. Why would socialists be goaded into such anger whenever they are reminded of these facts if, as they claim, they are not concerned about them?

And spare us also that other worn-out refrain: that Ethiopian Communism was nevertheless an improvement on the imperial *ancien régime*. This argument is as false in the case of Ethiopia as it is for Russia and Cuba. It is true that the emperors did not rule over paradise; food shortages were frequent and the poverty extreme. But the famines were not deliberately instigated, the population was not subjected to resettlement programs, and systematic mass murder was not the order of the day. And as we have seen, the Communists added their original contribution, that stylistic touch of murdering children.

No, as long as the left delays in clearing the threadbare rags out of its mental closet and as long as it persists in equivocating before the atrocious, it may be able to govern by trial and error, but it will not be able to lay claim to the key for understanding our times and building a viable future. Yves Santamaria tells us that in Ethiopia, as in the former USSR, "we continue to find mass graves with numerous bodies of the disappeared registered by Amnesty International. As in China, surviving family members were asked to defray the government's expenses for the executions, according to the principle of 'paying for the bullet.'" Evidently the parents had to reimburse the state for the ammunition expended in murdering their children. Or the son for the cartridge used in killing his father, or likewise the sister with respect to her brother. Here is proof positive that socialism means solidarity.

The left's complicity with deliberate, premeditated genocide is not just a phenomenon of the 1920s, of the generation that may perhaps be exonerated by their illusions, as François Furet suggested. On the contrary, it is constantly visible in today's mass media. Whereas the "disappeared" disgraced a regime such as Argentina's during the 1970s, in the land of Communism they are made to disappear from memory as well.

The world outside was quick to learn about the horrors of Ethiopian Communism. In 1986, André Glucksmann and Thierry Wolton set forth the tragic evidence, yet their book did nothing to shake the confidence of the Red Negus's admirers.[12] On one occasion Amadou-Mahtar M'Bow, the director-general of Unesco—an organization always at the cutting edge of progressivism—paid tribute to the tyrant by calling him a "great statesman." Indifference to the regime's crimes was one more confirmation of the rule of moral apathy that has worked to the advantage of all Communist states, and which is explained by what Glucksmann and Wolton accurately call "revolutionary immunity."

Mengistu, unlike Pinochet, was a full beneficiary of this immunity: no one called it into question, even after the Abyssinian serial killer was forced into exile. In 1991, abandoned by his moribund Soviet protector, Mengistu fled to Zimbabwe, whose "progressive" (and therefore irremovable) president, Robert Mugabe, the hero of so many humanitarian and anti-apartheid colloquia, immediately granted him political asylum. I have never heard the slightest mention of any organized initiative by the international left to have Mengistu extradited and hauled before an international tribunal. Eight years after the event, I continue to watch my mailbox for a petition from some anti-genocide association. In 1994, the Ethiopian judiciary undertook to serve summons on a few of the country's "great benefactors," asking Zimbabwe to extradite the foremost among these. Mugabe, ever more "progressive," refused. Yet to extradite Mengistu to his country of origin involved fewer legal headaches than to extradite a Chilean from one foreign country, Great Britain, to another foreign country, Spain.

Where was the wave of indignation across Europe calling for Mengistu Haile Mariam to pay for his crimes? Well, it would have been scandalous to drag this retired, peaceable philanthropist before a court. After all, in 1988 the Communist-oriented World Federation of Trade Unions—among them the French CGT—had awarded him a gold medal in recognition of "his contribution to the struggle for peace and collective security." A medal? By all means! It was worth no more than the people who offered it, or the person who received it. But today, after so much blood has flowed beneath the bridges of socialism, what value—what respect—should we accord a universal Sacred Conscience that is so scrupulously blind?

Here let me recount a revealing anecdote. In 1984, taking part in a broadcast debate, I was naïve enough to let slip the rather poor view I took of the news that the Ethiopian Communist Party, to celebrate the tenth anniversary of the revolution, had imported thousands of cases of the best whisky, champagne and foie gras—at a time when the nation was suffering one of those lethal famines for which Communism holds the patent. Next morning I saw myself brought to task by *L'Humanité* for my lack of common decency and proper awareness of my status as an unworthy, unqualified reactionary. This Ethiopian episode—the banquet of the chieftains surrounded by a famished populace and piles of still-warm corpses—forcibly recalls the famous passage in Orwell's *Animal Farm* in which Napoleon, the tyrant pig, lays down the doctrine: "All animals are equal, but some animals are more equal than others." What is remarkable about Communism, wherever it sprouts and in whatever cultural milieu, is how each regime unfolds according to an unvarying scenario, with each stage of development falling into place at the preordained moment. The only experimental verifications of historical materialism that we will ever witness, *faute de mieux*, are those it performs on itself.

Having done our "duty to forget" with respect to the Ethiopian "Khmer Noir," let us turn, at the risk of redundancy, to the celebratory mass in honor of the Khmer Rouge. Their crimes have been exposed, and the numbers are on the order of those encountered in geology or astronomy. But have we been able to register what the numbers represent? And have we done everything we can to punish the guilty? One has to admire the energetic inertia displayed by the absent-minded (except when it comes to the Pinochet dossier) international community: its demands for the extradition of the Khmer Rouge strongmen have been barely audible. I have kept my ears open, and the sound of cannon is faint. True, some of our socialist thinkers safely at home have argued that Pol Pot and his pals were never Communists, but instead were actually "rice-paddy" national socialists.[13] Here again is that old familiar trick of discovering that a Communist regime ceased to be Communist the moment its perfidies were revealed—on condition, of course, that it was no longer in power.

Let's suppose then, for the sake of argument, that they were National Socialists instead. The conversation might go something like this:

Question: Okay, given that they were Nazis, isn't that an additional reason to have them brought to justice?
Answer: Come again?

Question: You have on hand that rare commodity—an extant species of Nazi! And yet, despite such a windfall, you fail to act? Doesn't this prove that you yourselves are not at all convinced by the theories you are so eager to advance and that you know perfectly well, deep down, that your alleged Nazis are authentic Communists?

According to Ben Kiernan, an expert on Cambodian Communism, the number of genocide victims was between 1,700,000 and 1,900,000, or more than 20 percent of the original population of 7,900,000.[14] Nevertheless, Kiernan writes that twenty years after the regime was ended by the Vietnamese invasion in 1979, "the international power game has saved Pol Pot and his followers from any punishment for their crimes." The "game" here is the Western democracies' timorous dance away from anything that might displease China, which always supported the Khmer Rouge, even after they had taken to the jungle. As Jean-Claude Pomonti noted in *Le Monde,* "The crimes of the Khmer Rouge are not about to be put in the dock," and he spelled out why: "A trial before an international tribunal, even without Pol Pot, would besmirch not only his still-living immediate entourage—Khieu Samphan, Nuon Chea, Ta Mok—but also the countries that aided the Khmer Rouge, especially during the 1980s. Everyone would try to turn to their own advantage the revelations and accusations that could emerge. A number of regional governments probably don't want this to happen."[15]

Among these is Hanoi, for—contrary to the fable purveyed in the interests of international pro-Communist solidarity—the successors to the Khmer Rouge in Phnom Penh, installed by the Vietnamese in 1979, were not so irreproachable that they could not be summoned also to appear before an international court.* When in December 1998 two former lieutenants of the late lamented Pol Pot, Khieu Samphan and Nuon Chea, reappeared in Phnom Penh, Prime Minister Hun Sen hastened to greet them with reas-

---

* See Appendix E for my review of a book by an eyewitness to these events that came out in 1986.

surances that they would be "welcomed with bouquets of flowers and not with handcuffs." Khieu Samphan, for his part, gave an affecting press conference in which he confessed to being "distressed at the thought of all that he had caused the Cambodian people to suffer"; but he urged his compatriots—those who were still alive, that is—"to forget the past and work toward the future."[16]

Six months later, we saw a volte-face by Prime Minister Hun Sen: he contended all of a sudden that he had never promised to guarantee immunity for the two penitents and went on to blame the United Nations for delaying legal proceedings against the Khmer Rouge.[17] This was an outright calumny, since before you can delay proceedings you must first decide to initiate them. And who could possibly suspect the United Nations of being so base that they would take the initiative in prosecuting the perpetrators of a left-wing genocide? The "international community" in its passivity, or rather its good behavior, virtuously followed in the prudent course set by the UN. For twenty years I have been watching the press for a declaration—signed by our avenging high priesthood of accredited petitioners—calling for the Cambodian mass murderers to be put on trial and for their crimes to be exposed, exhaustively and in detail, to an appalled world; I have waited in vain.

★ ★ ★

The disparity in how the two totalitarianisms are treated is revealed in many other small ways. Thus the Italian *mani pulite* ("clean hands") judicial operations of the 1990s against corruption and bribery, and the "war against dirty money" in France, have miraculously avoided touching on Communist parties, or have dealt with them only in a most lenient and dilatory fashion. Their swindles have nevertheless come to light, from the "Red cooperatives" in Italy to the fictional "research departments"— devices for laundering stolen money—of the French Communist Party. In addition, there were the dummy companies, ostensibly set up for the purpose of trade with the USSR, that functioned as an indirect way for the Soviets to pay the Western CPs. And there were the sums directly but clandestinely sent by Moscow, undeclared currency paid either in cash or, for the Italian CP, to Swiss bank accounts, acceptance of which at the very least falls under tax evasion laws and may even be considered treasonous. Whenever new documents turned up confirming the scale of this illegal traffic—documents that since the fall of the Soviet Union have often been corroborated by the indiscretions of Soviet and East German participants—one couldn't fail to be impressed by the somnolent equanimity of the media and the conscientious inertia of the magistrates. These thieving practices had been described and were in full swing by the 1970s.[18]

Yet it wasn't until October 1996 that a national secretary of the French Communist Party, Robert Hue, was indicted for "participating in influence peddling." The investigation was engulfed in the depths of merciful amnesia until August 18, 1999, when the rumor went around that the Paris prosecutor's office had decided to call for adjournment of M. Hue's and the CP treasurer's case.[19] It turned out that this was a false alarm. That very afternoon came a formal denial: "The public prosecutor's summary is being prepared. We deny the reports being made about its content. It is too early to state what steps will be taken. The summary for the prosecution will be issued during the first week of September." In fact, we had to wait until the end of October.

Sometimes the unequal treatment meted out to those connected one way or another with the two competing totalitarian systems elicits behavior so derisory that it borders on the grotesque. In 1994, the Forza Italia (Forward Italy) coalition of parties won the Italian election. Silvio Berlusconi became president of the Council of Ministers and appointed as his minister of agriculture a leading figure of the National Alliance party, an offshoot of the old neo-Fascist Movimento Sociale Italiano (MSI) that had transformed itself by shaking off its past and repudiating Il Duce. Several formerly Fascist members of the old MSI had quit the party. Yet despite this democratic evolution, a number of European leaders, gathered in Brussels, refused to shake the new minister's hand.

Let's consider the semiotics of the incident for a moment. The leaders of the National Alliance had neither the intent nor the means to restore the Fascist dictatorship. On the contrary, they had broken with the Mussolini heritage and encouraged the departure of those nostalgic for it. They had hermetically sealed themselves off from such entities as the French National Front, the German Republikaners and the Jörg Haider's Freedom Party in Austria. If the Italian Communist Party—abjuring Marxist-Leninism and rebaptizing itself as the "Democratic Party of the Left"—has succeeded in restoring its status as an acceptable member of society, worthy of re-election, why shouldn't the same courtesy be extended to the National Alliance? As long as this asymmetry in dealing with converts from the left and converts from the right persists, high-flown talk of justice or morality or democratic progress will be merely an imposture. Rather than the moralization of politics, what we see today, more than ever before, is the politicization of morality.

Another manifestation of the refusal to acknowledge the obvious similarity between the two totalitarianisms is left-wing historians' lack of curiosity about the Soviet archives, which have been open for inspection for more than a decade. This torpor grows in direct proportion to the importance of the opened sources. Vladimir Bukovsky has eloquently described this singular intellectual laziness on the part of our subsidized ostriches, on both sides of the Atlantic, in *Reckoning with Moscow*.[20] Goaded to fury by the realization that they alone are returning empty-handed from the hunt—but what else can they expect when they never actually go hunting?—leftists do everything they can to perform "revisionist" editing, to the point of denying what others have discovered. In a *Le Monde* opinion piece, to take just one example, someone named Alain Blum mounted a counterattack by decreeing that *The Black Book of Communism* is "the negation of history." This inquisitor apparently forgot that François Furet, who had some understanding of historiography, was planning to give his endorsement to the travesty in question by writing the preface, and that only his sudden death kept him from doing so.

As soon as the tiniest glimmer of truth threatens to profane the Communist icons, the pit bulls of orthodoxy leap on the bringer of bad news, intent on ripping him to shreds. It is stunning to witness university professors, who likely as not perform admirably when they are working without their emotions in train, being so crude when they engage in polemics. We see them resorting to shameful tactics unworthy of them: false quotations; texts altered or cunningly turned upside down by being cited out of context; insults worse than those hurled by the Communists at Victor Kravchenko, the dissident Russian who, half a century ago, committed the sacrilege of writing *I Chose Freedom*.[21] An anthology of these exploits by the high intelligentsia can be found in Thierry Wolton's *L'Histoire interdite*.[22]

"God guard me against scorning any sincerity. But even the most open mind cannot accept everything," wrote Maurice Barrés in *Amori et dolori sacrum*. This Latin phrase, "Consecrated to Love and Sorrow," happens to be carved onto the façade of the church of Santa Maria della Passione in Milan.

There is a pendant: *Somno et quieti sacrum*. You can find these solemn words carved on another ancient monument, this one in Pisa. The meaning, "Consecrated to Sleep and Tranquility," is perhaps rather more suitable as a motto for most of the historians presumed to be chronicling our times.

And our times echo with the magical refrain "Remember! Remember!" Open, Sesame! The vaults of memory unlock, and they are filled with cheap trinkets. Is there anything of value that can yet be plucked uncorrupted from the caverns of forgetfulness?

CHAPTER TEN

A History without Meaning?

Communism has been granted an irrevocable absolution. As fresh crimes come to light, adding yet more pages to its dossier, the amnesty is reconfirmed, not only by the surviving Communist parties but by the non-Communist left and often by the right as well. Alluding to the Nazism-Communism comparison, even a Gaullist like Pierre Mazeaud, a talented politician and member of the Constitutional Council, says that "it is wrong to pose the question." The pretext for this verdict remains the same, whether it comes from Mazeaud or the CP secretary Robert Hue: "Communism has been led astray."

Such an eminent constitutionalist as Hue would do a great service to political science if he expounded to us how it happens that an intrinsically sound doctrine is everywhere and always "led astray." This pitiful explanation turns into aggressive accusations among the socialists themselves. Commenting on *The Black Book*'s publication in the fall of 1997, the first secretary of the Socialist Party, François Hollande, introduced a subtle note when he wondered, "Could it be that alliances with the extreme right are being prepared, with this book legitimizing them in advance?" You might have interpreted, the first secretary's words as meaning: The horrors described in *The Black Book* have nothing in common with our conception of socialism. But you would have been wrong. Instead, it's the same old song and dance: We must continue to combat anticommunism—and hence any honest account of Communism's past—because to inventory Communist atrocities, ostensibly in the course of objective research, is really a project to shore up the extreme right and rekindle fascism, which is now more threatening than ever, and launch a fresh apologia for the Vichy regime.

A more abject intellectual posture is hard to imagine. Eighty years of human suffering and all the historical documentation of it apparently count for nothing. Communism is progress; hence, those historians who tell the truth about it are enemies of progress. Does M. Hollande realize that by enjoining historians to falsify the record when it damages the socialist myth, he is acting like a Soviet cultural commissar?

Large sections of a vigilant left are eager to detect an implicit fascism among liberals and democrats who want only to let the unvarnished truth come to light. The same suspicion falls on the liberals' desire to see the laws occasionally enforced. In 1996, during Alain Juppé's government, when illegal immigrants occupied the Saint-Bernard church in Paris demanding that they be issued official residence permits, a broad spectrum of the left reacted in classic style. The ultra-left, followed by the Greens and a sizeable slice of the Reds, accused the authorities of employing Nazi methods and giving a repeat performance of the notorious wartime *rafle du Vél' d'Hiv** when they sent police vans to cart away the illegals. Since those responsible for spouting such inanities were not all imbeciles, it's hard not to think that they were guilty of bad faith. The fate of those rounded up in the Paris sports arena in 1942 was not to be returned to their country of origin or resi-

---

* *Translator's note:* The *rafle du Vél' d'Hiv* was a roundup of Jews in the Paris region during World War II. The Vélodrome d'Hiver bicycle stadium served as a transit camp for those deported to Auschwitz.

dence (an outcome they would surely have welcomed), but much the contrary. Conversely, we can be fairly certain that the squatters evicted from Saint-Bernard were not deported to death camps. As far as I know, France in 1996 was not occupied by a foreign army. Her president, parliament and government were chosen by means of an electoral process with universal suffrage, freely exercised by the citizens. The police were obeying orders deriving from laws that conform to a constitution ratified by the citizens.

This being the case, comparing the Pasqua-Debré laws on immigration to the "Vichy laws"—in effect, likening a democracy to a dictatorship under an enemy's thumb—shows either a grave debility in political analysis or a dangerous dishonesty on the part of those who deploy such an argument. It is dangerous because it is tainted with antidemocratic revisionism. Should it be unilaterally up to the immigrant whether or not he can stay in a country, especially one that provides costly social security to its residents? Shouldn't the authorities of the host country have a say in the matter? Defenders of the illegals' demands should attempt, if they are democrats, to persuade parliament to pass a law catering to those demands. If they succeed, they must be prepared to face the foreseeable consequences of such a drastic measure for the viability of France's already severely compromised integration policies. But they have no right to level charges of fascism or racism or Vichyism against citizens who have reason to fear the chaotic repercussions of automatic regularization for all illegal newcomers—in other words, the total removal of controls on immigration.

Let's not point an accusatory finger in the wrong direction. Who is responsible for the legal imbroglio when someone enters France fraudulently, and then brings in, again fraudulently, his wife or wives? Their children born in France are of French nationality, whereas the parents are not. It is not the Republic that must be blamed here, but those who have played fast and loose with her laws. Although we should evaluate this absurd situation with all possible humanity regarding the individuals concerned, the salient fact is clear: while to be born in France gives you the right to claim French nationality, this does not retroactively make all your ancestors French. And how can a state ask its citizens to respect the laws of the land if it simultaneously authorizes immigrants to violate them? There have never been civilizations without migratory movements, but when such movements are anarchic they may result in the sort of street wars and lawless zones that eat away at a nation.

The unconditional defense of undocumented immigrants is one of the numerous subterfuges in the design to relegate the average democratic citizen to the Vichyist camp with the insinuation that he would like to see a new genocide; never mind that the citizen simply wants to see the enforcement of democratically established laws. It is also an indirect means of fending off any scrutiny of Communism's record, and that of the left in general, by asserting the urgent priority of the "antifascist struggle."

From this perspective, the frontier between the two political regimes is clearly demarcated: on one side is liberal democracy, joined with fascism or Nazism; on the other is the left, of which Communism is always a part. Communism's great achievements have not been sufficient to expel it from the democratic community in the eyes of the left, whereas the liberal right, constantly and groundlessly accused of Vichyism, is denied a membership card. Since the dossier of Communism has apparently not established its fundamental incompatibility with democratic institutions, we must refrain from criticizing its past (and its present—Castro and his ilk), for it will have an important role in future battles. Communism, in the old bait and switch, must be judged only by what it promises, not by what it delivers.

The historian Pierre Vidal-Naquet spotlights this slippery ploy in his preface to the French edition of a book on the Holocaust by the American historian Arno Mayer.[1] He writes:

> Judeocide, as Arno Mayer calls it, by its very nature elicits pathological reactions. The events in question were already being denied even as they were taking place, and they have continued to be denied for reasons of self-interest or ideology. But while some have denied them, others have sacralized

them, making them the object of rituals and ceremonies, with a veritable religious orchestration.

Let me say plainly that I consider it a moral duty and an educational obligation that Judeocide, if not "sacralized" and "orchestrated," at least be called back to memory scrupulously and constantly. On the other hand, I find it repugnant when the genocide of the Jews is exploited as a diversionary feint to discourage recollection of other genocides. To denounce any inventory of the Communists' crimes as an insidious attempt to justify those of the Nazis is, in the vast majority of cases, not only a calumny as despicable as it is transparent, but an insult to the memory of the victims of the Holocaust. The victims deserve a better posthumous lot than to be enrolled in the service of a revisionism that is even more widespread than Holocaust revisionism, although just as "self-interested," "ideological" and "pathological."

In the effort to prove that the only crimes against humanity committed in the twentieth century were those of the Nazis, the conduct of the French during the Occupation is painted in the darkest possible colors. Whenever an event like the Papon trial plunges us back into memories of the Occupation, we are told that the facts being dredged up are compelling the French to confront "for the first time" what happened during the Vichy era. According to this endlessly repeated tale, we French since the Liberation have been rejoicing in the exhilarating myth that all the French took part in the Resistance, and somehow we haven't troubled ourselves sufficiently to bring all the *collabos* to justice. Well then, even if some Vichyist sharks were able to elude punishment, the purges nonetheless made for an immense national affair. Between 1944 and 1951 there were tens of thousands of trials and close to 7,000 death sentences (most of these, admittedly, in absentia, for most of the accused were in flight). To these must be added around 5,000 summary executions before and after the Liberation, nearly 14,000 sentences to hard labor and about 25,000 to life in prison, not to mention the 50,000 condemned to national disgrace, which forced many former collaborators out of their professions.[2] This was hardly a case, then, of letting bygones be bygones. The Papon trial was important because it put into focus this question: To what extent can actions taken by officials or military personnel in the service of a tyrannical regime be excused on the grounds that they were merely "obeying orders"? But the trial brought no new revelations to light.

It is false to assert that the majority of the French supported Vichy. While it is undeniable that only a minority were active members of the Resistance, to use this obvious fact as grounds for inferring that all the rest were likely to be *collabos* bears witness to an astounding incomprehension of real life. From 1941 onward, large numbers of French people were hostile to Vichy and to the Germans without being active Resistance fighters. And let us not forget that the French under the Occupation showed themselves to be one of the least anti-Semitic of European nations, as (among others) Marek Halter showed in his film *Les Justes* and Emmanuel Todd discussed in his book *Le Destin des immigrés.*[3] Among the fifteen countries aside from Germany and Austria for which we have accurate figures relating to the genocides, France ranks with two others—Italy and Bulgaria—as having the fewest victims in proportion to its Jewish population. Would this have been possible if the citizenry had not by and large assisted their Jewish compatriots, giving them places to hide and often supplying them with false documents such as forged baptismal certificates?

Another calumny designed to shore up the indictment "You have all been pro-Nazi so leave Communism alone" concerns the French national museums. It is alleged that they neglected to publicize the list of artworks stolen by the Nazis from Jewish collectors and subsequently recovered after 1945; and that by keeping silent about their existence, the Direction des Musées de France, which is supposed to be merely a depository for such works, sought to appropriate them. Thus the highest levels of our administration, our most respected conservators, turn out to be heirs of Hitler, as it were. How then can one have the effrontery to mention other injustices or supposed injustices?

In 1997, journals of every political stripe joined in a campaign with the ARTE television channel in reaction to a report by the

Revenue Court concerning the aftermath of the extortion or sale of artworks. I will let Philippe Meyer summarize the report and refute the misinterpretations that were made of it, voluntarily or involuntarily:

> As a matter of fact, it was a routine enquiry of the court that reopened the question of the 2,000—out of 61,000—as yet unrecovered works of art and their unidentified owners. This is the same court that absolved the museums of the charge of having dragged their feet in searching for the owners (a task delegated in 1949 to a department of the Ministry of Foreign Affairs) and credited the conservators for their ongoing efforts to publicize the works in question. Exhibition of some of the paintings and *objets d'art* (and their exhaustive display over the Internet) has shown that their artistic interest is almost always minor, that a large number of them were not stolen but bought (by dealers who understandably were not eager to boast about their connections with Nazis), and that many of them did not come from the collections of despoiled Jewish owners: out of thirty-eight pictures exhibited in Beaubourg, only one belongs to this category. Finally, it is established that the museums have never presented themselves as owners of works that were simply on loan to them and have consistently acknowledged the works' provenance.[4]

All right, then, but shouldn't we still try to prove that the democracies, beneath their angelic masks, conceal a twin-horned demon of totalitarianism and incurable anti-Semitism brooding at their core? As soon as this secret is laid bare, it will be hard to bring an outdated suit against the left in general and Communism in particular for deviations that, however regrettable, are irrelevant. In the hour of danger, shouldn't we remind ourselves that the left alone, with the aid of a reformed Communism, is still the champion of authentic democracy?

Here is an enigma of our era: the post-Communist left is more zealous to whitewash the Communist past than even the Soviet leaders themselves in their heyday. We know from such sources as

Beria, My Father that the bosses, even before the pivotal admission by Khrushchev in 1956, were all "aware that they were participating in a criminal regime and were committing infamies."[5] They all maintained dossiers on the crimes of their comrades so as to make them sing in the event of their own arrest—Lavrenti Beria foremost among them as chief of the NKVD after 1938 and then of its successor, the KGB. Will the French CP first secretary François Hollande, whom I quoted early in this chapter, seize upon Beria's precautionary measure so as to accuse him of seeking to forge an alliance with the extreme right? But never mind: the alliance was tightly knotted very early on. Well before the Hitler-Stalin Pact in 1939, the USSR had begun to hand over German Communists, agents of the Comintern flushed out on Soviet territory, to the Gestapo. These are facts of history, not entirely conforming to the censored version that M. Hollande and his like wish to inscribe in stone.

* * *

Once the intrinsic criminality of Communism has been airbrushed away, or at least larded over with layers of cosmetic innocence, the second phase of *l'opération "grande parade"* can be initiated: the *democratic* rehabilitation of Communism, which, as sound Marxist analysis requires, must come through its economic rehabilitation.

Communism retains its economic superiority because it opposes capitalism, the market, neoliberalism and their outcome: globalization, or the free worldwide circulation of goods, capital, people, technologies and ideas. It's true that the left has given up trying to maintain that socialist economies work better than capitalist economies, a thesis that used to be commonly advanced and was defended in the 1950s even by "bourgeois" economics. Today, leftists no longer broach the subject, limiting themselves to noting that the real world is afflicted with poverty, inequality, crisis, corruption, economic stagnation and underdevelopment. How to explain this regrettable situation? It can only be due to capitalism, now that actually existing socialism has abandoned the field. The argument is familiar: Communists promised a perfect society but didn't succeed in constructing it; so they decree that capitalism is absolute evil because it prevented their ideological phantasm from taking form. They conclude that liberals are the real totalitarians, prepared to use the barbaric methods of a "Stalinism of the right," as Jean-François Kahn put it, in order to impose their alleged *pensée unique.** The truth, of course, is that liberalism is not a conformist ideology, for liberal societies acknowledge contradictions and entail a multiplicity of viewpoints by their very nature. But for the left and the ultra-left, a regime is totalitarian if it does not guarantee *them* a monopoly on free expression.

Moreover, the claim that the world's poverty is solely attributable to liberal practices rests on the naïve hypothesis that the entire world follows such practices. But the majority of countries mired in poverty have been—and many remain—*dirigiste.* They are likely to have been ruined by copying the Soviet model: statism, collective farms, unprofitable industries, and corrupt leaders who, holding the reins of both political and economic power, are free to indulge in systematic institutional theft. Extreme backwardness frequently has political causes, particularly in Africa, where the incessant civil wars and cross-border wars, the tribal genocides and massacres driven by fanaticism have combined to render useless all the international aid that has been poured into the continent—aid more generous than in any other part of the world but almost entirely misappropriated by governments. If it remains true that since 1990, broadly speaking, the ebb of centrally planned economies and the flow of market globalization are pushing economies little by little to open up and privatize, this recent and tentative evolution toward the market has gone but a short way, and "totalitarian" liberalism is far from reigning supreme.

Nevertheless, the denunciations continue and extend well beyond the ranks of the paleo-left, since in Europe, and above all in France, both the right and—despite many a denial—the

---

* In left-wing parlance, *la pensée unique* refers to a putative doctrinaire conformity of thought—the "ideology" of the free market. See Appendix A.

social-democratic left are imbued with the *dirigiste* illusion. I have already quoted the antiliberal profession of faith that came from the Gaullist Philippe Séguin in January 1997. In the same month, the General Council of the Socialist International sounded the charge against "the neoliberal fundamentalism that covets world hegemony as a modern totalitarianism."[6] And a woman as worthy as Geneviève de Gaulle-Anthonioz, who presides over Aide à toute Détresse Quart Monde (International Fourth World Movement), an NGO, opined that "Society is threatened by the totalitarianism of money." A former deportee to Nazi camps, she clarified, "I have experienced two totalitarianisms in my life."[7] Don't think for a moment that the other totalitarianism could have been Communism. Of course not: it's *money,* here presented as equivalent to Nazism, or even worse. For "the totalitarianism of money is not the least dangerous form," concludes Mme de Gaulle-Anthonioz, seeing proof in the increasing number of people that the French economy is leaving behind. Evidently she has never asked herself why the number of homeless people in France has increased by a factor of three or four over the last fifteen years: Is it because of too much liberalism, or rather too much of its opposite? This is a question that is systematically brushed aside, for even to pose it amounts to bowing in the direction of the American devil.

So those who remain faithful to Marxism are getting reinforcements from all sides. They no longer pretend that Communism as an economic system was good in itself, in the absolute sense, nor that it remains an ideal to be concretized. Communism's merits are gauged in relation to the execrated capitalist system, the old adversary against which it wages eternal warfare. Thereby it has gained this definitive advantage: it does not have to exist in order to be true.

Then comes the corollary, part two of an entirely fanciful argument: Not only is Communism defensible in the domain of economics, but it represents the only truly democratic force in the world today. Here again, Communism is democratic not in itself, but in opposition to the fundamentally antidemocratic essence of liberalism and capitalist market economics. On April

30, 1996, the French CP and the Greens published a joint declaration in which they warned about "the necessity to checkmate the economic and financial theories in the name of which present and future generations are pitilessly sacrificed. . . . The survival of humanity is at stake." This rhetorical flight leads to a summons for "democracy to take wing," which suggests that democracy has never yet arisen anywhere, or that it is mortally threatened by liberalism.[8] As an excellent historian of Communism, Marc Lazar, writes, "Communism was supposed to establish a superior model of democracy, notably because it would not be bound to market forces."[9] This "supposition" was professed not only in France by the CP, the ultra-left and the Greens (who thereby revealed themselves to be ideologues more than environmentalists), but also by the Communist Refoundation Party in Italy (Partito della Rifondazione Comunista, the faction made up of Communists who were unwilling to follow the Democratic Party of the Left, the virginal denomination of the "de-Marxized" Italian CP), by the East German Communists, and by most of the dead or moribund European CPs (Scandinavian, Belgian, Portuguese, etc.). All pointed an accusing finger at the "dictatorship of capitalism" and "market totalitarianism."[10]

Most of these parties are nowadays minuscule and their electorate continues to melt away. Yet their ideology spreads beyond Europe. The discourse that dominates and terrorizes university campuses in the United States makes the affable Robert Hue, national secretary of the French CP, seem almost tolerant in comparison. You would have to go to the ultra-left, among Pierre Bourdieu and his acolytes—we will visit them in a subsequent chapter—to find a French equivalent to such murderous academic sectarianism. The American campus phenomenon, which extends also into some American newspapers, magazines, radio and television channels, is a reminder that the Marxist mentality can flourish and have considerable effect on public debate even in nations where Communism did not succeed in forming a party with electoral clout or influence in the unions. Communism can be an ideological presence even where it has never been a political player.

With regard to Communist crimes, the American moral dilemma differs fundamentally from that of Europe. In the United States, the deeds of Stalin and Mao never drew the active complicity or the massive approbation that Europeans bestowed on them. Today, in those American circles where the Marxist delusion still flourishes, it is for the most part theoretical and abstract, or the posture of a minority of "liberal" intellectuals. On our side of the Atlantic, we may ask ourselves if indeed "Europeans are capable of reflecting on the tragedies of their past," in Marc Lazar's words. Europeans can do so with regard to the Nazi tragedy—but largely, alas, because it throws up a smokescreen against a clear view of the Communist tragedy.

In their heart of hearts, of course, the revisionists of Communist history are not unaware of the realities they deny or explain away as unrepresentative accidents. As Jean-Paul Sartre, a connoisseur, put the matter, "There exists a faith of bad faith." Between outright lying and blind belief lies a fog of hybrid awareness that takes something from both extremes without being reducible to either. When Communists or their friends claim they didn't know that the Prague trials were rigged, they are lying. But they now acknowledge that the trials were rigged, something they long refused to admit. And they admit the existence of the gulag, although when *The Gulag Archipelago* came out in 1973 they did all they could to discredit Solzhenitsyn. No one these days is willing to extol—as did the complaisant pilgrims of yesteryear—the radiant health of the populations of the Ukraine or China during the genocidal, deliberately engineered famines. But still there is an uncrossable line: any conclusion that can be drawn from the facts must not point to a condemnation of Communism as such, nor, above all, allow us to uphold democratic capitalism as superior in every way.

In the mid-1970s, the publisher Jean-Claude Lattès announced his intention to bring out a new edition of Jan Valtin's *Sans patrie ni frontières*,[11] the autobiography of a German Communist who became utterly disillusioned after living in the USSR. The editor of a big evening newspaper retaliated with the accusation, "You will be serving the cause of the wealthy (*les possédants*)." Anything rather than praise for private property, which takes us quickly from the right to the ultra-right. In a revealing and comic scene that I have already described but is worth mentioning again, during a television broadcast of *La Marche du siècle*, Robert Hue, having protested that Communism had nothing to do with the "monstrosities"—only too real, alas—described in *The Black Book* and *The Gulag Handbook*, suddenly dived into his pocket and produced an issue of the National Front's publication, waving it under the noses of Stéphane Courtois, Jacques Rossi and myself. With this theatrical gesture, the CP's national secretary was saying, "Let's suppose, for the sake of argument, that what you are saying is true. That doesn't make you any the less servants of fascism." I mention this little vignette again because it illustrates the mixture of vague acknowledgment of the facts and refusal to draw the consequences therefrom that constitutes *bad faith*. All anticommunists (and the most neutral of historians fall into this category insofar as they describe what has actually happened) are "objectively" in the service of the extreme right—or, not much better, simply the right.

The claim that the crimes of actually existing socialism are unrepresentative continues to be the story we hear today, and it is accepted by right and left alike. Whereas dictators classified as fascists (the Greek colonels from 1968 to 1974, Augusto Pinochet, the Argentine generals before 1982, etc.) are rightly pilloried, the dictators who perpetrated the judicial murders in Havana, who set up Vietnamese and Chinese concentration camps, who inflicted famine on the North Koreans—to mention a few of their recent exploits—are not treated as pariahs; they are honored with many invitations as well as flattering visits by obsequious guests. The Paris Transport Authority (RATP) gives Castro princely gifts that the taxpayers subsidize without their consent. In *L'Humanité* we find this delightful paragraph:

A fine Christmas gift for Cuba. Tomorrow, twenty-five spanking new buses will leave Le Havre on a cargo ship bound for Havana. Solidarity with this West Indies island, a victim of the blockade [sic] imposed by the United States, is made possible thanks to the combined efforts of the RATP—which is offering the vehicles—and the Cuba Cooperation Association, whose driving force is Roger Grevoul, vice president of the Val-de-Marne departmental council. The buses will come with replacement parts as well as basic toolkits for repairs. Shipping costs will be covered by the Cuban state and harbor charges by Cuba Cooperation.[12]

So the Association for Encouraging Marxist Mass Murderers is not relaxing its zeal in the least, despite all the devastating historical facts that have come to light. The reader will have noticed the typical gaffe about a "blockade." Proof that there is no blockade: the buses duly arrived in Havana. Without being aware of it, *L'Humanité* in one and the same article is offering up a lie and its refutation.

Indulgence for Communists still in business extends even into such a taboo area as anti-Semitism. In 1998, Gennady Zyuganov, Russian Communist Party boss and head of the largest parliamentary bloc in the Duma, published an open letter in which he accused Zionism of "conspiring to seize power in Russia," and "Zionist capital" of causing the economic catastrophe in Russia, which was being pushed ever closer to the brink since the stock market crash of August 17, 1998. Zyuganov compared Zionism to Nazism: both, he said, were seeking "world domination." The only difference was that Hitler openly advertised his ambition, whereas the Zionists operated behind the scenes. This is essentially the message of that famous anti-Semitic forgery, *The Protocols of the Elders of Zion,* the work of a Russian who subsequently became a Leninist. Naturally, Zyuganov deployed that old sleight of hand inherited from the Stalin and Brezhnev eras: he swore that he was attacking only Zionism, not the Jews. But his party comrade and Duma colleague Albert Makashov, disdaining the anti-Zionist fig leaf, made no bones about his anti-Semitism.[13]

Now imagine that Gianfranco Fini, the leader of the Italian National Alliance party, had come out with similar words. The National Alliance, with roots in the old Movimento Sociale Italiano (MSI), is routinely called a "neo-Fascist" party, although it broke with the surviving diehards of the Mussolini cult and was founded under the auspices of center-right neoliberalism. What storms of indignation, what avalanches of lawsuits would have swept over Signor Fini if he had expressed himself in like fashion!

We may conclude that the left at least partially concedes the true history of Communism, while depriving it of its meaning. Facts are considered in isolation, not as parts of a larger picture that can reveal their significance. That is why Communism's defenders shrink from integrating the separate elements, the long series of failures and crimes, into a synoptic, global view that permits the underlying logic to be pieced together. Hence the violent hatred directed toward *The Black Book*. By the cumulative effect of its mountainous information, it militates against the fragmenting of Communist history into a hodgepodge of isolated phenomena with no relation to their common source.

The swings exhibited by the left in their reception of Solzhenitsyn's books had already given ample illustration of this principle. His books could be accepted if his criticisms dealt simply with "regrettable" facts that could be presented as mere malfunctioning of the system, but not if they pointed to the conclusion that socialism is intrinsically destructive of humanity. In 1962 it was Pierre Daix, editor-in-chief of the Communist Party's literary weekly, *Les Lettres françaises,* who devoted his energy and talent to *One Day in the Life of Ivan Denisovich,* drawing attention to the book's importance as a historical document and as a work of art. It's true that Nikita Khrushchev had authorized its publication in the USSR, since Solzhenitsyn's short novel lent support to the Soviet premier's "secret" report of 1956 denouncing Stalin's crimes; and the Soviet ambassador to Paris, under orders from his master, put pressure on the French CP to bring out an edition of *Ivan Denisovich* as soon as possible. The non-Communist left therefore felt they had been authorized to heap praises on its author. The tone changed after 1964 when, under Brezhnev, Solzhenitsyn became the object of attacks and censorship in his homeland—without, however, losing the support of Pierre Daix. For this failure to toe the party line, Daix himself came under increasing criticism from the French CP until, after *Les Lettres françaises* closed down in 1972, he quit the party. Then, a year later, Solzhenitsyn became a leper in the eyes of the left with the publication of *The Gulag Archipelago*.

These oscillations are not hard to explain. The sufferings of Ivan Denisovich could be classified in the "mistakes" category, but *The Gulag Archipelago* exposed the regime itself as a mistake. So its author became the enemy. Between the small masterpiece of *Ivan Denisovich* and the larger one a decade later, there had been an evolution: from a description of "mistakes" that could be dismissed as anomalous, to a description of a political system whose galaxy of concentration camps was a necessary feature of its existence. It was this general conclusion that the left could not endure and that it continues to reject even after the collapse of Communism.

The first task on the agenda, then, is to pick apart any attempt at synthesis. Once this precaution has been taken, a declaration of penitence—or at least of regret—can be made more easily than in the past. *Le Monde* takes note:

> The French Communist Party resembles one of those prudes of Molière who embrace virtue when they are no longer capable of sinning. Since the ascension of Robert Hue to party leadership, we have lost track of the acts of contrition, the public proclamations of regret, if not of remorse, for all those who were ignominiously chased from the ranks for the only reason that they wouldn't toe the Stalinist "line" imposed by Moscow during the Twenties.[14]

The party still balks, however, at admitting its complete lack of autonomy with respect to Moscow during its entire history. This absolute dependency, ferociously denied by the Communists and gladly "relativized" by the non-Communist left, and even by the right, has by now been definitively established thanks to the opening of the Soviet archives.[15] What has come to light demolishes the party's defense—the claim that it had no knowledge of and was not a party to the atrocities of Lenin, Stalin and their successors. Once again, the shell game of partial confession: the

French Communists belatedly acknowledge the crimes but not the support they gave to the criminals when, in full knowledge of the truth, they placed themselves in the service of the criminals' lying propaganda.

Likewise with economics: reluctant acknowledgments of failure are made, ambiguously and equivocally, but such failure is not taken as evidence of Communism's fundamental unfitness in this domain, as Marc Lazar writes:

> Some parties—those of Spain, Greece and Portugal, for instance—have come around to suggest that economic catastrophe owes much to the assimilation of capitalist values by Gorbachev and many other East Bloc leaders. In other words, the fall of the Communist regimes was due not so much to the fact that they were Communist as to their abandonment of Communism. They gave in to the lure of capitalism, which thus is made responsible for their fate.[16]

So the bankruptcy of Communism proves the bankruptcy of capitalism. Skeptics who look askance at this ingenious argument must be denied the opportunity to exploit the disappointments of collectivized economies in order to tout the superiority, or the less toxic character, of capitalism. They won't be allowed a say in the matter, for the left also claims the distinction of being the first to mount a critique of Communism. Following the principle that valid criticism of the left can come only from within (why? shouldn't the same privilege be extended to the right? the Mafia or the Gestapo?), the left feigns amnesia about those who criticized it from the outside at a time when doing so was not without risk. Better to pass them over in silence.

Yet I can remember how outside observers from time to time were secretly approached by Communists and asked, in order to influence public opinion, to give a helping tactical shove in support of some party faction or other. Nothing could better illustrate human absurdity than the air of self-importance and the sententious tones of these Communists, true believers in revolution and the struggle against capitalism, as they uttered their sibylline *sous-entendus* condemning the sectarians of their own party. Like Louis Althusser, they would sometimes appeal to me for a discreet piece of journalistic propaganda in behalf of their heroic resistance, never doubting that I would be wildly enthusiastic for their hermetic struggles. On these occasions, it was not a matter of Communism saving humanity from bourgeois oppression, but of the humanity of the bourgeois press saving Communism.

Whatever the outcome of these laughable internecine skirmishes, which continue to restructure factions and alliances, and whatever the final judgment on the past, which the left concedes may not always have lived up to the myth, Communism will stay with us because it continues to be an engine of protest against social injustice and the antidemocratic, ultraliberal onslaught. With its new allies on the far left—the Trotskyists not excluded!—it remains the central motor of "resistance" against liberalism. Anticapitalist ideas have taken wing over much vaster expanses than those occupied by openly declared Marxist forces, and will therefore, the Marxists believe, be the guiding ideas of the future.

This is what leftists believe, but are they really convinced? They clearly perceive that the world is evolving in the opposite direction to their own. Every day they are reminded of the fact that their ideological passion, even if it attracts a clientele and a public, cannot reverse the worldwide drift toward privatization, free enterprise, free trade and the free market. The only sources of resistance to this tide are the benefits dispensed from the public trough, the "entitlements" that Mendès France said were, more often than not, undeserved privileges.

The Europeans themselves, so *dirigiste* by tradition, have lately rediscovered a well-established truth, one that analysts who foresaw the pernicious consequences of large-scale nationalizations had tried in vain for half a century to warn against: that public services and public planning are not synonymous. The choice is not (at least in most cases) between public services obedient to bureaucratic planning, on the one hand, and private enterprise answering only to market forces on the other. There can be, indeed there always have been, private enterprises burdened with public service obligations, reconciling the demands of economic efficiency with those of the public interest. Despite all the antiliberal hysteria, this understanding of liberalization has guided the development of European public services during the last decade of the century. Alongside government-run public services, we have seen an expansion of privately administered services, subject to market forces, in transportation (most notably in the airline industry), telecommunications, postal carriers and energy utilities. This trend is strongly in evidence worldwide. In response, the left can do little more than wage a delaying action. The fantasy of a neo-Bolshevism advancing triumphantly over the ruins of neoliberalism exists only in the imagination of the left. It is true that socialist economics, whether of the First or the Third Way, can continue to inflict much harm, and taxpayers will continue to bear the heavy cost. But its inherent defects are leading inexorably to its demise everywhere.

At the same time, it is certain that blindness to the lessons of history must be accompanied by blindness to present realities. Minds are slower to change than events. One subterfuge in the art of eluding reality—as I point out several times in this book—consists in blaming liberalism for the ravages caused by planned economies. This deception is not exclusive to the left, which has scattered its ideological seeds far beyond its own ranks.

For example, an article on Mongolia in the right-leaning *Le Figaro* bears the title "Les Pétards mouilles du libéralisme" (The Damp Squibs of Liberalism).[17] Well, Mongolia is a country with a very primitive economy largely based on livestock; in addition, it has been subjected to sixty-eight years of Soviet Communism, with the usual sterilizing results. *Le Figaro*'s reporter notes that ten years after the fall of Communism, Mongolia was still vegetating in poverty. He blames this unhappy situation entirely on the advent of liberalism. But how could ten years of "democracy" and "liberalism," of a highly theoretical kind moreover, have been sufficient to create a miracle of modern capitalism? How could this country, where none of the cultural or economic pre-requisites for capitalist development are found—a country that has been wedded to its ancient ways for thousands of years and further crippled by socialism—be expected to improvise in the space of a decade the complex mix of methods and know-how that the West, starting from a much higher level, took seven centuries to build? Apparently it is no longer *le sens de l'histoire* but its *contresens* ("nonsense") that impresses itself upon so many disturbed minds as a frame of reference or an intellectual lifeboat.

A quiver of joy thrilled through antiliberals when Asia was hit by an economic crisis in 1997. Was this the first spasm of capitalism's death agony, a harbinger of its approaching end? True, Marx and Engels had already predicted this demise for January 1848, or February at the latest. In the summer of 1999, accursed capitalism was struggling back to its feet again. And Europe was awakening from its torpor, despite Maastricht and the single currency, despite the vicious penchant for neoliberalism displayed by some European Socialist parties!

Even in the realm of ideology, however remote from reality, the antiliberals' position is less secure than one might suppose judging from their noisy displays. Analyzing a series of polls taken by the Centre d'Études et de Connaissances sur l'Opinion Publique (Cecop) during the second half of 1999, the organization's director, Jérôme Jaffré, notes that globalization—frequently condemned as the "great Satan" in ideological debates and in the media—is regarded as a good thing by 53 percent of French people, as opposed to 35 percent who view it unfavorably. Among the center-right electorate, 53 percent think well of it, while among those of the left—oh, rage and despair!—the figure rises to 57 percent.[18] Whoever has experienced the heavy hand of the right's statism in France since 1945 will hardly be surprised. Worse still, between 1995 and 1998 the proportion of left-wing voters who viewed the concept of nationalization favorably dropped from 57 percent to 44 percent; and privatization rose in popularity from 32 percent to 39 percent.

Although the Communist Party (supported by the far left, with which it has formed ties, and by all the free market's adversaries), claims to be an avatar of the future, this opinion of itself is shared by few. In *L'État de l'opinion 1997*,[19] a summary of polls taken throughout 1996, we learn:

> In all groups questioned, the word "communism" has frightening associations, because it is inevitably linked to the experiences of the so-called "socialist" countries: mentioned are massacres, loss of liberty, tyranny, poverty, caste privileges, etc. In other words, a total reversal of image has taken effect. . . . In the absence of a sufficiently clear demarcation between the CP and Stalinism, a vote for this party brings with it an ideological cost that puts the brakes on electoral mobilization.

One of the authors invited to comment on these statistics, the future minister of education Claude Allegre, drew attention to another finding that tends to dampen the revolutionary left's hopes for the future: "Marxism has positive connotations for 7 percent of respondents, negative for 76 percent; Communism has positive connotations for 20 percent, negative for 66 percent." So Marxism has been even more discredited than Communism. Thus the plea for "a return to Marx," the attempt to blame Communism's crimes and disasters on an alleged betrayal of authentic Marxism, does not convince the popular jury in the slightest: unlike the intellectuals, the average French citizen would impose an even heavier sentence on Marx than on Stalin.

But figures like these will not discourage our post-Communist revolutionaries. Having never based their convictions on an examination of history, nor their conclusions on the study of societies, they will feel all the more convinced that they alone are capable of restoring—sorry, I mean *establishing*—democracy and justice.

CHAPTER ELEVEN

The Highest Stage of Democracy?

So far we have been looking at the flimsiness, not to say the dishonesty, of exculpatory arguments based on nobility of intentions or the beguiling power of illusions. Perhaps we may accept these excuses for the earliest years of the Bolshevik regime, when information concerning its true nature had not yet reached the multitude of the USSR's foreign admirers, although the political intelligentsia was *au courant* with everything from the very beginning. But even for the man in the street, the time of innocence was necessarily brief. From roughly the mid-1920s onward, there could be no good-faith misunderstanding. Those in the West who clung to their Communist allegiance, or who signed on to it anew, were henceforth knowingly choosing lies over truth, tyranny over democracy.

In a personal letter commenting on my book *Democracy Against Itself: The Future of the Democratic Impulse*, in which I developed this idea, a close friend and renowned historian offered this counsel:

You know better than I do that Communism, which was greatly nourished and justified by the antifascist form it took in the West at least, is historically a version of democracy: its radicalized form. This is what differentiates it from Nazism, even if its consequences have actually been much worse and even if the parallels between the two systems are obvious in hindsight. If it were not a version of democracy, it would be hard to understand why so many people subscribed to it. I believe it is antifascism that was the real key to Communism's success in Europe.

Well, there are numerous objections that could be raised against my friend's crucial objection. First is the general point that dictatorships can wage war on each other without for that reason ceasing to be dictatorships. When Saddam Hussein embarked on a conflict with the ayatollahs in 1980, this undertaking hardly turned Iraq into a democracy, nor was Iran similarly transmogrified.

Second, and more specifically, the Popular Front of the anti-fascist left was consolidated only after Hitler seized power in 1934, when the campaign of lies defending the USSR had been in full force for sixteen years and every countervailing attempt to bring attention to the reality of Communism had been neutralized according to the standard, well-tried methods. Moreover, the Soviet antifascist posture was equivocal and wavering. After helping Hitler win the 1933 elections by ordering the German CP to concentrate its efforts on crushing the Social Democrats— whom he regarded as the real "fascists"—Stalin secretly continued to forge collaborative links that culminated in the openly proclaimed Nazi-Soviet Nonaggression Pact of 1939.* Similarly, during the Spanish Civil War, while they ostensibly fought on the Republican, antifascist side, the Communists' overriding zeal to liquidate their socialist and anarchist allies was an important

---

* Even after the war, Stalin went about recruiting Nazi technicians who specialized in the construction of gas chambers. See Pierre de Villemarest, "Les spécialistes nazis du génocide ont aussi travaillé pour Staline," *Le Quotidien de Paris*, July 13, 1993.

factor in Franco's victory. A bizarre way to combat "fascism"! And of course the Soviet Union was dragged into World War II despite itself when, to Stalin's stupefaction, Hitler suddenly attacked him.

These are well-established facts—contrary to the simplifications of the credulous non-Communist left, which allowed itself to be domesticated by the CPs when it swallowed the intimidating slogan that any criticism of the Communists was a sign of pro-fascist complicity. The short era between 1934 and 1939, when Moscow ordained the policy of a Popular Front against "fascism," does not suffice as the key to understanding the whole of Communist history, nor as an explanation for the servility of the left, and often of the right. What fascist threat explains or excuses the Mao cult during the Sixties and Seventies? Or in the same decades, the *cordon sanitaire* of lies that was set up as a way to prevent the truth about Communism from being known? Or the preferential treatment accorded to domestic Communist parties in the West?

It is traditional for the left to put "fascism" and Nazism in the same political basket. The prewar "antifascist front" placed equal or even greater emphasis on the struggle against Hitler than on that against Mussolini or Franco. Thus set in the habit of using the term "fascism" as a synonym for Nazism and as a designation for all totalitarian or authoritarian regimes of the right.* This confounding served to put Germany, Italy and Francoist Spain on one side; and on the other, the democracies along with the Soviet Union, which was magically converted into a democracy with one stroke of the ideological wand. It was in those prewar years that a conditioned reflex developed to inhibit

---

* I found myself stupidly committing the same misusage in an article published in the Spring 1998 issue of *Commentaire* with the title "L'essentielle identité du fascisme rouge et du fascisme noir." Neither Nazism nor Communism was fascist in the exact meaning of the word defined by history. Both systems were far further advanced on the path of evil.

any denunciation of Communist totalitarianism: to condemn it, or even merely to describe it, was to see oneself lumped in with the "fascists"—in effect, accused of having pro-Nazi sympathies.

Since then, historical and political analysis has made some progress, even if vocabulary has not followed. Recent work has demonstrated that the kinship between Nazism and Communism is much closer than that between Nazism and the historical—not the metaphorical—Fascist regime that existed in Italy between 1922 and 1945. Granted, the word "totalitarian" was coined in the context of Benito Mussolini's dictatorship, which was far from being a democracy; yet it was not totalitarian in the strict sense of the word, as were the USSR and Mao's China and their various offshoots.

The Nazis and the Communists recognized no limits: beyond strictly political control, they sought to dictate every aspect of substance and style in the arts, philosophy, even science. Italy was never subjected to the same degree of tyranny. "Mussolini's regime," wrote Raymond Aron, "was never totalitarian: universities and intellectuals were not forced to toe the line, even if their freedom of expression was restricted."[1] The Fascist writers—Malaparte, Pirandello, Ungaretti—wrote their works as they chose, without having to obey the diktats of a state aesthetic. Malaparte had been a Communist before switching to Fascism, and Ungaretti followed the opposite trajectory, becoming a Communist after Mussolini's fall, as did numerous other Italian intellectuals. Il Duce did what he could to promote an architectural style called Novocento (by analogy with Quattrocento, Cinquecento, etc.); but to his personal taste we owe, thankfully, only a few bombastic edifices, and he made no attempt to prevent a highly elegant modernist architecture from flourishing. Futurist painters—they were ardent Fascists—likewise were permitted to do what they wanted without interference.

But what above all separated the Fascist state from the out-and-out totalitarian state was that it never practiced mass murder, and it never felt the need to exterminate its own people as an imperative springing from its very nature. The Italian Fascists' political crimes were limited to the killing of a few of the regime's adversaries, or imprisoning them, or placing them under house arrest in remote mountain locales or on islands. They never set about "liquidating" harmless citizens by the millions, or constructing networks of concentration camps and labor camps where huge numbers of their own people would be reduced to serfdom.*

Pierre Milza (like Raymond Aron) points out that in 1929 a group of antifascist intellectuals, led by the illustrious dissident Benedetto Croce, were free to publish their response to a "Manifesto of Fascist Intellectuals."[2] They vented their dismay at their colleagues' regrettable *engagement*, censuring them in terms that Julian Benda, author of *La Trahison des clercs*, would not have disavowed. Publication of such a counter-manifesto would of course have been inconceivable in Nazi Germany or the Soviet Union. Likewise, Fascist censorship of the creative Italian cinema was never especially vigilant.

Agreeing with Renzo De Felice,[3] Pierre Milza notes that Mussolini, a disciple of Georges Sorel more than of Karl Marx, conceived Fascism as a revolutionary movement—hostile not only to liberalism but also to capitalism, parliamentary systems and reformist socialism. For example, the creation of the Istituto per la Recostruzione Industriale, an organization tasked with nationalizing businesses, was an economic catastrophe whose dimensions would have made any socialist state proud, and whose costly outcome is still being felt today.

It was only after 1936 that the Fascist state began to take on a more sinister totalitarian hue. Discriminatory policies against Jews were adopted after 1938, but they evidently owed more to Mussolini's desire to please his new ally, Hitler, than to any animus against Jews that he may have harbored. Previously, Il Duce had maintained good relations with his Jewish compatriots and had even pursued a foreign policy supporting Zionism. But this dark turn by the Fascists would never approach the depths of criminality that the Nazis and the Soviets attained.

---

* Some commentators, no doubt stressed by our ever-enlarging knowledge of Communism, have ventured to compare Italian Fascism to the Khmer Rouge. See, for example, the opinion piece by Alain Blum in *Le Monde*, November 18, 1997.

Without playing down post-1936 developments, De Felice continued to insist on the incommensurability of Fascism and Nazism, even during the years leading up to the war. Indro Montanelli made the same diagnosis in his great *Storia d'Italia*.[4] Many of the country's institutions—the universities, the Church, a large number of enterprises (in the rich and varied Italian textile industry above all), small-scale craft and trading businesses, farms—were allowed to remain essentially independent. The constitutional structure of parliamentary monarchy was kept standing in principle, ready to be reactivated. It was King Victor Emmanuel who eventually informed Mussolini of his dismissal from office and had him arrested. Who was there in Germany with the legal and constitutional power to do likewise vis-à-vis the Führer at the moment when the Nazis were collapsing militarily?

With regard to the anti-Semitic laws of 1938, several Italian historians have recently contested the view that these were strictly imputable to opportunism in connection with the Nazi-Fascist alliance. Instead, they have looked for causes deep within Italy's past. Undoubtedly such causes exist, but Pierre Milza's research has established that, to the slight extent that Italian anti-Semitic ideas were formulated at the end of the nineteenth century or the beginning of the twentieth, they were mainly borrowings from the abundant French literature on this theme. In practice, the Italians are among the least anti-Semitic peoples in the world. Mussolini's laws did not lead to genocide, and Italy was the European country where the Jewish population suffered the least.[5] In the matter of homicide, an abyss separates Fascism from the far higher levels of productivity achieved by the Nazis and the Soviets, whose regimes belong to the same criminal galaxy. Fascism belongs to another galaxy—not that of the democracies, of course, but not that of totalitarianism either. If we haven't yet demarcated the true frontiers between Nazism and Communism, it is because de-Nazification was effected after 1945 but there has been no de-Communization after 1989.

In summary, when it comes to the domain of action, which is generally conceded to be not merely tangential to politics, Italian Fascism never practiced mass extermination, forced displacement of populations or their internment in camps, bloody purges and the like—which are common traits of Nazism and Communism, and which give us grounds to define them as regimes based on permanent terror. Both represented a great and unprecedented threat to humanity during the twentieth century, despite all the efforts at dissimulation and sleight of hand deployed by the contortionists of pro-Communist *distinguo*. The term "fascism" is therefore improperly used in designating anything but the Italian dictatorship and its replicas, for example in Latin America.

In the realm of theory, on the other hand, analogies and exchanges between the three regimes abound: they agreed in defining themselves as revolutionary, as enemies of the "bourgeois" mentality and of parliamentary democracy, and as anticapitalist. Not long before the end, when he saw that defeat was inescapable, Adolf Hitler began to regret not having imitated Stalin by nationalizing the entire German economy. Contrary to the favorite thesis of the Marxists—a thesis that, as per custom, is never made to confront the facts—Big Capital financed neither Hitler's nor Mussolini's accession to power.[6] The Nazi "revolution" shared the Fascist "revolution's" detestation of bourgeois parliamentarianism, but was more oriented toward the past, vaunting a revival of the pure Germanic ethos that was supposed to have prevailed before the "Aryan race" was corrupted by the admixture of "inferior races." Mussolini's intellectual background, like that of the Bolsheviks, owes more to the legacy of the French Revolution and, surprisingly enough, to Gracchus Babeuf. Following his example and that of the Communists, Il Duce believed that a "new man" could be created through appropriate education. And Communists and Fascists alike were pursuing progress—or believed they were doing so.

According to both the latter ideologies, humanity in the nineteenth century made the mistake of trying to achieve progress by means of democratic institutions, a course conducive only to factionalism and corruption. To avoid such an outcome, we should turn instead to the concept of an omnipotent state, with power concentrated in one individual. Luigi Pirandello explained the theory in his 1904 novel *Il Fu Mattia Pascal*: "When power is held in the hands of a single man, he knows that he is alone and that he is there to serve many people; but when there are many people who govern, they only want to satisfy themselves and we are left with the most idiotic and odious of tyrannies: tyranny under the mask of liberty."[7] But the tenure of power by a single person can be justified—according to Mussolini, that great expert in mobilizing the masses—only if that person enjoys the support of the entire people. This is the dictatorship of the proletariat, as it were, in its Fascist version. Moreover, the Fascists were aware of certain similarities between their agenda and that of the Bolsheviks. Giuseppe Ungaretti, in an article in *Il Popolo d'Italia,* a daily newspaper that came under Mussolini's directorship after he quit editing *L'Avanti,* wrote, "The federative organization of soviets, all in all very close to our own in its conception of the state's authority, is a program that deserves to survive."

In his pro-Fascist *Storia delle origini del fascismo,* published in 1939, the eminent historian Gioacchino Volpe explained the emergence of Fascism by the overriding need to remedy the decadence and decay of the liberal state, divided and undermined by special interests associated with the squabbles between political parties. A book by Paolo Simoncelli, *Cantimori, Gentile e la normale di Pisa,*[8] deals with the group of intellectuals who gravitated around Giovanni Gentile, the most celebrated prewar Fascist philosopher, in that center of Italian culture which is the teacher training college of Pisa. Simoncelli describes how, after Mussolini's fall, these intellectuals generally abandoned Fascism for Communism—Gentile for Antonio Gramsci—while continuing to serve the antiliberal ideal that had always been theirs. Simoncelli's testimony makes it easier to understand why Palmiro Togliatti, secretary-general of the Italian Communist Party, in 1944 launched an appeal to young Fascists to join the party "so that they might realize their ideals." I will leave to historians the task of explaining why Italian Fascism as a political system and means of wielding power—although it became ever more intolerant over the years—did not evolve toward perpetrating the mass butcheries seen in genuinely totalitarian regimes.

Finally, this time in the domain of ideas, there is a central kernel common to Fascism, Nazism and Communism: their shared hatred for the liberal order.

★ ★ ★

The argument that the essence of Communism is democratic by virtue of being antifascist is therefore a flimsy one. Wasn't Communism a totalitarian engine of extermination before Fascism arrived on the scene, and didn't it remain so after Fascism disappeared? This fact remains a given over the very long term and in widely varied countries—a stubborn reality that historians and political scientists must take into account when they try to describe and define the Communist phenomenon.

Surprisingly, none other than François Furet wavers between the idea that Nazism and Communism are equivalent, and the view that Communism despite everything is related to the democratic tradition. In *The Passing of an Illusion,* he subscribes to the underlying thesis of Vasily Grossman's masterpiece, *Life and Fate,*[9] namely the "secret connivance that links Nazism and Communism, even in war." On the sensitive area relating to the uniqueness of the Shoah, Furet goes so far as to say, in agreement with Grossman, "However exceptional the massacre of the Jewish people, it does not cancel out what is comparable between the two regimes in their philosophies of power and their suppression of liberty."

But elsewhere, as Claude Lefort points out with some astonishment in a penetrating essay, Furet believes he can discern a kinship between Communism and democracy.[10] He maintains in classic fashion that revolution, according to Marx and Lenin, "prepares the realization of a democratic *promise* by emancipating the exploited workers." (My italics.) It is stupefying to see such a sharp thinker relapsing into confusion between promises and actions—as if the entire structure of Communism were not organized around Utopia, that is, around the demand to let intentions pass for actions. As for "emancipating the exploited workers," let me say a few words about this democratic achievement of Communism.

The art of *"penser socialiste"* consists in perceiving the exact opposite of what emerges transparently from the data. Thus we can keep harking back to the notion that Communism, despite all its shortcomings, at least advanced workers' rights. Those who make this claim choose to overlook monumentally obvious facts: that the most important workers' rights—the right of association and coalition, the right to form unions and strike, for example— were introduced between 1850 and 1914 in and by the liberal societies, and that these same rights were all suppressed in socialist states without exception. In all socialist states, the only union was the state itself, which, far from being an instrument for defending workers' interests, was a monopoly designed to regiment, surveil and control the working class. Arrests and executions of strikers, like the mass executions and concentration camps, date from the very beginning of the Bolshevik revolution. In June 1920, strikers at the weapons factory at Tula, including many female workers, were interned in camps. To gain their freedom and be re-employed, they had to sign the following statement: "I, the undersigned, a stinking dog and criminal, repent before the revolutionary tribunal and the Red Army, confess my sins and promise to work conscientiously."[11] It is doubtful if even the most infamous of capitalist bosses has held humanity in so much contempt that he made striking employees sign such an appalling document; he would in any case incur the strictures of the law—that "bourgeois" law established precisely to protect human dignity. In the strict light of history, socialism may be defined as the regime that abolishes all the rights of workers.

We often hear the rejoinder that in capitalist countries the Communist parties were, at the very least, agencies of protest whose "struggles" for workers' rights compelled the bourgeois states to extend those rights. This also is a false assertion. Once again: the most fundamental of those rights, relating to unionization and strikes, were established in the industrialized nations prior to the Great War and the birth of the Communist parties. As for social welfare—medical insurance, family benefits, retirement security, unemployment protection, paid vacations and so on—it was put into place between the wars or after 1945 in those countries where Communist parties were nonexistent or negligible (Sweden, Great Britain, Holland, Germany), as well as those where they were strong (France and Italy). We owe these policies as much to conservative as to social-democratic governments. It was a reformist Democrat, Franklin Roosevelt, who created the Social Security and welfare systems in the United States, which were enormously expanded thirty years later by Kennedy and Johnson. In Britain, it was Lord Beveridge, a Liberal economist, who became the architect of the entire social welfare system that was adopted during World War II and only grudgingly accepted by the Labor Party afterward because they feared that it would put a damper on the proletariat's revolutionary ardor.[12] In France, the politicization of the central trade union, Confédération Générale du Travail (CGT), which in 1947 became purely and simply an appendage of the French Communist Party, simultaneously decreased the rate at which workers became unionized and the effectiveness of the unions.

With firsthand knowledge of François Furet's intelligence and erudition, I find it implausible that he was in any danger of falling into the crowd of dupes and hypocrites, or of preaching some sort of equivalence between intentions and actions—that shell game where theory is slyly made to stand in for practice. Furet nevertheless, possibly beguiled by his own past illusions or pulled leftward by one last, tenuous thread, would still grasp fitfully for that Raft of the Medusa: democratic Communism!*

Why would a leading savant of "quantitative history" not be willing to admit that the Communist thinkers and masters were entirely successful in achieving the *quantity* of what they set out to accomplish? Possessing absolute power, would they have

---

* *Translator's note:* "Raft of the Medusa" refers to a disastrous 1816 shipwreck made famous by Théodore Géricault's dramatic painting. Survivors on a makeshift raft fought and murdered each other and resorted to cannibalism. After thirteen days they were rescued, but by then their number had been reduced from 150 to 15.

been so masochistic as to inflict on themselves, for a hundred years, accomplishments contrary to the convictions their lackeys attributed to them? Why be so cruel to themselves?

The reason for Furet's paradoxical swings of opinion regarding Communism's true pedigree—totalitarian or democratic—is no doubt partly due to his decision to treat Communism essentially as an "idea": an idea, he said, that was an "illusion." But can you really discuss Marxism-Leninism, which determined the fate and completely transformed the lives of billions of human beings over so many years, as if you were debating Cartesianism or utilitarianism or existentialism? In other words, is it just one philosophical theory among others, a harmless system of thought that you may or may not adhere to intellectually, perhaps moving on after an episode of disillusionment that affects no one but the crestfallen disciple?

I have already mentioned how far the very concept of "illusion" is a restrictive one, in my view. Communism cannot be reduced to an abstract credo, or Hitlerism to the scientific plausibility of Nazi racial doctrines. Both regimes were above all systems of power in practice—power without precedent in history, if not without ideological precursors.[13]

Powerful minds have lent their support to the theory that Communism and democracy spring from the same ground, even if their fruits are different—and even if Communism's record is "quantitatively" as bad or worse than that of Nazism. The link between Communism and democracy, according to Simon Leys in an article in *Commentaire,* may explain why "our historical memory treats Communism and Nazism unequally." He adduces "disquieting evidence" such as this: "The friends of *Commentaire,* I am happy to say, have quite naturally included some repentant Communists, but I doubt that many ex-Nazis have ever numbered among them."[14] And Pierre Nora, for his part, on an episode of the television forum *Caractères* featuring a discussion with Francis Fukuyama, asserted that Communism was a struggle for democracy—to the evident bewilderment of *The End of History's* author.[15]

Leys and Nora are not so naïve as to fall into the trap of confusing intentions and actions, nor so underhand as to try pushing others into it. One reason for this controversy (or rather, muddle) concerning Communism's fundamental sources of inspiration is apparently that CPs in liberal societies are perforce aligned with the left-wing opposition, with agendas touting advances in democracy and expansions of social justice. The choice of Communism may therefore be dictated by worthy theoretical motives. Unfortunately, it comes with the false postulate that in order for democracy to be fulfilled, capitalism must be abolished.

The adepts of historical materialism, whose culture is paradoxically founded on a superb indifference to history, studiously avoid taking into account the simple fact that the *only* democratic societies that have ever existed are capitalist societies—or at least societies where the rights to private property, free trade and cultural liberty prevail. Thus the next step in their argument, which for them is decisive, is the gratuitous claim that Communism within liberal societies is "on the left" because it aims to destroy capitalism and therefore fights to advance democracy. This postulate also is refuted by the facts, though it allows leftists to assert that they are more democratic than liberals. Insofar as this is the official line, let us concede that many ingenuous neophytes of Communist parties as opposition forces may be sincere in claiming allegiance to democracy.

But lest we get mired in endless confusion over the existent versus the nonexistent—which would make a mockery of the historian's task—we must wrap up the debate about Communism's democratic or antidemocratic vocation by considering not what Communists in opposition say, but what Communists in power do. Well, there is massive and indisputable evidence that all Communist parties everywhere, once they are in power, begin business by wiping out every freedom. There is no exception to this rule. The alleged democratic dimension of Communism cannot be discerned in the history of real regimes; it has to do rather with the history of political sensibilities, with currents of thought in capitalist countries. In fact, the Furetian concept of an "illusion"—

the illusion of perfecting democracy in particular—applies only to Communists affiliated with opposition CPs in liberal societies, who operate under the protective umbrella of the bourgeois rule of law. It doesn't work at all for Communist governments, which were not at all illusory for those they reduced to slavery.

Should we then refrain from questioning the genuineness of the Western Communists' commitment to democratic ideals? We could refrain, if not for the quantity of reliable information about the system in power that has poured down upon them since its beginnings, which makes their sincerity in error implausible. We should take care, of course, not to lump together the deceivers and the dupes, the conscious accomplices to crime and the willfully blind. The latter were guilty merely of giving full rein to the vast human capacity to deny disturbing truths. But the others, the deceivers, professed to be the knowing architects of a system whose tyrannical and criminogenic character they knew from close up. Maurice Thorez and his Comintern-appointed mentor, Eugen Fried, habitués of the Paris-Moscow beat during the 1930s—that decade of engineered famines and great purges—obviously suffered from no illusions about the radically, congenitally and irremediably antidemocratic nature of the regime they were serving in the USSR and machinating to establish in France. And Palmiro Togliatti, who was living in the Soviet Union during the same period under the name Ercoli (and whose false testimony at the trial of Bukharin helped bring his former friend before the firing squad), had a very clear understanding of the sort of regime he would try to set up in Italy after Mussolini's fall. He would have been highly amused if someone had lauded the "democratic" inspiration of his vision, when he in fact intended to replicate the Stalinist prototype.

Let's look for a moment into the mental world of the Communist International's leadership. According to them—or, at least, according to the argument they used in front of Western audiences—Soviet totalitarianism represented the highest developmental stage of authentic democracy. It was the triumph of the proletariat, as embodied in Stalin, and the ultimate goal of the historical process under the guidance of the CPUSSR. If you want to write history by taking literally the self-serving declarations of despots, then by all means Communism was a struggle for democracy. But if historians are willing to endorse such slogans, they should do likewise for those trumpeted by the Nazi and Fascist leaders. After all, Hitler and Mussolini also boasted that they personified the aspirations of the vast majority of their subject peoples. Concentrating every power in their own hands, they were convinced that they were creating a form of democracy far superior to parliamentary polities, which are always subject to unstable majorities, party rivalries, dubious coalitions and shifting alliances. Moreover, this conviction of theirs was less unfounded than the Bolsheviks' pretensions, since the Fascists and the Nazis came into power by means of the ballot box, unlike the Soviet Communists.

With regard to the Communist reality, even the crowd of militants, voters and sympathizers, though not privy to Comintern secrets, could not forever remain uninformed. As time went by, they could hardly avoid forming a fairly accurate picture of the totalitarian logic of Communist regimes, if only because they could see the same logic at work in the internal functioning of the Western CPs. The sincere democrats among them understood their mistake and quit. Those who remained—from the most unpolished proletarians to the most sophisticated intellectuals—did so because within their heart of hearts they wanted not a democratic society but the Total State. At the end of the day, wasn't this the form taken by Communism in all its manifestations? In the long run, it was difficult for even the most poorly informed of the rank and file to overlook this salient fact.

Again and again, the blueprint was passed on: from Stalin to Mao, Kim Il Sung, Ho Chi Minh, Pol Pot, Ceausescu, Castro and Mengistu, accompanied by material and military aid, producing the same form of society by the same means—by enslaving, degrading, starving, imprisoning and exterminating. How can anyone maintain that Communist leaders have always aimed to create the opposite of what Communist parties in power have always and everywhere accomplished, pursuing their goal with implacable resolve? Is it conceivable that the champions of

Communism in the West could have remained unaware, for the greater part of a century, that the system could follow no other pattern? And how can we avoid concluding that this was precisely the model they sought to realize in their own countries, whatever lip service they gave to democracy? If you went looking for a perfect instance of what Karl Marx called an "ideological superstructure," you would be hard-pressed to find something better than the myth of Communism's "democratic" essence.

You might think that the Communists had deliberately gone to absurd lengths to provide us with examples of the contradiction between their theory and their practice. As Claude Lefort points out, the Stalinist constitution of 1936, which grants on paper all sorts of democratic guarantees to the Soviet people, coincided with the beginning of the great purges. As this constitution was doomed to remain a dead letter—for to have applied it in practice would have instantly brought down the regime—we must assume that it was intended as a cruel joke and a creative form of sadism: a juridical sadism. Reading to a prisoner undergoing torture the articles in the Universal Declaration of Human Rights that forbid torture reveals an exceptional totalitarian genius. But for a witness of this performance to take it as proof of the torturer's democratic credentials illustrates the unbounded human capacity to move comfortably within the elastic realm of misconception. The behavior of Communists in democratic societies, although kept within limits by bourgeois laws, was no less totalitarian. The 1955 "trial" of Maurice Merleau-Ponty in the hall of the Mutualité in Paris, with a spectacular bunch of CP philosophers as the "tribunal," ended predictably in a verdict condemning his book Les Aventures de la dialectique, in which he criticized Marxism.[16] In a capitalist context it was inconvenient for them to take the logical next step: the physical liquidation of the author.

In a classic work telling the story of his own condemnation, Charles Tillon has aptly described the machinery of these mock examinations, or "Moscow trials in Paris." And Claude Lefort recalls a splendidly "democratic" episode of Stalinist violence that took place during the first hours of the Fourth Republic. During an electoral meeting he attended in support of a Trotskyist candidate, a gang of thugs from the Stalinist CPF suddenly burst in. Lefort describes what happened:

> I had barely finished my short speech—before a packed hall, to our pleasant surprise—when chairs came flying onto the platform and fighting broke out. The incident was not unforeseeable, but I got embroiled in a scene that left me feeling confused. Noticing a young woman being roughly handled by an angry group, I went to help her. They were holding her fast, shouting to her face: *"Hitléro-trotskiste!"* She kept on repeating as loudly as she could: "I was at Ravensbrück!" They yelled back: "Liar! Slut!" Just as I reached her, she held up a card, crying "Here's the proof! Here's the proof! My prison card!" The ID was torn from her hands, ripped to shreds and hurled back into her face before I managed to extricate her from the hysterical mob.[17]

I am not a historian, but I seem to remember that Fascism and Nazism had vanished by 1946. Yet on that evening, the CP Chekists were physically assaulting peaceful citizens who were merely exercising their constitutional right to set forth their political positions during an election campaign. If Fascist and Nazi methods still survived among us in 1947, they belonged to the Communist Party and to it alone.

Again, I agree with Claude Lefort when he insists that "we cannot conclude, as does Furet, that Communist illusions have their roots in the heritage of democratic ideas."[18] Furet's interpretation fails to recognize the fact that many people harbor a desire for totalitarianism, succumbing to what I have called "the totalitarian temptation." Totalitarian man, the "new man" of Communist regimes, is manufactured by the systematic annihilation of the last vestiges of autonomy for civil society. In this organized engine of destruction, the new man is but a cog in the machine— usually against his will, but sometimes not.

According to Yuri Orlov, the system can be reduced to simple, fundamental features: There is but one party holding power, and it monopolizes the economic, political and cultural spheres.

This monopolization is accompanied, naturally, by the creation of a repressive police apparatus, total ideological control and a mythology of the monolithic state. These features are found in all Communist regimes. They are reproduced with such exact conformity that it's hard to see why anyone would still insist on asking whether or not they correspond to the intentions of their creators. Unless the study of history consists in seeing what is not and not seeing what is, the question is an idle one.

A useful addendum to Orlov's criteria is that Communist repression has invariably fallen not only on declared enemies of the regime but also on millions of harmless folk who never meant to attack or even criticize it. Witness, from 1918 on, the innumerable instructions, flowing from the Cheka and from Lenin himself, not to seek proofs of the "guilt" of such-and-such a social or ethnic group, but to liquidate it simply because of what it was. For its subsistence, Communism apparently needs a regular diet of executions. The collective extermination of innocent people, not for what they do but merely for what they are, culminates in a sort of physical hatred resembling the Nazis' pathological loathing of the Jews. According to Maxim Gorki, "Class hatred must be cultivated with feelings of organic revulsion toward the enemy as an inferior being, a degenerate physically and also morally."

The tropism toward totalitarianism on the part of certain individuals explains the 1968 generation. They have been credited with a spirit of libertarian idealism, but in reality they nurtured hatred for liberal democracy and indulgence toward Marxist regimes and agendas. In Germany, they got it into their heads that the supreme model to emulate was the German Democratic Republic. "These young people," wrote Ernst Nolte, "were manifestly guided by the conviction that the socialist GDR, despite a few 'deformations,' incarnated the finest potentialities of Germany, and that on some distant day it would be the foundation on which a reunited socialist Germany would be built in the heart of a socialist Europe."[19] Nolte observes that from this time on in Germany, attention was focused almost exclusively on Nazi crimes while any mention of the word "totalitarian" in connection with East Germany became *verboten.*

I vividly remember dining in West Berlin, in the autumn of 1975, with Willy Brandt and Marion Countess Dönhoff, founder of *Die Zeit*, an excellent left-wing intellectual weekly that was favorable toward détente with the USSR. The countess asked me if I was working on a book. I replied that I was about to publish *The Totalitarian Temptation*. Visibly surprised, she asked me sharply, "How can you use such an outmoded concept as totalitarianism?" Brandt smiled in quiet amusement; after his fall from power, which had been contrived by the East German espionage agency, he suffered from no such illusions.

The GDR cult, a curious feature of the 1970s and 1980s, sheds light on the staggering absurdity of some demonstrations that took place in West Germany when the Wall came down. Their object was to protest the "imperialist annexation" of the GDR by the capitalist penal colony that is the Federal Republic.

In France also, the philosophizing of the "sixty-eighters"—which originally did not lack an occasional anticommunist, or rather anti-CP, inflexion—quickly mutated into a particularly virulent strain of rehabilitated paleo-Marxism. The degrading cult of Mao, the labor union federation with its "shared" program of mainly Communist inspiration, the pro-Marxist militancy of public education, the support given to the Baader-Meinhof Gang and the Red Brigades (which also sprang from the '68 movement), the calumnies heaped on Solzhenitsyn—all these marked a new era of Cold War reglaciation. A slew of leftists even thought that the Soviet and French Communisms, in comparison with the Chinese variety, were not sufficiently totalitarian: they were "revisionist." But there was no longer any need to build an antifascist front, since the last European regimes of fascist coloration were then giving way to democracies—in Greece, Portugal and Spain. So it was not in response to any actual danger, but rather through attachment to the totalitarian idea *as such* that a suffocating intolerance began to spread through the Western democracies in the years following 1968.

You sometimes have to ask yourself if the deepest need of quite a large number of intellectuals is not a predilection for serfdom, to which they owe their propensity and talent for creating a species of informal totalitarianism in the heart of free civilizations. Absent any external political dictatorship, they like to reproduce in their relations with one another, as a sort of *in vitro* experiment, the effects of the phantom tyranny they long for: the condemnations, exclusions, excommunications, defamatory campaigns—the whole gamut, right up to that old socialist-style bugaboo of "fascism," a charge lodged against anyone who hesitates to join the prescribed rites of veneration and execration.

It's a truism that in every airless dungeon where freedom of thought is stifled, a mutual tyranny is established between prisoner and jailer. Each player (as Hegel understood) takes his turn at being master and slave, or plays both roles simultaneously. But the astounding thing is that the invisible re-education camps embedded within free societies are created by *intellectuals* for their own use, while other citizens for the most part decline to let themselves be imprisoned.

No historian, in my view, has yet managed to elucidate convincingly the mystery of the paradoxical pro-Communism of the 1970s and 1980s. So we are poorly equipped to understand the reasons for the resistance, during the 1990s, to acknowledging Communism's true nature. One hypothesis is that this flight into denial has been dictated by fear of having to accept evidence of the consanguinity of Nazism and Communism. It is not pleasant to have to confess that you have supported, for almost a century, a type of political regime essentially identical to the one you fought against as the supreme embodiment of evil. The pain of having to do so is dreaded throughout the left, far beyond Communist Party circles, and also by complacent or foolish people on the right. Alain Poher, for example, is a Christian Democratic politician, a moderate centrist, president of the Senate and twice acting president of the Republic, yet he saw nothing amiss in supplying the preface to the French edition of the works of a totalitarian brute: the "genius of the Carpathians," none other than the *Conducator* Ceausescu. And numerous Western universities conferred honorary doctoral degrees on the Romanian tyrant's wife, Elena, who liked to pass herself off as a scientist of high achievement although in point of fact she was notoriously illiterate. Why so much servility? Of course, there were all those little treats showered on our progressive intellectuals by the East Bloc states (travel opportunities, colloquia, banquets, seaside vacations), but these fringe benefits of ideological kowtowing are not the final explanation.

The politico-intellectual community reacts as though it were being flayed alive if anyone ventures to draw parallels, however obvious and factual, between Nazism and Communism. Their sensitivity quickly turns to anger if you draw attention not only to the kinship in criminality of the two regimes but also to cultural affinities. During the summer of 1999, the Weimar Museum presented two parallel exhibitions, one consisting of paintings from Adolf Hitler's personal collection, the other a representative selection of East German art. What leapt right out in the most glaring fashion from these displays—and came as no surprise to anyone familiar with "socialist realism"—was what they had in common: the most vulgar and ridiculous pomposity. Needing to hold absolute control over creativity, and reactionary as regards literature and the arts, totalitarian regimes specialize in official *bien pensant* work as insipid as it is bombastic.

The juxtaposition of the two sets of dreadful paintings, spotlighting their similarity in political and cultural stupidity and in kitschy bad taste, provoked an indignant response from ex-Communists. Their exasperation was whipped up all the more by the Weimar curator's decision to display—alongside the paintings exalting the permanent felicity that the people were supposed to be swimming in thanks to Communism—a series of photographs by visitors from the West, which showed daily life in East Germany as it actually was: poor and dreary. Reacting to this exhibit, a former GDR minister of culture, Klaus Hopcke, did not mince words: he called the museum's curator, Achim Press, "a complete idiot."[20] Here is the typical socialist mentality on display: the "idiots" are not the perpetrators of the wretched productions, but those who exhibit them years later for public viewing. Herr Press, originally from West Germany, was also accused of reflecting the "colonialist" scorn felt by the West for the formerly Communist territory of East Germany.

As usual, the left had no intention of dealing with the facts, nor of determining whether the works in question manifested a likeness of style and purpose. For the Marxists, the scandal consisted in staging an exhibition that provided museum-goers with an opportunity to perceive this similarity for themselves. (In effect they are saying: Okay, perhaps the convergence exists; but don't *show* us that it exists!)

Totalitarian kitsch is universal. True, there is no pleasure in being reminded that through four decades, in the name of art, you promoted the fabrication of rubbish by the cartload. But note how former Communists, far from trying to understand the how and why of their mistakes, seek only to conceal them and prohibit any mention of them. This, too, shows post-Communism to be alien to the democratic spirit of free expression, which in the cultural domain, even years after the events, entails the freedom to gather information and form judgments.

Was this spirit foreign to Karl Marx himself? Some of the severest critics of Communism stop short of tracing the totalitarian reality of Communist regimes all the way back to Marx. But whether or not Marx explicitly desired or foresaw this outcome, the suppression of liberty has been an ineluctable consequence of his economic system wherever it has been applied. If Marx was unaware of his program's antidemocratic logic, then he was guilty of a lapse that doesn't say much for someone who set out. to understand the historical interdependencies linking economic, political, social and cultural structures. What's more, Marx's democratic sensibility does not seem to have been particularly well developed, a point attested by the texts cited in Chapter 6. To those I would like to add the following, which clearly reveals that Lenin's methods originated in Marx: "In a sense, good is evil. It is good that must be eliminated. That is what obstructs progress in human relations. And 'evil' is good, since it produces the movement that makes history by sustaining the struggle."[21] What this passage means is that attachment to human rights is evil if it resists the revolution. In the pursuit of revolutionary struggle, it is permissible to commit acts that in our everyday vocabulary are mistakenly called "evil." This line of argument was taken up and brilliantly developed by Leon Trotsky in his book *Their Morals and Ours.*[22]

Marx's words, with their inversion of morality, encapsulate the very essence of the logic that served as justification for Robespierre's Terror and Stalin's purges. Truth and justice can and must be sacrificed to the necessities of revolutionary combat. In 1864, after the International Workingmen's Association adopted the motion he had drawn up, Marx confided to Engels, "In the preamble to the statutes, I have been obliged to agree to two phrases where mention was made of *duty* and *right,* as well as *truth* and *morality* and *justice.* I have positioned them in such a way that they won't do too much harm."[23] Did Marx invent the notion of the dictatorship of the proletariat? This has often been contested. Boris Souvarine, for example, maintains that the few lines that Marx wrote about the subject hardly amount to a formal theory or an explicit recommendation. Yet the theme is clearly developed in the second section of *The Communist Manifesto,* "Proletarians and Communists." It's true that the question is only of academic interest, since the dictatorship of the proletariat has never been seen, and what has always prevailed in Communist regimes has been the dictatorship of an oligarchy.

The oligarchy always proclaims itself mandated by "the whole people," but this is a ruse common to all despots. A much better definition of Communism in practice is Nicolas Werth's phrase: A state against its people.

CHAPTER TWELVE

Fearing Liberalism

Toward the end of 1999, the television network ARTE aired a long made-for-TV police drama featuring a Spanish private eye based in Barcelona. The story begins with a homicide in that city and goes on to Paris, where the hero speedily tracks down those guilty of the murder and a whole series of related crimes.

Without going into the tedious details of the monotonously banal plot, I will merely draw attention to the following: 1) The hero has been a hardcore leftist or card-carrying Communist and remains a man of the left, a fact that we are not allowed to forget for a minute. 2) The guilty parties turn out to be in the pay of a firm that sells armaments to Iraq, a racket that mightily displeases our leftist hero. 3) The organization in question is neo-Nazi. The woman who turns out to be the criminal mastermind, before being gunned down by an ex-accomplice, unmasked by the detective, cries out, "Why are you doing this, at the very moment we're finally winning the war for a liberal world order?" In short, it's a magnificent example of socialist realism.

Here was a major television network—one that sets itself up as "cultural"—offering prime-time fare that, apart from its stunning mediocrity, was an exercise in unalloyed political propaganda based on two gross factual errors. First, in reality it was the left, in lockstep with the extreme right—sharing a hatred of the United States and preferring the Butcher of Baghdad to American democracy and to the United Nations—who lent their support to Saddam Hussein. Second, even a cursory reading of Hitler's writings should demonstrate that real Nazis were as antiliberal in their ideology as the Marxists. But for the scriptwriters who turned out this drivel, the important thing was to drum into the viewers' heads an imaginary equivalence between neoliberalism and Nazism.[1]

The fact that such a canard could be advanced in a film financed by Franco-German sources—in a vehicle, moreover, without the slightest redeeming aesthetic value—tells us more about the abiding manias of the post-Communist left, fixated on rescuing its past, and about its methods and propaganda techniques, than many a highbrow dispute among the intellectuals or historians.

Revealing likewise are some of the media's knee-jerk responses to events. Thus on the morning of October 5, 1999, two trains collided in the London district of Paddington, killing twenty passengers and injuring several hundred. The instant reaction to this accident by the French media was predictable. From every side rose the unanimous buzz, the same commentary repeated all day long: since the privatization of Britain's railways, the new companies, motivated only by their quest for profit, had slashed their spending on safety improvements, especially with regard to infrastructure and signaling technology. The conclusion was obvious: the killed and injured were victims of liberal excess.

Were that true, then the 122 victims of the 1952 railway accident in Harrow were slain by socialism, since British Rail was then nationalized. Likewise, in France on June 27, 1988, a collision between trains at the Gare de Lyon, which killed fifty-six people and injured thirty-two, was imputable to France's nationalization of her railways in 1937 and therefore to the Popular Front. And on June 16, 1972, the tunnel at Vierzy, in L'Aisne, collapsed on two trains, killing eight hundred passengers. Structural integrity was not exemplary here either, even though the company responsible for the tunnel's maintenance was state-run.

After a few hours' investigation of the Paddington disaster, authorities determined that the driver of one of the trains had ignored two yellow lights that were warning him to slow down and had run through another light that was telling him to stop. It seemed that human error, not human greed, explained the tragedy. "So what?" the antiliberals were quick to retort: the equipment was still at fault because the train was not fitted with an automatic braking system that would have come into play when the driver failed to stop. No doubt, but a system of this sort would not have prevented the French driver's error in the Gare de Lyon accident; nor would it have helped much on April 2, 1990, at the Austerlitz station in Paris, when a train smashed through a barrier, careened across the platform and plunged into the refreshment lounge. As for infrastructure, the antiquated state of French grade crossings, with poor signaling and flimsy barriers that drop only at the last second, causes between fifty and one hundred deaths every year. The infallibility of public services *à la française* is not altogether obvious, although facts like these are never permitted to cross the antiliberals' threshold of consciousness.

It should be pointed out also that the British railway system, even when it was state-owned, had a reputation throughout Europe for inadequate performance; and it wasn't privatized until 1997. Were two years of alleged mismanagement really long enough to have caused such deficiencies in infrastructure and rolling stock? In reality, British Rail had bequeathed to the private companies a thoroughly degraded system that had been jeopardizing the safety of passengers for several decades. The accusations directed against market liberalism on account of the 1999 tragedy issue less from rational analysis than from the abiding *idée fixe*.

Let me clarify my position here. Liberalism should not be considered the obverse of socialism; it is not a fabulous recipe that guarantees perfect solutions at all times. A society dominated by the private sector is quite capable of compromising the well-being of consumers in the quest for profits. It is up to the state to prevent such excesses, and vigilance in this respect should be a function of its true role—a role that, for the most part, it does not fulfill. But when blindly obsessive antiliberals claim that negligence, incompetence and corruption can never pose a risk to users of nationalized transportation systems, they are making an assumption that might be disputed by thirty passengers on two trains that collided in Norway on January 4, 2000, if these souls still numbered among the living.

It's the same story when it comes to automobiles. When Renault's sole shareholder was the French state, its products were neither more nor less safe to drive than Peugots, Citroëns, Fiats or Mercedes, which were manufactured by private companies. If anything, they were less safe, since the Dauphine model, for example, quickly became known for its tendency to flip over. When Renault was a nationalized concern it was permanently in the red; so the cars emerging from its factories, since they produced no profit, ought to have been peerless specimens of design and manufacture, and accidents caused by defects should have been impossible.

Such examples illustrate the ubiquity of a more-or-less unconscious fund of antiliberal culture that bursts out like a cri de coeur and is all the more astonishing in that it persists in spite of all we have learned during the twentieth century and in spite of prevailing trends throughout most of the world. Practice diverges from theory, for it seems that our instinctive reactions are more open than our intellect to the lessons of the past. The antiliberal is a like a magus who claims to be able to walk on water but takes care to demand a boat before setting forth. How are we to explain this enigma?

One reason is the intellectual inertia that I have called "ideological persistence of vision."[2] An ideology can survive long after its political and social embodiments have disappeared. In France, for example, at the close of the 1930s—a century and a half after the Revolution—an active royalist movement boasted numerous partisans of absolute monarchy. Without taking a direct role in parliamentary politics or government, it exerted a pronounced influence through its publications and the work of talented authors who propagated ideas hostile to the Republic. Despite its unrealistic agenda of monarchic restoration, this school of thought played a far from marginal role in public debate and cultural life. Similarly, after the tectonic shift of 1989, the socialist mindset persists even though the world is moving in the opposite direction.

Daniel Bell was ridiculed after he published *The End of Ideology* in 1960.[3] Over the next twenty years, there was nary a colloquium without some participant or other asking him sarcastically about the end of ideology at a time when ideologies seemed to be flourishing more than ever. Indeed they were, but to what purpose? The cults of Mao and Che Guevara were essentially phantasmagoric. Never has the falsity of Marx's famous pronouncement, "Man never poses problems that he can't resolve," been so thoroughly exposed. If the history of the twentieth century has shown one thing, it is that man is likely to spend his time posing problems that he cannot resolve—because they are essentially beyond solution—while refusing to tackle numerous genuine problems whose solutions are well within reach. There are two ways for an ideology to spend its final days: in the concrete world or in the conceptual domain. It may very well be terminated in the former and persist in the latter, exerting no more influence on actions—except perhaps as an impeding force—but continuing to wield enormous influence in the realm of words. In this case, ideologues obey their supreme rule: never admit that you have been mistaken, especially if your mistakes have caused people to lose their lives.

When ideologies that have been refuted and disgraced by the actions of their zealots continue to exert influence, it is chiefly in the echo chamber of the public media. I have given several examples from television, the medium that in our era has above all dominated the art of "communicating"—which subsumes the art of misleading.

Such impostures will vanish only with the passing of time. They will be inflicted on us as long as the former adulators of great crimes remain ensconced in our intellectual and media establishments. These persons' avoidance of truth is not hard to understand. They are obedient to the basic human drive for self-preservation and the need to flee from the past, from that famous "duty of remembrance" that is honored with respect to the Nazis but not the Communists. So the defensive counterattack against liberalism is a diversionary strategy, a way of avoiding the truth about Communism and more generally about socialism. "Those who want to bring happiness to humanity never bring happiness to actual people," said Claude Imbert. "Those who dream of an ideal egalitarian system start out as bricklayers and end up as nomen-klatura."[4] One might add: and bounce back into successful third careers as authors and hosts of history programs on television.

Hammering away with imprecations against "the ravages of liberalism" is a surreptitious way of insinuating: "Hey, Communism wasn't really so bad, apart from a few 'deviations' from its true nature." Antiliberalism, however, has functions that go beyond mere justification of an unjustifiable past, and are rather more concrete. These relate to warding off two fears that are present in each of us: the fear of competition and the fear of responsibility. These feelings are not just vague apprehensions; they are dominating anxieties. Membership in a redistributive economy allays these fears and reduces stress. The statist machine promises the psychological comfort of not having to bear the burdens of responsibility for oneself.

★ ★ ★

In the spring of 1890, Émile Zola, installed in his new apartment on the rue de Bruxelles, received a journalist from the *New York Herald Tribune* (now the *International Herald Tribune*) and told him:

I am presently working on a novel, *L'Argent* ("Money") which will deal with issues concerning capital, labor and so on, that are being debated these days by Europe's discontented classes. I will argue that speculation is a good thing. Without it the world's great industries would die out, just as without sexual passion people would die out. The grumbles and growls emanating from socialist sources are the prelude to an eruption that will change existing social conditions to some extent. But

has the world been made a better place by our great Revolution? Are men more equal in any respect than they were a
hundred years ago? Can you guarantee to any man that his
wife will never cheat on him? Can you make everyone equally
happy and wise? No! So stop talking about equality! Liberty,
yes; fraternity, yes; but equality, never![5]

A man of the left—which he proved at a heavy price—and
a venerated idol of twentieth-century French socialists, Zola was
insightful enough to see that there can be no society without
inequalities. These may derive either from differences between
individual performance or from disparities in advantages conferred by the state—or more simply from the wall separating those
who have one or more state privileges and those who have none.
Here I am using the word "privilege" in the exact sense defined
by Littré as "an advantage granted to an individual or to a group
and enjoyed to the exclusion of others, to the detriment of the
common law." I feel obliged to point out this primary meaning
because *privilège,* in politically but not semantically correct French
usage, has become synonymous with "rich." As a corollary, poor
people must be "disadvantaged."

Now, one can be rich without ever having enjoyed the slightest
privilege, or with an ostensibly modest income that is fortified
by remunerative advantages. The nomenklaturist may be rich
because his political connections are worth the presidency of a
large state monopoly. On the other hand, he may struggle along
in a bureaucracy or a *mutuelle,** thanks to some smalltime, mostly
fictive employment that nonetheless constitutes a "privilege."

The inequalities within productive liberal societies are constantly subject to a mixing process and are always in flux. In

---

* *Translator's note:* "In addition to standard health coverage provided by the
'Sécurité sociale', many French people contribute to complementary insurance
schemes run by mutual-benefit organizations known as *mutuelles,* often linked
to specific professions. The *mutuelle* reimburses some or all the medical expenses that cannot be met by the 'Sécurité sociale'." From the *Collins Robert Dictionary,*
unabridged, 5th ed. (2001).

statist, redistributionist societies, the inequalities are frozen in place; whatever the talents and energies of someone in the French private sector, he or she will never have the benefits that are granted as an entitlement to an official of Électricité de France. Nor those of an employee of the French National Railway Company (SNCF, Societé Nationale des Chemins de Fer Français), which has been described as "a world champion in terms of hours, days and kilometers of work stoppage."[6] (Translation in socialist language: "Public service *à la française*.") In societies of this type, well exemplified by France, the state creates the special privileges that generate inequalities, beginning with those that members of parliament confer on themselves. After only twenty years, they collect full retirement benefits—of which 70 percent is funded by the taxpayers and not by the sacrosanct socialist *répartition* pension scheme, which can never be adequate and which, with respect to parliamentarians and other public employees, amounts to a con game, intellectually and financially.[7] France has no fewer than 532 special retirement plans, which amount to so many state-bestowed entitlements: a touching restoration of the *ancien régime,* in practice if not in theory.

Privileges are not manna that falls only on public servants. In France, overproduction of fruit and vegetables of poor quality—blotting-paper lettuce, tasteless tomatoes, radishes devoid of pungency, peaches so hard they might be serviceable as *boules de pétanque**—is the automatic result of the piling-up of national and EU subsidies that make it advantageous. Farmers know by experience that their destructive protests, their assaults on public buildings, arson, roadblocks and interruptions of railway service, will not incur the wrath of the law but instead will garner additional financial handouts. When several categories of citizens are exempt from the obligation to respect the law and may violate it with impunity, that is the very definition of *privilèges* in the most precise etymological sense of the word. Farmers have actually

---

* *Translator's note: Boules de pétanque* refers to a game of bowls from the south of France, played with steel *boules.* M. Revel's judgments here reflect his renowned expertise as a gastronome and culinary historian.

enjoyed legal and pecuniary special dispensations for a long time. Already in 1963, de Gaulle was lamenting the passivity, not to say cowardice, of his ministers in the face of rural violence. Addressing the problem of cattle overproduction, the general grumbled that "the gendarmes are sheep, the prefects are sheep, the ministers are sheep—the state is served by gutless sheep!"[8] In 1999, public conduct deteriorated still further. Although overproduction in reality is caused by the "European social-agricultural model," French farmers in a stroke of genius hit on the plan of fingering a scapegoat: the United States of America, land of McDonald's.

By sacking some McDonald's outlets, the farmers were giving clear proof of their acumen, for the fast-food chain purchases virtually all its basic foodstuffs from local providers and employs thousands of French people. The restaurants were destroyed, to nationwide acclamation, in the name of the war against *malbouffe* (junk food)* and in defense of the *terroir* (the local "soil" of culinary and wine-making traditions)—never mind that for forty years the righteous husbandmen had been giving us insipid fruit and hormone-crammed chickens with a fishy smell. Their real motive was a refusal to accept competition. The French never ask themselves, "Why does McDonald's have so many customers? Do their low prices have something to do with it?" And, by the way, I can't quite see how the McDonald's menu, with its ground-beef hamburgers, French fries and salads, is so very far from standard French fare or in what way it represents American imperialism.

Every summer, French agriculturalists set fire to trucks carrying fruit and vegetables not from the United States but from Spain, a fellow member of the EU. So anti-American demagoguery

---

* *Translator's note:* In her illuminating chapter on José Bové, Claire Berlinski writes: "*Malbouffe*. This concept is important. Bové coined this neologism. As Gilles Luneau correctly observes, there is no word in English that captures its full meaning. It is generally translated as 'junk food,' but that dismissive, vaguely ironical Americanism does not capture the full *horror* of bad *bouffe*, with its intimation of contamination, pollution, poison. The word *mal* in French should in this case be translated as 'evil.'" From *Menace in Europe* (New York: Crown Forum, 2006).

serves as a mask for a broader protectionist agenda: the war against globalization. It aims at perpetuating an agricultural model based upon taxpayer subvention combined with subsidies for exports and barriers against imports. The servile French government hurries to accommodate the farmers and persists in economic folly. Jumping onto the "Hate the United States" bandwagon, it makes every effort and invokes every pretext to beat back imported products, even from Europe or Latin America, as it demonstrated at the Rio Summit in 1999. The valiant knights of this crusade lose sight of the fact (if they ever knew it at all) that the United States imports more than it exports—hence the chronic American trade deficit—whereas the EU exports more than it imports. In particular, France ranks first in the world as an exporter of agricultural products, just ahead of the United States. Attacking international free trade is therefore, from France's point of view, a suicidal policy. Yet in 1999 the national hero of the moment for the French intelligentsia was José Bové, "*alter*-globalization" activist and dismantler of McDonald's restaurants. Meanwhile, nearly all the Nobel Prizes in the sciences went to Americans, or to European scientists who had relocated to the United States—a fact that should be worrisome to us Europeans. They have their Nobel laureates, and we have our Bové.

For some years now, the "Bové model" has been fervently embraced in the cultural domain as well. The French government marches with our cinematographers and audiovisual artists under the banner of "cultural exceptionalism." While the elimination of competition is a bad idea in purely economic terms, leading to poor quality and high prices, one can understand how it might seem attractive at first glance. On the other hand, coming from artistic and literary creators, appeals to the state for protection against works produced abroad amount to confessions of a talent deficit. "Shield us," said Baudelaire, "from the humiliation of comparisons!" This, in essence, is what our "creators" are ordering the government to do. Their principal bugbears are the same as those of our farmers: the United States above all, followed by the World Trade Organization—i.e., the rest of the world. Their dearest wish is that the public should be as poorly informed as possible about the competition's achievements, that they should be deprived of cultural choice, and—most important—that the state should subsidize their "creations," just in case their compatriots are reluctant to open their wallets. The state, in other words, should compensate for the poor attendance by squeezing money from people who don't want to pay the price of admission. Inequalities like this are typically disguised as resistance to "the dictatorship of the market" and to "ultraliberal globalization." The best part is that this campaign to isolate and standardize French culture should be conducted in the interests of "acknowledging cultural diversity in the world," to quote the French minister of foreign affairs.[9] We can only regret that our European ancestors did not hasten to squash the insufferable dominance of Italian painting during the fifteenth and sixteenth centuries, or French literature's invasive influence during the eighteenth, under the guise of protecting the "diversity"—or rather, the provincialism—of European culture.

In a society where inequalities result not from markets and competition but from state policies, the art of economics is reduced to getting public authorities to rob my neighbor for my own profit, if possible without the victim knowing whose pocket the pilfered resources will end up lining. Hence those societies— of which France is an outstanding example—where roughly half the population subsists, entirely or partly, directly or indirectly, on money seized from the heavily burdened other half. A large portion of state-derived revenues may very well constitute fair pay for honest work, but an equally large portion is payment of privileges and financing of clientage. In short, the political class exchanges money for votes.

Dozens of books and thousands of articles have dealt with the waste of public money in France; but the state refuses to do anything about it, instead constantly increasing both taxes and deficits. Among the beneficiaries of the squandered sums— which often seem more like embezzlements—are the innumerable *associations* that our accommodating legal system allows virtually unrestricted freedom of action. Pierre-Patrick Kaltenbach has ably shown how this works. Writing about nonprofit associations in the journal *Le Débat,* he says, "When you lack conviction enough to convince and courage enough to command, all that is left to you is to corrupt." And he adds, "Along with the deficits and the debt that have permitted the financing of the status quo and social entitlements, the associations have been the era's main expedient." The growing deficits, debt and taxation levels can only be favorably viewed by those whose privileges they finance, in a country where the tax base is restricted to half the population and where 20 percent of households contribute 80 percent of revenue. If you counter that this 20 percent consists of the richest among us, you would be mistaken. The truly rich have been transferring their wealth abroad for a long time. Those who are saddled with the heavily progressive direct taxes are the highest-paid salaried employees— that is, the upper middle classes, who are likely to owe what they have to talent. For them, tax evasion is out of the question and emigration an increasingly tempting option.[10]

The assertion is made that the continually increasing social security deductions, deficit spending and debt are justified by social policies designed to help the unemployed and the needy and those who have been "excluded." This would be a good argument if, on the one hand, the economic policies of various French governments and several other European governments since 1980 had not done everything possible to multiply the numbers of unemployed and destitute; and if, on the other hand, the resources made available by deductions had been efficiently put to work without corruption. This has not been the case. *Le Point,* a center-right publication, has presented a detailed investigative report on "Les Profiteurs de la banlieue."[11] The billions of francs poured into the *quartiers* and "free zones" (the businesses that dare to set up shop in the chaotic *banlieues* are generously subsidized) have for the most part been hijacked by bogus—indeed, Mafia-like—associations, by do-nothing urban-planning bureaucracies that gorge themselves on honoraria for projects doomed to be mothballed. Once again the state does everything except what it's supposed to do, which is (after deducting and redistributing) to monitor, discipline and sanction. But then it would lose its clientele.

A genuinely social policy consists not in taxing and wasting vast sums in order to indemnify more and more of the unemployed, but in doing what is necessary to ensure that there are fewer people out of work. A report by the Conseil Économique et Social recalls that the actual or potential workforce rose from 22 million in 1973 to 26 million in 1994.[12] But two-thirds of this additional four million joined the ranks of the unemployed or became beneficiaries of publicly subsidized make-work jobs. In fact, the actual number of workers receiving economically justified salaries in the commercial sector dropped by 900,000 over a period of twenty years.

The Cologne summit of June 1999 served up a rehash of that old concoction, the European Employment Pact. This was nothing more than a tissue of platitudes and an avowal of failure and impotence, for to need an "employment pact" at all is itself an admission of failure. The "pink" nations deem themselves morally and socially superior because they can boast of employment pacts, but this is rather like someone with a broken leg in a cast who considers himself a better athlete than someone in good shape because at least he has a physical therapy program. When there is an average of 10 percent unemployment and perhaps ten million people working illegally, as in Europe at the end of the century, it is only human to prefer perorating about plans for the future rather than about successes in the present. And to pass the time you can always make sardonic comments about American-style "hamburger-flipping" jobs. (Read: full employment.) While there has been some improvement recently in France, unemployment still stood at two and a half times the level in the United States.

In Europe, and particularly in France, the prevailing way of looking at the employment situation is to view each business sector in isolation—like a ministerial department—rather than to consider the nation as a whole. This explains the demand by Communists and ultra-leftists in the October 16, 1999, demonstration in Paris to suspend workforce-reduction "social planning" in favor of the socialist model of the thirty-five-hour workweek.

Élie Halevy, in his obituary for Georges Sorel, reminded us that Charles Maurras (to whom the inconsistent Sorel had once

granted his approval) was "the theoretician of social peace protected by the state."[13] In this debate, the left gives proof again
that it is unconsciously defending right-wing theses; it wants
to guarantee permanent employment to *every* employee in *every*
business enterprise, thus condemning economies to stasis and
ensuring high levels of unemployment worldwide; and it refuses
to notice that the nation on our southern border, with its flexible
employment policies, *taken as a whole* has been enjoying full
employment. The left seems unaware that it is beating the drum
for the protectionist policies followed by Franco until 1959; when
Spain's economy collapsed, he was forced to seek aid from the
International Monetary Fund and advice from the liberal Opus
Dei economists. In France it is still sacrilege to say that job flexibility causes employment levels to rise in the active population
as a whole. Contrast the position taken by Massimo D'Alema,
a former Communist, elected prime minister of Italy in 1998.
In September 1999 he saw nothing amiss in devoting an entire
speech to "the end of the 'employment for life' myth" and to the
benefits of "flexibility," without thereby arousing the anger of the
Italians.

With us, trade protectionism is linked to the protection of
special statutory rights and the right to waste public funds. That's
why the winter strikes of 1995–1996, intended to keep in place
the benefits enjoyed by the civil service and public utilities, were
enthusiastically supported both by the ultra-left and by a large
number of private-sector salaried employees who do not receive
these benefits. The leftist mindset condemns economic gain if it is
obtained within the framework of the market and therefore subject
to risk and competition. But gain is allowed—even admired—
if it is a statutory benefit, obtained without effort, imagination
or talent. And "ultraliberal globalization" fills the left-wing heart
with anxiety.

I wrote "the leftist mindset," but I ought to have written "French
public opinion in general." A National Assembly debate of June
23, 1999, in anticipation of the World Trade Organization conference scheduled for the following November in Seattle, showed
that the antiliberal and anti-American attitudes of the right-wing

politicians were just as pronounced as those of the Communist ministers and parliamentary deputies or the environmentalists.

Along with the fear of competition, fear of responsibility is another reason for clinging to a statist society. These associated fears have exerted a powerful influence on the feelings of those who refuse to acknowledge the failure of Communist societies, in which both competition and responsibility were eliminated.

All collectivism is intrinsically irresponsible and is recognized as such, even in societies that are only partly collectivized. In the statist way of looking at things, nationalized companies do not have to account for their mistakes, nor do their employees. In 1986, the French government outlined a plan for public transport: the idea was to scale salaries partly according to merit. It was a right-wing government, but the concept had begun to take shape under the previous government, which was socialist. There was a revolt by the 21,000 drivers of the SNCF (French National Railway Company) and the 3,249 members of the RATP (Paris Transport Authority). The state immediately beat a heroic retreat, in full acknowledgment that the state itself enjoys the privileges of irresponsibility. Here is the grandiose tradition of the "strong" French state—essentially a strong runner "whose swiftness is its renown," as Père Ubu quipped of his own horse, so quick to bolt.*

The left is scandalized by the perks awarded to CEOs in the form of stock options and by the size of their retirement packages. These prerogatives are open to criticism—they reveal a sort of "nomenklaturist" capitalism à la française—but they do not compete with the 150 billion French francs that vanished into the vaults of the "national" Crédit Lyonnais, losses attributable to a combination of incompetence and dishonesty. In the private sector, the gifts are funded by the shareholders, whom no one has forced into making their investments. But the resources swallowed up by the nationalized black hole came from the taxpayers, extorted by the chief culprit, the state, almost without their awareness.

---

* *Translator's note:* *"dont la célérité fait la célébrité"* is a quotation from *Ubu roi*, a satirical farce by the absurdist playwright Alfred Jarry (1873–1907).

Alarmed by the depredations that were bleeding Crédit Lyonnais dry, bureaucrats from the Ministry of Finance sent a note about the affair to their minister, Pierre Bérégovoy. The minister returned it with a dry comment in the margin: "*Laissez faire M. Haberer*" ("Let Mr. Haberer handle it"). M. Haberer happened to be the president of Crédit Lyonnais, a bank that had been raided by friends of the president of the Republic and of the Socialist Party. In this case, "laissez faire" sounds good to socialist ears. But when "laissez faire!" applies to an entrepreneur who builds and manages a wealth-producing business, the left reads it as an atrocious exploitation of the proletariat.

Most piquant is how the state, wanting to correct its economic blunders (*read*: sweep them under the carpet), instead sets about aggravating them. It's like an ambulance that has been summoned to the scene of a traffic accident but plunges into the crowd when it gets there, mowing down the survivors. To cover up as best it could the damage done to Crédit Lyonnais by its stupidity and dirty tricks, the state in 1995 created a committee baptized Consortium de Réalisation (CDR), tasked with liquidating the bank's dubious debts. Instead, CDR managed to increase the losses by at least one hundred billion francs.[14] It was a right-wing government that invented this burlesque *pompe à phynances,** faithfully trailing after the left and trying to clean up its gaffes and swindles. The cost to the public for this miracle: an average of three thousand francs per capita, and in reality much more for the minority that bears the major part of the tax burden. At least the French had the satisfaction of being able to say they had escaped the dangers of neoliberalism.

But it wasn't over yet. In 1999, Crédit Lyonnais—now privatized—had to shed four million dollars just to rescue itself from the legal proceedings started against it by American justice. The culprit in this affair was an Italian crook named Giancarlo Parretti, who bought up the movie giant Metro-Goldwyn-Mayer only to plunge it into fraudulent collapse. Lyonnais had loaned Parretti

---

* *Translator's note*: pompe à phynances, or "financial pump," is another period joke of Alfred Jarry's.

two billion dollars, a sum that had to be completely written off by the bank, and hence by us. The bank's managers claimed they were victims of an abuse of trust. But according to the American prosecutor handling the case, "Close examination of documents relating to some of the transactions makes clear that this explanation doesn't hold water."[15] Lyonnais was not the victim; it was an accomplice, doubtless at the behest of political forces. Didn't Giancarlo Parretti have a Paris office on the rue de Solférino, in the headquarters of the French Socialist Party, where he allegedly represented the Italian Socialist Party?

A masterstroke of high finance like this aptly illustrates the perennial methodology of statism. Conservative estimates are unanimous that for several decades four hundred billion French francs (in 1999 values) have been squandered every year by the state and the regional authorities. This spectacular wastefulness—it is also plundering—is equaled only by the vigorous efforts of our leaders to maintain it at a satisfactorily astronomical level. There have been unsparing breakdowns of the scandal by the Court of Accounts and the regional chambers of accounts, and by the books, articles, academic studies and whole issues of weekly magazines devoted to it. These exposés could not have failed to land on the desks of our presidents, our ministers and our regional representatives, yet these worthies have not made the slightest attempt to staunch the hemorrhaging flow of patronage—a patronage that has nothing to do with genuine solidarity or with "Social Europe." The ruthless imposition of taxes is hardly designed to create jobs or bring relief to those who don't have them, or to promote solidarity or stimulate productivity; its purpose is to rescue the state from its own corruption, waste and incompetence. The state refuses to mend its ways; likewise the local authorities, guilty also of extravagant follies and scorn for the taxpayer. The current renewal of economic growth will help France endure a few more years of its sickness. But will it effect a cure?

In any event, there is unlikely to be a change of attitude in France's tax advisory council, where ideology trumps proficiency and where the members, sounding more like politicians than technical experts, seem to have learned their economics from the likes of Trotskyists such as Alain Krivine or Arlette Laguiller. The public should ask itself if the abnormally high numbers of outcasts in French society does not derive from our debilitating prodigality rather than from the so-called *horreur ultralibérale*. But the public is too naïve and too well trained to consider the possibility, for it is constantly being taught over the airwaves that liberalism is the source of all evil. I grant that France is a rather extreme case, but for this reason it is interesting and instructive. For many of us French, the state never has to answer for the consequences of its actions. Any mistakes, thefts, infractions, injustices and tragedies must only be laid at the door of the private sector.

The dream of a society devoid of accountability, in which the prerogatives of those who govern and the earnings of those who are governed have no direct relation to ability or productivity, is a constant temptation lurking in the heart of each of us. It's a dream that explains the nostalgia for Communism, or the hope for an absurdly impossible post-Communist equivalent. Whence the paradox, in some countries of the former East Bloc, that it's sometimes harder for people to extract themselves mentally from the post-Communist muddle than it was for them to escape bodily from the prison of Communism.

Yuri Orlov has given us the most concise and illuminating description of what could be called totalitarian socialism's secondary benefits (to borrow an expression from psychoanalysis). In his words, "the citizen is in large part freed from responsibility for the results of his work." But, "For this lack of accountability in the professional domain to be condoned, ideological loyalty is *de rigueur*." Ideological loyalty, besides, is what confers the right to employment in the first place. In exchange for self-annihilation before the party, the individual is assured of a job. Of course it will be a miserably paid job—the average monthly wage in Cuba is currently around six dollars—but then, very little work is required. Lifelong employment is guaranteed: employment involving almost no work and almost no pay, a situation pithily summed up in the joke so often heard by travelers to the Soviet Union: "They pretend to pay us and we pretend to work."

A career scientist, Yuri Orlov cites instances of colleagues who absented themselves from their labs for months at a time or who produced sham results, all without the slightest penalty. Promotions depended more on ideological dependability than on professional competency. Among the rewards granted to the servile: "Appointment of people to better-paid positions unrelated to their qualifications, exaggeration of their accomplishments when bonuses are calculated." Political toadying meant the sacrifice of liberty and dignity, but the trade-off was a certain peace of mind. It is easy to understand, then, how a people raised for several generations in cozy, docile mediocrity finds it hard to adapt to the turbulent waters of a competitive society where actions have consequences.

Listening to the testimonies of some citizens of central Europe, you realize they expected that democratization and liberalization would not entail loss of their inefficient, lifelong sinecures, and that they would be handed a Californian or Swiss standard of living on a plate. Apparently it never occurred to such people that, given a choice between a jalopy like the Trabant, manufactured in East Germany, and a Western-built or Japanese car of comparable price, shoppers (especially those from East Germany) would always go for the latter. It wasn't long before the Trabant factories closed for good.

The discontents of the East Germans and Berliners translated, in 1999, into the electoral rise of the old Communist Party, now rebaptized the "Party of Democratic Socialism" (PDS), to the detriment of Gerhard Schröder's Social Democratic Party (SPD). But in West Germany, although the SPD lost votes there also, it was to the advantage of the center-right Christian Democrats. Aversion to the pale pink of Schröder's brand of socialism and the "watermelon" green of the environmentalists had prompted a swing toward liberalism in West Germany, but in the East a nostalgia for the encompassing state.

This was despite the fact that no other population emerging from Communism had received, or could dream of receiving, the credit that was advanced to the former German Democratic Republic. When reunification was under way, Helmut Kohl's decision (made for political and psychological reasons and against the advice of the Bundesbank) to fix an exchange rate of one East German mark for one West German mark was a sumptuous gift. Imagine if everyone in France could exchange their savings in francs into an equal number of dollars, or even Swiss francs. In addition, between 1989 and 1990, the West Germans earmarked for their compatriots' economic recovery sums equivalent to 5,000 billion francs, or roughly 765 billion euros. For a population of fifteen million, this wasn't too shabby. Even so, the Ossis keep up their accusations of Wessi stinginess! Investment does not preclude resentment. Investments, if they are to be fruitful, presuppose liberal norms: acceptance of competition and a willingness to shoulder responsibility for one's own destiny. This is the price one must pay for a high standard of living.

* * *

"It is not by means of laws and regulations that you are going to bring order to the economy." When Lionel Jospin, prime minister of the so-called "plural left," made this sensible remark in the course of a televised speech, the Communists, the Greens, a large number of Socialists and of course the far left rose up in protest. To them it smacked of a scandalous turn toward liberalism. During the weeks that followed, the prime minister backpedaled, and his Socialist colleagues fell all over themselves in their efforts to tone down his imprudent—indeed, impudent—words and to mitigate their unfortunate effect.

"No, we aren't liberals!" cried the finance minister, Dominique Strauss-Kahn.[16] (Given the evisceration-by-taxation that this gentleman inflicted on us, we were in no danger of thinking that he was.) "French socialists want to be modern, but not liberal," echoed a headline in Les Échos, summarizing several proclamations from our desk-bound crusaders.[17] The same newspaper had already told us, fifteen days earlier, that "The Socialist Party maintains that the government has not taken a liberal turn," a statement that reflected only half the truth. Similar professions of faith were heard from every side in the press and on the airwaves, sounding for all the world as if the believers were being summoned to the reconsecration of a profaned church.

The explanation most frequently offered for the French rejection of liberalism—a rejection joined in by the right, or most of the right anyway—invokes an alleged statist tradition deeply rooted in our psyches. The refrain is that France has always been a *dirigiste* nation; therein lies her ancestral vocation, her innermost nature and cultural identity; and this quality, fortunately, distinguishes and shields her from liberal chaos and "Anglo-Saxon" barbarism. From Louis XIV's powerful minister Colbert to de Gaulle, from Robespierre to Mitterrand, from Jacobinism to Bonapartism, from *planisme* (economic planning) to socialism: we French worship the state and clamor for its ministrations.

The trouble with this interpretation of our history is that it is a fable, and one of recent making. Concocted during the second half of the twentieth century, it has been intended mainly to confer patents of nobility on bulimic and megalomanic French authorities since 1945. So Colbert was opposed to the market? These are the minister's own words: "A state-supported enterprise, if it is still unprofitable after five years, must be abandoned." Has our contemporary French state abandoned SNCF, Air France, Crédit Lyonnais or other bottomless pits? Obviously not, although their breakup is long overdue. Let Colbert rest in peace.

Colbert is not alone in being traduced by such tendentious revisionists. So we must welcome, as a work of intellectual and historical hygiene, the publication of *Aux sources du modèle libéral français*.[18] This major work, well researched and containing a wealth of information, is a collaborative effort of thirty-one contributors, all of them eminent economists, historians and philosophers.

Three lessons stand out. The first is that there were as many great eighteenth-century precursors of liberalism to be found in France as in Scotland or America, some of them writing at an earlier date. The primary source of modern liberalism, of course, remains John Locke's seminal work, *Two Treatises on Civil Government* (1690). But it was French thinkers, with Turgot in the lead, who influenced Adam Smith, the Scottish author of *The Wealth of Nations* (1776), and likewise the American leader Thomas Jefferson—not the other way around. It was the physiocrats who, in a celebrated article in the *Encyclopédie,* were the first to argue in favor of free trade.

Second, whatever the champions of the "Bolshevik" version of the French Revolution may prefer to think—focusing on the thirteen months of the Jacobin tyranny and slighting the other nine years involved—the unexpurgated historical account tells us that the Revolution, in its philosophical principles and its legal reforms, was essentially liberal. It was opposed to collective ownership and uncompromising on private property rights. It constructed a legislative edifice devoid of all the corporatist and statutory shackles of the *ancien régime* in order to establish unrestricted liberty with respect to entrepreneurship, work, trade and banking. Montagnardist *dirigisme*—price fixing, confiscation of harvests, monetary laxity—was but a parenthetical episode that ended in shortages and bankruptcy.*

Finally, and as I have already pointed out, it was the nineteenth-century liberals who were the first to pose what was then called "the social question," answering it by laying down several of the founding laws of modern civil rights. And it was in the liberal nations that trade-unionism was strongest. On this subject, two articles by Armand Laferrère, "Droit du travail, justice de classe" and "L'argument de la justice sociale," are illuminating.[19]

For Laferrère, the French choice of "equality over liberty" amounts to hypocrisy. The French enjoy less liberty than the Americans and the British, but inequality in France is no less. Our inequalities are different from theirs, flowing from preferential treatment by the state and local authorities. The only inequalities that the French condemn are those due to private

---

* *Translator's note:* The Montagnards ("Mountain Men"—so-called because they sat on the higher benches of the Assembly) were an extreme faction during the French Revolution who were opponents of the moderate Girondins and became associated with the radical Jacobins. They effectively ruled France in 1793–1794. A later movement, from 1830 to 1848, was inspired by the *montagnard* Reign of Terror.

incomes or inheritances. Services and perks allocated by and to the political-administrative-unionist-NGO class are accepted and even respected: cars and apartments, transportation, free mail and telephone services, special retirement policies and such. Benefits like these may often be the rewards of honest, useful work, but they are also not unlikely to be manna showered down on hordes of domesticated parasites and paid for by taxpayers judged as "privileged"—that is, those who have no privileges and earn what they have by their labors.

French resistance to liberalism stems partly from the elevation of equality over liberty, as Alexis de Tocqueville saw clearly in *The Old Regime and the Revolution*. What he was less perceptive about was the French acceptance of state-derived inequalities and rejection of those arising from competition. This is easiest to verify in the cultural domain, where our left-wing artists and intellectuals, tirelessly fighting for financial handouts and strenuously defending the *préférence nationale* so dear to Le Pen, modestly take cover behind the fig leaf of "cultural exceptionalism."

If, for example, a dramatist teams up with a producer, and with the help of private capital, they succeed in staging a play that finds favor with theatergoers and earns, let's say, a million or so francs within the first year, they are putting themselves at serious risk of being ostracized for having made concessions to crass commercialism. But if another author and another producer, with the aid of public subventions to the tune of a comparable sum, present something that is performed once or twice before invited audiences and then falls into oblivion, they are viewed as great creators who sacrifice before the altar of a "demanding" (and how!) conception of their art. The first-mentioned, the risk-taking entrepreneurs, were able to provide compensation for the actors, stagehands, scene painters, lighting technicians, bartenders, box-office assistants, accountants, ushers and other supporting staff over a space of twelve months, on top of which they have, of course, paid rent to the owner of the theater and taxes to the government. Philistines, both of them! The creators, on the other hand, enjoying the favor of some well-placed functionary or politician and picking the pockets of the taxpayers, are promoted by the ruling coterie of critics and invited to the July 14 garden party at the Élysée.

What the French detest is not inequality as such but inequalities that cannot be credited to the state. Nothing reveals this truth better than the popular support accorded to the series of strikes that froze the public services during the winter of 1995–1996. These were motivated by the fear that the unjustified prerogatives enjoyed by public-sector employees might be subject to revision. The strikers were egged on both by private-sector workers— simultaneously victims of and providers for this inequitable arrangement—and by the preening sociologists of the ultra-left who in theory are champions of egalitarianism but in practice are creatures of privilege. In exchange for doing a modicum of work, the professors are tenured and invulnerable, subsidized for life by the very same society they ostensibly want to destroy.

In the chapter of his *Souvenirs* where he relates the activities of the 1848 Committee for the Constitution, Tocqueville notes that a conservative such as Vivien showed himself to be just as keen to defend administrative centralization as Marrast, who "belonged to the ordinary type of French revolutionaries, who have always understood the liberty of the people to mean despotism exercised in the name of the people." After saying that this unlikely harmony between a man of the right and a man of the extreme left was surprising to him, Tocqueville goes on to explain:

> I was used to the phenomenon, and I had long remarked that the only way to bring a conservative and a radical together was to attack the power of the central government—not in application, but in principle. That was a sure way of throwing them into each other's arms. So when people say that nothing is safe from revolutions, I tell them they are wrong: centralization is safe. In France there is only one thing we cannot establish: namely, a free government. And only one institution we cannot destroy: centralization. How could it ever perish? The government's enemies love it, and those who govern cherish it. The latter, it's true, from time to time perceive that centralization exposes them to sudden and irremediable disasters;

but this doesn't fill them with disgust for it. The pleasure it provides them of being able to meddle with everything and hold everyone's fate in their hands is reason enough to bear with its perils.

Tocqueville's observations here are as valid today as they were in 1848. He is telling us where the French heart lies: more with the state than with liberty. This and similar references of his to the French taste for centralization of power in some respects support the claim that this trait goes far back in our past. But French liberal thinking also goes a long way back, even if we have applied it much less than the Americans and the British. Economic *dirigisme,* strictly speaking, took center stage in our affairs mainly during and after the Second World War. Once in power after 1981, the united left—the Socialists allied with the Communists—gave more emphasis to this model, even as it crashed upon the rocks.[20]

But socialism can never be the cause of its own constantly repeating failures. "Employment policies" that achieve record levels of unemployment never elicit the slightest twinge of doubt; nor are lessons learned when liberalization makes some progress and employment levels recover. According to the propagandists of the left, it is liberalism that is responsible for socialist failures; democracy for the chaos left behind by Communism; the UN for ethnic hatreds that have spurred on African holocausts; the World Bank and the International Monetary Fund for embezzlement of aid by Third World dictators; and the World Trade Organization for the reluctance of developing nations—China, for instance—to enforce standards for working conditions that the WTO would like to see adopted universally.

★ ★ ★

The ritual imprecations against classical liberalism are all the more surprising in that, since the extinction of socialism, the world's governments are all advancing rapidly in the direction of freedom. Governments that vociferate the loudest against liberalism are in fact doing the opposite of what they preach. Some of them—like the leftist French administrations that are condemned to carry around the millstone of their Communist allies and other political blocs as "plural" as they are vacuous— do so grudgingly or belatedly, thus garnering fewer benefits than governments that are quicker to fall into step with global evolution. But none are able to offer any real and lasting resistance to liberalism, while acknowledgments of its inevitability come from every quarter.

"In Brazil, going backwards is not an option," proclaimed Gustavo Franco, formerly governor of his country's central bank. He went on to say that liberalization, bringing profitable privatizations and a return of investments from abroad, had stabilized and opened up an economy that used to be heavily protectionist and *dirigiste*.[21] The same could be said about Argentina, which during the ten years of Carlos Menem's presidency (1989–1999) went through a similar stabilizing process. Although the closing year of his presidency saw a recession, this was in no way comparable to the chaos Menem had to confront on his accession to power. It is interesting to note, however, that the media laid emphasis on that final recession. The message: This is where liberalism takes us! There was a voluntary loss of memory at work here: Menem's achievements were being ignored.

When Menem took office, inflation stood at a spectacular 28,000 percent. In Buenos Aires, shops were posting in their windows the hourly changes in prices and exchange rates. Ten years later, inflation was 2 percent and the gross domestic product had increased by 40 percent. Disgraced by years of dictatorship, Argentina had become respectable again in the community of nations. There is still unemployment and poverty, but less than there was. When critics complain that Menem "sacrificed the social dimension of Perónism," it should be recalled that Juan Perón, over the nine years of his presidency (1946–1955), managed to transform Argentina, which in 1939 enjoyed the same per capita income as Great Britain, into an underdeveloped nation. To applaud this exploit, which hit the poor most of all, reveals a strange conception of social policy. Menem's successor,

Fernando de la Rúa, elected in October 1999, intends to follow the path of Tony Blair.

Algeria, an African country that, without actually being a Soviet satellite, had copied the USSR's recipes for economic failure in the most servile manner, chimed in with a timely *Adieu au socialisme!*[22] Economic liberalization has been proceeding apace in Algeria since 1998 and is changing public attitudes. "At all levels of society," writes a *Jeune Afrique* correspondent, "including among the poorest, and above all among young people, opening up to the outside is more than a wish. It is a passion."

In the Southern Hemisphere, two Labor parties—one in Australia and the other in New Zealand—had already taken notice of "Old" Labor's shortcomings and had invented "Blairism" ten years *avant la lettre*. Robert Hawke's Australian Labor Party lowered taxes, kept a check on public-sector salaries and deregulated the economy just as much as did the "conservative" Ronald Reagan in the United States during the same years. The prime minister maintained that these steps were the necessary basis for real job creation and assistance for the poor: "You would have to be an idiot or blinded by prejudice," he said, "not to understand that you must have a vigorous private sector and growth if you want to get serious about improving the lot of the greatest number of people."[23] New Zealand's liberalization was the work of a Labor prime minister, David Lange, who between 1984 and 1989 privatized most of the public sector, including airlines, mining and petroleum concerns, forest products and electric utilities. Lange put the matter plainly in terms of classical engineering: "Social democrats must come to terms with economic inequalities because they are the motor that drives the economy as a whole."[24] Was it to punish such insolence that François Mitterrand in 1985 ordered the blowing-up of Greenpeace's vessel *Rainbow Warrior* in the New Zealand port of Auckland? This attack caused two deaths, those of a Portuguese photographer and the honor of France, but did nothing to slow down New Zealand's economic ascent, which was skyrocketing at a time when France, with indomitable progressive energy, was sinking into unemployment, recession and monetary collapse.[25]

The mistake made by the archaic left is that it fails to recognize that liberalization does not compel the abandonment of social programs, but better management of them. For French socialists, the main requirement for sound social policy is expenditure, not wise implementation. Results are of secondary importance. In France there are eleven hundred lawless neighborhoods, a record without equivalent in the other EU nations. But we reckon our social arrangements to be better than theirs because we "release" enormous sums of money for the *banlieues*. What is this money used for? Are we making the most of it? Whom does it profit? Is it being wasted—or misappropriated? Why such a gulf between the scale of the funding and the slenderness of the results? To ask such questions would be to make concessions to a "liberal logic," a sordid productivity-oriented mentality. The important thing is that "the rich" pay up, even if the poor get hardly anything out of it.

The Netherlands and Sweden (which was practically bankrupt in 1994) have succeeded in liberalizing their economies in ways that partly resemble New Zealand's approach, yet without abandoning their generous social budgets, which they have found ways to manage more efficiently. Sweden has above all freed up production by launching into competitive enterprise, privatizing industries including telecommunications, energy, banking and transportation. The nation's renewed growth is fueled by technology startups that for the most part didn't exist in 1990. Holland has achieved full employment once again, to the point that a workforce shortage necessitates the importation of workers from Great Britain, Ireland and Poland. The economic recovery here is not the fruit of privatization alone; it stems also from reducing the state's budget deficit and tightening control over social expenditures. The Dutch system was being abused by fraudulent unemployment claimants and by those who were making government assistance a way of life.

In Europe as elsewhere, the curtain is falling not only on classical socialism but on the Third Way. What a cemetery for Third Ways, or "mixed economies," the twentieth century has been! French socialists who in 1981 were calling for a "rupture with capitalism" have become social democrats, and those who were social democrats have become liberals, even if they have rebaptized themselves as "social" liberals. You have to make a living, after all! In the 1990s the old Italian Communists, with their new "Democratic Party of the Left" (PDS), became more liberal than both the left and the right wing of French politics. The outcome is that the "pink Europe" that was so enthusiastically extolled after Prodi, Blair and Schröder came to power very quickly revealed itself to be contradictory, incoherent and mythical. Coming on top of the Swedish, Dutch and Danish liberalizations, the developments led by Blair in the UK and by Schröder in Germany showed that while socialists might still be in the majority in Europe, they were divided among themselves.

Their disunity came out into the open in June 1999 when Blair and Schröder made public a manifesto titled "Europe: The Third Way / Die Neue Mitte." They were advocating financial discipline, stricter control over public spending, reducing the crushing tax burdens on businesses and individuals, flexible employment laws, going from a welfare society to a work-oriented one, pruning of public bureaucracies and redefinition of the state's responsibilities. In short, Blair and Schröder were recommending the exact opposite of what the French government was doing.

France's leadership resented the manifesto as an aggressive critique directed against it. "BLAIR-JOSPIN: CLASH ON THE LEFT," headlined Le Nouvel Observateur, which also published the ruminations of the minister for European affairs, Pierre Moscovici, a "close advisor" of Lionel Jospin's, in an interview titled "No to Tony Blair!"[26] Britain's prime minister never possessed an odor of sanctity for France's left, always contemptuous of what they call the "American left," a term they use to label such un-American figures as Mario Soares and Michel Rocard. After all, Blair had pushed the spirit of *double* collaboration—of class collaboration and of collaboration with the United States—to the point of proposing that the Socialist parties of Europe unite with the American Democratic Party so as to create a global confederation of the center-left, which would replace the Socialist International. In other words, under the pretext of modernizing the left, he was selling it down the river. When Blair was invited to give a speech before France's National Assembly, in the background you could hear groans from several of the Socialist deputies. *"Lamentable! Lamentable!"* was the refrain, loud enough to be audible in the public galleries. Is Blairism anything else but "Thatcherism with a human face?" asked Philippe Marlière in an excellent *Temps modernes* article. He recounted the following highly instructive anecdote:

> During the 1997 Franco-British summit in London, Tony Blair was chatting with Jacques Chirac. The British prime minister was singing the advantages of economic deregulation and "flexibility." Chirac listened, puzzled, and by way of reply launched into a description of a more interventionist state. When his host refused to back down, an amused Jacques Chirac conceded that he hadn't expected that he would have to defend a moderate social-democratic model against a Labor prime minister.[27]

What would the French left become were there no right?

Enraged by the Blair-Schröder manifesto, French Socialists felt avenged and reassured when, in the autumn of 1999, the German chancellor suffered a succession of electoral catastrophes in which the Social Democratic Party lost some of its traditionally safest seats. The left-wing French press and the media read in this development proof of the German public's rejection of the "new SPD's" concessions to neoliberalism. This explanation ignores a small detail: except for the special case of the ex-Communist Party's progress in East Germany (analyzed above), everywhere else Schröder was defeated not by the forces to his left or by the Greens but by those on his right, namely the liberals of the Christian Democratic Union (CDU).[28] So the voters were not showing any desire for a return to paleosocialism. What stood revealed were the political contradictions of a "pink" Europe, and particularly of a "pink" France, which was being drawn into the current of liberalism while desperately clutching at the broken branches of bygone ideologies littering the banks.

The "turn to liberalism" had been taken years before by the leftist parties of southern Europe, more sharply even than by those of Western and Eastern Europe.[29] The Spanish Socialist Workers' Party (PSOE) of Felipe Gonzalez, right at the beginning of Spain's democratic transition, had cancelled the nationalizations on its agenda, as did the Portuguese socialists upon their return to power after the liberal decade of Cavaco Silva, from 1985 to 1995. But it is on the subject of Italy that Europe's leftist theoreticians are most amusingly wrongheaded, the April 1996 general elections being a case in point.

Contrary to what is vigorously maintained in France, these elections were not a historic turnaround, the left's first victory since the war. The elected majority was center-left, and its leadership was positioned more at the center than on the left. In fact, Italian political history has been punctuated with center-left governments since the Sixties—that is, since the Socialist Party started forming alliances with the Christian Democrats. An example: in 1965, Pietro Nenni, the historic Socialist Party chief, was vice president of the Council of State in a cabinet led by Aldo Moro, the Christian Democratic leader who was assassinated in 1978 by the Red Brigades. And from 1983 to 1986, it was a Socialist, Bettino Craxi, who led the government that held the record for duration in the First Republic's history.

Should we see a historic watershed in the fact that Communists participated in a government led by the centrist Romano Prodi? No, because they were no longer Communists. In 1991—to point out again what the French seem to have difficulty acknowledging—the Italian CP embraced market economics, changing their name to Democratic Party of the Left (PDS) and becoming a member of the Socialist International. Politicians coming from the ranks of the PDS and entering Prodi's government at the ministerial level have been moving toward the center-left for five years already.

Another misapprehension of the blinkered French left is that the 1996 results did not represent a crushing victory for the center-left. Far from being a landslide, the so-called Olive Tree coalition was able to gather fewer votes than the total for right-leaning parties: 428,894 fewer, to be exact. If the coalition was nevertheless able to obtain, quite legitimately, more seats than its adversaries, it is because three-quarters of Italian parliamentarians are elected on a majority basis by a one-time vote for a single candidate; on this occasion the left knew how to keep tight ranks and put forward only one candidate per district. In contrast, a divided right advanced several candidates in almost every district, a misguided strategy that is not forgiving in this type of election.

Finally, Romano Prodi's agenda was not different from the programs of deficit reduction and currency protection that had prevailed throughout Europe since the Treaty of Maastricht. It was expressly modeled on Chancellor Kohl's policies in Germany, with the goal of entering the lira into the European monetary system and satisfying the Maastricht requirements with regard to a single currency. Prodi also carried out privatizations, beginning with the telecom industry.

The only two Italian parties opposed to this European trend were, on the right, the formerly Fascist National Alliance and, on the left, the Communist Refoundation Party, formed by the Italian CP minority who in 1991 rejected social democracy in favor of remaining faithful to Marxism.

At the close of 1998, Prodi's government was followed with one led by Massimo D'Alema of the PDS, a development that unleashed foot-stamping jubilation among the paleosocialists. Just think! Italy's head of state—a Communist! It seems that blindness to historical reality is an ineluctable consequence of Marxist convictions. In his preface to a book by Dominique Lecourt on Lysenko, Louis Althusser wrote, "Marx has equipped Communist parties, for the very first time, with the scientific means to understand history."[30] Poor Louis! How sorry I am that you are not here to share a laugh as I read aloud that sentence, which you doubtless wrote to gratify the ayatollahs who surrounded you.*

---

* *Translator's note*: Louis Althusser, a French Marxist intellectual, supported Ayatollah Khomeini's fundamentalist bid for power in Iran. Althusser subsequently became mentally ill and, after murdering his wife, was confined to an institution for some years.

These unprecedented "scientific means to understand history" bequeathed to the left by Marxism were scarcely in evidence when continuity was perceived between the Italian Communist Party of 1948 and the PDS of 1998. In an action emblematic of the change of heart, the PDS turned over to private hands a third of Enel's capital. (Enel is the Italian equivalent of Électricité de France.) Along with his adoption of market solutions and his acceptance of NATO (of which Italy was the most operationally effective and dedicated European member during the Kosovo intervention), Massimo D'Alema gave his support to employment flexibility in terms that even politicians of the French right would not have dared to emulate: "The era of guaranteed lifelong employment is over," he said at the Levant Trade Show in Bari, taking up his favorite leitmotif.[31] Earlier in the year, at the Milan stock exchange, he had proclaimed that "More flexibility creates more jobs."[32] The Italian experience bore him out. Although Italy's *average* unemployment level is more or less the same as France's, around 11 percent in 1999, its geographic distribution is highly uneven. The northern provinces—Friuli, Venice, Lombardy, Piedmont, Emilia Romagna and, to a lesser degree, Umbria and the Marches—boast employment levels *à l'américaine,* or between 3 and 6 percent. It is not without reason that Bologna, a municipality that since the war had every appearance of being an unassailable Communist bastion, went over to the right in 1999. After all, since liberalism was working for the city, why not elect an actual liberal rather than a repentant Communist? What makes Italian unemployment statistics shoot up so high in the nation taken as a whole are the rates prevailing in the provinces to the south of Latium. The reasons for this disparity are rooted in the social "culture" and inherited attitudes of the Mezzogiorno, which make it an ancient "exception" and outweigh economic factors when it comes to the question of job creation.

When the Socialist French government sets itself up as advisor to the other EU countries, lecturing them for failing to adopt France's wonderful "employment pact," it verges on the ridiculous. Among the Fifteen, as regards employment France ranks in the bottom three—joining the company of Finland and

Spain. In 1998 and 1999, unemployment levels seemed to be going down in France, as they were in Spain also, but even so, our dogged devotion to social-welfarism would hardly place us among the leaders.

What's more, the improvements of which Jospin's government boasted may largely be artifacts of highly questionable statistics. Marc Nexon, in a long and amply documented article in *Le Point,* went so far as to use the accusatory term "cooked-up figures." This journalist concluded:

> Behind the encouraging figures that the government releases every month is fudging that borders on outright lying. The only statistical categories used are those that show a significant lowering of unemployment. But there are others that point in the opposite direction. People being struck off the lists right and left, others who have long been out of work and have reached the limits of state benefits, and thousands of state-created jobs for the young—all this serves to prettify statistics that have only a distant relation to the depressing facts.[33]

Even without such cookery, the official account hardly compels admiration, since average unemployment in the G7 nations stood at 6.2 percent and in the Republic it was 10.8 percent. So it's not surprising if the "French solution" doesn't attract many disciples.

The Italian left's warming to liberalism—or, more exactly, its fresh perception of liberalism, not as the antithesis of leftist politics but as its condition—contrasts with the passé reveries of the French leftists, who as usual are several steps behind the rest of Europe. In the same way, the critique of Communism is more radical coming from Italian ex-Communists than from the French "plural left" socialists.

As an example of this lag, a recent article by the PDS secretary Walter Veltroni is worth quoting.[34] Veltroni begins by saying that, in the document he had prepared for the forthcoming PDS congress, he had defined the twentieth century as "the century of bloodshed, the century in which mankind could conceive and execute the genocide of the Jewish people, the century of Auschwitz and the Nazi persecutions, and also the century of the Communist tragedy, of Ian Palach,* of the gulag and the horrors of Stalinism." To those who reproach the PDS for the coyness of its self-criticism, Veltroni replies, "We have put Stalinism on the same plane as Nazism, the gulag on the same plane as Auschwitz, and we have named Communism as the tragedy of the century. How could we state it any more clearly?" Assimilation of the two great totalitarianisms—still sacrilege in France—is here being officially sanctioned by the second most highly placed PDS leader, who continues, "Justice and liberty are two inseparable values. . . . Communism and liberty have proved to be incompatible—that was the great tragedy of post-Auschwitz Europe." To those who clamored for the PDS to "break every tie with the past politics of the Italian Communist Party," the secretary said, "We have gone further than that. We have *dissolved* the party. And we did it ten years ago." And the president of the PDS, Massimo D'Alema himself, had stated in his closing speech at the party congress of the previous year, "Communism changed into an oppressive force, a totalitarianism capable of gigantic crimes."

Such frankness contrasts with the cunning pigheadedness of someone like Robert Hue, loudly proclaiming that he refused to renounce the appellation "Communist" for his party. Questioned about allegedly fraudulent financing of the French CP, he denounced what he called a "political plot." This visionary elaborated, "There is an intense class war in this country. We are in a situation where there is a Communist Party confronted by aggressive liberal forces."[35] Between the two national party secretaries there is a gulf of a hundred years, at the very least.

An article like Walter Veltroni's could not please everyone. It aroused cries of joy as well as vociferous polemics. But the latter were on quite a different level from the French counterattacks. Two years earlier, the publication of *The Black Book of Communism*

---

* *Translator's note*: Ian Palach was a Czech student who burned himself to death in Wenceslas Square in 1968, as a protest against the Prague Spring invasion by the Red Army.

245

in Italian had already provoked a lively debate in which, alongside the usual clumsy subterfuges and hackneyed platitudes, there was a sense of historical accountability that has become rare in France. In *La Repubblica*, a center-left daily comparable to *Le Monde*, Sandro Viola wrote, "May this book cause us never to forget that in our youth we flirted with an infamous Idea, that we admired detestable men and avoided seeing that the Idea in question was producing an infinite number of crimes."[36]

And what Walter Veltroni had the decency to admit in his famous *La Stampa* piece was that there had always existed, throughout the century, a *democratic* anticommunism. He was refuting the worn-out lie that the French Communists and their friends were attempting to refloat: namely that anyone who was anticommunist necessarily had to belong to the extreme right—to be a "fascist" and therefore a "dog," in Jean-Paul Sartre's formulation.

That the two top officials of a party that is both the heir to and gravedigger of its Communist predecessor could be so frank in their analysis is a clear indication that "pink" Europe is far from being homogeneous. And it is getting less and less pink in coloration, drawn as it is toward the market by the liberal tendencies inherent in the logic of the EU and by globalization, a process that the EU must participate in if it wants to become the counterweight to America's economic power that it aspires to be. Socialism survives among us in the guise of so-called "voluntarist" measures, which usually have effects opposite to those desired, or in the form of political patronage disguised as "solidarity." Both forms will prove less and less compatible with the market as time progresses.

At the summit of the European leaders of the democratic left—joined by the presidents of the United States and Brazil—held in Florence in November 1999, expressly to debate "progressivism in the twenty-first century," Lionel Jospin drew a distinction between "market economies" and "market societies," assenting to the former while rejecting the latter. But to accept the marketplace is already to repudiate socialism—a meaningless word if its primary meaning of "collective ownership of the means of production and exchange" is not retained.

To reject the "market society" doesn't commit you to very much, for such an entity has never existed and could never exist. In every society since the beginning of time there have been activities, values and institutions that by their very nature escape from market forces. The important thing is to leave to the market what properly belongs to it; but not everything belongs to it. Socialism wants to assign to the state what properly belongs to the market, and to regulate what should be controlled by the free individual. The liberal order, on the other hand, has no intention of assigning to market forces those matters that do not concern it.

To assert that you can prolong the faltering life of socialism with the aid of a state that "regulates" the market is little more than verbal consolation. Why didn't the French state "regulate" Crédit Lyonnais and Elf Aquitaine in the era when they were nationalized, rather than let them continue to rot in mismanagement and corruption, incurring the prodigious losses that taxpayers were forced to indemnify? Why doesn't the state begin to "regulate" itself and its bloated parasitic extensions: the Mutuelle Nationale des Étudiants de France, for instance, or the Caisse des Retraites Complémentaires des Cadres, or the Comité d'Entreprise d'EDF, or the ten thousand subsidized nonprofit associations— "profitable without limit"?[37]

The whole concept of "market socialism" is a contradiction in terms and a bad play on words. It recalls nothing so much as the description of his economic policies given by General Velasco Alvarado, Peru's socialist dictator, when he said that "the revolutionary government of the armed forces is neither capitalist nor Communist, but just the opposite."

CHAPTER THIRTEEN

The Ultra-Left
and Anti-Americanism

"RIOTERS TERRORIZING GENEVA!" headlined the Swiss Sunday newspaper *Info-Dimanche* on May 17, 1998. The previous day, five thousand demonstrators had invaded the city to protest, not against Fidel Castro's presence—Communist enthusiasts for the firing squad being generally received as welcome guests by the democracies—but against globalization, free trade and the World Trade Organization's upcoming meeting on Monday. The protesters proceeded to smash windows, set fire to cars and loot shops. In this merry month of May, the ideologues of the ultra-left were renewing their assault on capitalism, and doing so in one of capitalism's greatest bastions.

Since 1994, in Mexico's southern region of Chiapas, the Zapatista Army had been reviving the rural revolt in its most primitive form.[1] What a contrast with the rest of the country, which was modernizing, liberalizing and even democratizing more than at any other time in Mexico's history. And in October 1997, all over the world, the left—at least in academic circles—had celebrated the thirtieth anniversary of the passing of Ernesto "Che" Guevara, that wretched symbol of failed guerrilla strategies. But isn't failure an exemplar for the ultra-left?

In Germany, the Greens at their March 1998 convention had been shouting for the elimination of all nuclear energy, for the dissolution of NATO, and for raising the price of a liter of gasoline from 1.70 to 5.00 marks. Realizing, however, that this last demand would be a sure way to alienate voters, they scratched it from their program three months later. In Italy, the fate of Romano Prodi's government, since its birth, had hung on a group of thirty-four deputies belonging to the Communist Refoundation Party, a group of paleo-Marxist-Leninists who had refused to follow the Italian Communist Party's majority on the path to modernity. (As we have seen, the Communist Party changed its name to Democratic Party of the Left and became a reformist coalition that narrowly managed to win the 1996 elections.) This small faction of "radical reformers" had for months been blocking the move by Prodi, the Europe-minded prime minister, to support the bids of Poland, Hungary and Czechoslovakia to join NATO. Refusal by a splinter group of these "radicals" to vote in favor of the government budget would result in the fall of Prodi's government in the autumn of 1998.

In France, what has been called the "Red left" or the "left of the left" offers the paradoxical case of an elitism that could be described as "populist." The principal inspirers of the movement belong to the high intelligentsia, even the academic nobility: the Collège de France, the École des Hautes Études en Sciences Sociales, and the Centre National de la Recherche Scientifique. Privileged and invulnerable, these people, in exchange for very little work, are granted lifelong stipends by the society they aim to destroy. But their books, far from remaining confined to rarified circles, enjoy huge sales. *Sur la télévision* and *Contre-feux* (Counterfire)—by the school's leading light, Pierre Bourdieu—and Serge Halimi's *Nouveaux Chiens de garde* (The New Guard Dogs), for instance, have been national bestsellers for months.[2] The group has its own publishing house, Liber-Raisons d'agir.

These authors influence public opinion in ways that go beyond the academic. Their support for the winter strikes of 1995–1996, for the demands of the *sans-papiers* (illegal immigrants), and for the demands made around Christmas 1997 by the unemployed who were no longer entitled to receive benefits, conferred on these demonstrations an ideological rationale and wide publicity that embarrassed governments of right and left, but above all Lionel Jospin's Socialist government. The weekly *L'Evénement du jeudi,* reporting on the "Bourdieu network," awarded him the title of "most influential of the French *intellos.*"

So ultra-Red theorizing translated into political consequences: it stirred the electoral hopes of Trotskyists and other extreme factions, who erupted in frenzied activity, infiltrating the unions and threatening the Communists with outflanking maneuvers to the left. After the regional elections in the spring of 1998, commentary focused mainly on the extreme right's electoral results, which nevertheless failed to improve upon the 15 percent reached ten years earlier. Less noted was the novelty of an upsurge by the extreme left, which tripled its strength relative to the regional elections in 1993. Meanwhile, the Communists seemed irremediably frozen at less than 10 percent of actual votes. Would they sink lower? Panicked, the CP national secretary Robert Hue launched into competition with his rivals on the far left, loudly calling, in the vocabulary of another age, for "higher taxes on employers" and falling into ecstasies over Marxism—"a breath of fresh air," as he described it in an interview with *Libération.* To regard Marxism as a breath of fresh air in 1998, you would have to be stifling indeed.

Some might object that in 1998, after all, twelve or thirteen EU governments and a fair number of governments on other continents claimed to be of the left, and that the ultra-left therefore was once more going in "the direction of history." That would be a superficial impression. As we have already seen, most governments of the "left" today bear little resemblance to what was understood by the term two or three decades ago. Portugal and Holland are governed by socialists, but there is a gulf separating them from the French socialists—who themselves are evolving toward "pragmatism"; and only nuances of difference separate them from the Spanish government of José Maria Aznar, classed on the right. The Italian and British governments are attached to the left only by a tenuous and mostly verbal thread. The Soviet collapse and the liberal turns of several venerable social-democratic parties (such as Gerhard Schröder's SPD, the Swedish Socialist Party, the Peronist Party of a veteran *dirigiste* country like Argentina, as well as Mexico's Institutional Revolutionary Party), combined with China's conversion to an increasingly relaxed capitalism—all these developments show that the classifications and political vocabulary of the twentieth century have been smashed to pieces. Even the "Revolutionary Party" of a country like the Dominican Republic is actually a peaceful social-democratic affair, every bit as prudently reformist as its European and South American counterparts. In politics as in everything else, reading the label is not enough to tell what the bottle's contents taste like. The real fracture in contemporary politics is the divide between the liberalized left and the radicalized ultra-left.

The ultra-left is now all the more visible because it is more isolated. It has ceased to consist of radical factions within governments of the left, since these profess reformist ideas that twenty years ago were the province of the right; so it is benefiting from the sort of optical illusion that makes coastal islets seem larger at low tide. The ultra-left has collected under its wing those nostalgia-haunted reactionaries who have abandoned all hope of influencing, from the inside, the actions of the parties that once upon a time formed the classical left. The simplism of their ideas is amazing when you consider that these are intellectuals who have at their disposal every means of accessing information about twentieth-century history and society: We must compel the rich to pay up, but also prevent them from making money; journalists without exception are lackeys of Big Capital and the Establishment; the failure of international Communism does not prove that it was a bad system.

Moreover, the ultra-left remains confined to the intellectual world. In France, their gains in the 1998 regional elections were followed by setbacks in the 1999 European elections, which also showed a further weakening of the Communist Party as it fell a point below its already depressing result (8.6 percent) in the 1995 presidential election. Thus, while it hasn't lost its undeniable savoir-faire when it comes to organizing demonstrations, especially in support of corporatist rearguard battles, the far left, Communists included, is no longer a popular movement. Its assault force—or what remains of it—issues forth almost exclusively from a fortress in the heart of the intellectual and journalistic milieu.

So yet again, at the end of that century in which they led humanity so far astray, a significant number of intellectuals have failed in their mission. Instead of helping the public understand what is going on, they persist, under the pretext of helping the most powerless among us, in clinging to their calamitous prejudices. Lavish in handing out the worst possible advice, in particular the counsel to reject the modern world outright, they are actually promoting the creation of poverty. Pierre Bourdieu's *Contre-feux* is subtitled *Propos pour servir à la résistance contre l'invasion néo-libérale* (Remarks in Behalf of Resistance to the Neoliberal Invasion). The Mexican author Carlos Fuentes hurried down to Chiapas so as to encourage the unfortunate peasants of that region to commit acts of violence that would achieve nothing—his real motive being to glorify himself as a "revolutionary" intellectual. Here, reaction reaches its nadir.

It has often been remarked that an ideology becomes most virulent when it is on the point of disappearing. The ultra-left provides a case in point. Its increasingly marginal electoral status—in contrast to the commercial success of some of the books produced by its theoreticians—shows that its audience is not among the "masses" but among the elites, broadly speaking: the full gamut of the intelligentsia, from top to bottom, that conducts or passionately follows the ideological debates. The authors and journalists of the ultra-left are supplying a large proportion of these people with what they evidently want to hear.

So what is this message? You will search their writings in vain for fresh ideas. Instead, you will find only the hoary Marxist vulgate, served up this time in a version that is even more intellectually impoverished than in the past. It can be summed up in a few words: Capitalism must be destroyed; the press and other media have sold out to the neoliberal *pensée unique;* a conspiracy—heir to the old "anticommunist plot"—is intent on muzzling the ultra-left or trapping it into rigged discussions while constantly depriving it of the right to speak.

The latter was one of the favorite mantras of Georges Marchais, who every year spent dozens of hours on television complaining that he was being excluded from the airwaves. He made a major fuss. But Pierre Bourdieu goes one better: he refuses invitations on the pretense that no one ever invites him. Or, more precisely, he claims that he would not be allowed to express himself anyway. In other words, he might have to face a few objections, as in any debate. In comparison with Bourdieu's outright refusal to participate, the monologuing dialogue of the late, lamented Marchais (with whom I often had the pleasure of participating in forums) seems in retrospect to be a model of tolerance, finesse and generosity of spirit.

Speaking from experience, in his essay *Du journalisme après Bourdieu,* Daniel Schneidermann smartly dissects how this circular *idée fixe* operates—how it manufactures proofs of what it denounces, and then says, "Look, I'm not going to debate you because you actually want to have a discussion rather than just listen to me."[3] This kind of self-fulfilling prophecy is a favorite stratagem in the leftist repertoire. Thus, when capitalism is not wreaking sufficient havoc, the far left inserts itself into the system to ensure that such havoc is done. This is what has happened in the domain of education, with consequences far more tragic than being deprived of hearing M. Bourdieu more often.

Already by the 1970s the ultra-left ideologues were perfectly aware that the theory of education set out by Bourdieu in *La Reproduction*[4] was false, and that the so-called "Jules Ferry" schools of the republican French model had always been social elevators for children from families of modest means. So the ideologues did what they could to make public schooling dysfunctional by reorganizing it in such a way that children—all children—would be unable to get a good education, however diligently they applied themselves. For thirty years now, militants of the Bourdieu movement have endeavored to take control of *pédagogisme,* which is an ideology and not to be confused with pedagogy, which is an art. And their coup has largely succeeded: *they have made French public education conform to Bourdieu's theories.* By applying his methods, they have confirmed his thesis, transforming into realities the evils that previously had been figments of his imagination. Today, since our schools are no longer capable of educating, they no longer function as social elevators. Instead, they are engaged in mass-producing "failure at school," churning out unemployable illiterates. As a crowning touch, the "Bourdivin" ideologues blame these disastrous results on the ravages of neoliberalism, whereas in fact the outcome was a predictable consequence of their own totalitarian doctrine.

It is striking to see the extent to which Bourdieu's range of ideas coincides with that of the Communist intellectuals of the Seventies. In 1980, for example, four Communists published a book dealing with cultural topics.[5] After boasting that "cultural action with a Communist orientation on the part of the municipalities has contributed to enlarging the need for culture," the authors accused the reigning powers of having "turned culture into a commodity." What originality! A Socialist minister haranguing the World Trade Organization in 1999 could have sounded much the same—which tends to confirm that French socialism has been influenced much more by the obsolete Communism of 1980 than by liberalism. The Communist writers continued, "The establishment policy in this area aims at maximally desocializing cultural life, to promote withdrawal into the self and individualism." On display here is the anti-individualistic phobia of all totalitarians, all reactionaries, for whom individual autonomy must be eradicated in favor of collective indoctrination. What must be done to throttle "the ideological counteroffensive waged in France by the forces of Big Capital"? Well, we must eliminate "those commodities manufactured by the cultural industries: radios, stereos, television sets, tape recorders, video recorders, cameras, music recordings, paperbacks, etc." In short, if we are going to save culture, we must suppress culture. There is an unmistakable similarity between these reactionary excommunications and the imprecations of Bourdieu and his disciples, twenty years later, against television, publishing, journalism—the whole cultural gamut. They display the same lofty tone one would expect to hear in the philosophizing of a party cell secretary, circa 1950.

How did television, or audiovisual media generally, come to be regarded as an assassin of culture? And of liberty itself? The answer is that in 1979, Régis Debray established an equivalence between the police-state repression of Eastern Europe and "the gigantic symbolic panoply of the capitalist countries," namely the omnipresent clusters of television antennas.[6] Here are two parallel totalitarian entities: Yuri Andropov and his special psychiatric hospitals on one side, Bernard Pivot and *Apostrophes* on the other.*

Pierre Boncenne, in a deliciously ironic book published in 1996, evaluates Debray's indictment.[7] The author—as it happens, a colleague of Bernard Pivot's on *Apostrophes* and subsequently on *Bouillon de culture*—was also editor-in-chief of the journal *Lire* and founder-editor of *Écrivain*, which only goes to show that one and the same individual can serve the cause of literature on television as well as on the printed page. It's just this sort of cross-fertilization between the old and new media that violates the terms of the "revolutionary" *sharia*, if you believe the "beautiful souls" whose scandalized modesty Boncenne depicts with such wit.

The trouble is that all too frequently the arguments of the anointed ones rest on a flat ignorance of the facts. Pierre Bourdieu, for example, asserts that "Never have moralism and conformism been imposed via television with such violence and relentlessness, and it is significant that literary prizes are increasingly awarded to journalists, confirming them in their role as the poor man's *maîtres à penser.*" Here is a Collège de France professor, director

---

* *Translator's note:* Bernard Pivot hosted the influential television program *Apostrophes* (1975–1990), consisting of a studio discussion among six authors and sometimes described as "a cross between a literary salon and a boxing match." Régis Debray accused Pivot of exercising a dictatorial influence over book sales through *Apostrophes* and other ventures.

of studies at the École des Hautes Études en Sciences Sociales, making an error so clumsy that it would be unacceptable if committed by an apprentice journalist. Is this how sociologists do their fact checking? If Bourdieu had taken five minutes to consult the list of literary laureates since 1970 (with the exception of Inter-allié, formally established as an award for journalists), he would have seen that his thesis is unsustainable; Pierre Boncenne has fun demolishing it in the space of ten lines. What's more, since the beginning of the nineteenth century, writers of distinction have been strongly represented in the pages of journals, from Chateaubriand to Zola, Maupassant to Montherlant, right up to Nourissier, Rinaldi, Buzzati and Vargas Llosa.

Pierre Bourdieu is not a serious sociologist; he is a fanatical ideologue. The "facts" buttressing his deductions often derive from a cascade of elementary errors that could have been avoided with a small effort on his part—or on the part of the "teams" he "directs," who are no more likely than he to respect the data. We can only deplore the waste of public funds involved in financing the "surveys" of so-called researchers who can be so insouciant about the task of fact checking, when publications like *Le Petit Larousse* or *Quid* are readily at hand.

We had a right to expect a little more subtlety in the rehabilitation of Marxism with its indictment of capitalism, especially in view of Communism's seventy-five-year history of cultural devastation and capitalism's not entirely sterile record during the same era. The prowess of Bourdieu and his disciples consists in constantly reasserting an a priori principle. They proceed as if history never happened. This radical denial spares them from having to labor at the kind of special pleading that one hears from Communism's more timid advocates—who at least are not entirely oblivious to reality when they invoke a list of attenuating circumstances.

In the name of their exalted *science*, Bourdieu and the Bour-divins scornfully dismiss common knowledge. Their method is to make assertions, never arguments. In an issue of *Esprit*, Olivier Mongin and Joël Roman, respectively publisher and editor of a review that can hardly by classified as right-wing, expose Bourdieu's "deliberate practice of lying and falsification," which "fails even a minimal code of intellectual ethics . . . combined with strange excesses that betray the mentality of a bad cop rather than a scrupulous sociologist." Bourdieu "incarnates the most obsolete type of *engagé*"; he invokes "a pure argument from authority," starting with the postulate: "I am *la science,* because I say so, because I am a professor at the Collège de France and that's where *l'esprit scientifique* reigns."[8] Circular reasoning of this sort, where the reasoner derives the truth of what he is saying from the simple fact that it is he who is saying it, is reincarnated—in aggravated form, naturally—among the sage's disciples.

A nice example of this method is found in Serge Halimi's libelous pamphlet *Les Nouveaux Chiens de garde*.[9] Pronouncing François Furet's *The Passing of an Illusion* to be "bad history," the only argument he offers is that it was "definitively refuted" in an article in *Le Monde diplomatique*.[10] But as Daniel Schneidermann has pointed out, Halimi just happens to be a contributor to that publication,[11] a coincidence that makes his fulminations against what he calls "market editorialists" rather ridiculous. An author, it goes without saying, is permitted to quote from an article in a journal to which he also contributes; but he should do so for the purpose of adducing arguments, not dispensing with them altogether and offering up an assertion as proof. Had Furet in fact been "definitively refuted" by *Le Monde diplomatique,* a publication no one is required to learn by heart, we would like to know the substance of the refutation. If there is a scourge worse than a "market editorialist," it is one who editorializes by diktat. And a dictatorship is apparently the only political system in which the acolytes of M. Bourdieu could breathe easily, for a dictatorship alone would grant them what they yearn for in every fiber of their dogmatic minds: monopolistic control over speech and the silencing of dissent.

The intolerance of a small coterie of intellectuals, when it is held up as a model, ends up imbuing what might be called the "lower clergy" with the same spirit. So in 1997 we saw a librarian of the Lycée Edmond Rostand at Saint-Ouen-l'Aumône—with the backing, alarmingly enough, of a "teachers' association"—

purging the school library. She withdrew the works of authors she regards as belonging to the "extreme right"—i.e. fascists—including those of two eminent historians, Marc Fumaroli and Jean Tulard. Worse, the Pointoise court dismissed the lawsuit by the censored authors, who had lodged a complaint of damage to reputation; the court's pretext was that it did not "believe that Mme Chaïkhoui was transgressing when she drew up a list of titles that she judged to be dangerous." In what way are books like Fumaroli's *Heros et orateurs* and Tulard's *Napoléon* dangerous?[12] On what authority or mandate or competency is Mme Chaïkhoui qualified to pronounce on some "danger" or other and ban it from the shelves of a publicly funded library? Has the Inquisition been re-established in France?

Acts like this librarian's are unjustifiable and dishonorable. When the judges dismissed the plaintiffs' charges, did they realize the type of society they were ushering in? But the judiciary would never dare come down on a "teachers' association," and hence against censorship from the left, even if all the laws of the Republic were being broken. On the other hand, when in 1995 the National Front mayor of Orange sought to restore "ideological equilibrium" in the municipal library, which in his view had too many left-wing books on its shelves, almost the entire press was justified in comparing such sectarianism to the autos-da-fé of books in Hitler's Germany. But when the auto-da-fé is perpetrated by the left, even if it springs from a crass lack of education and flagrant ignorance of the works being censored, the national educational system and the judicial authorities grant their benediction.

We are living in a country where a low-level employee can purge a library on the utterly implausible grounds that certain works reflect fascist or racist sympathies and—why not?—are responsible for the Holocaust. Our elites condemn censorship and false accusations when they come from the National Front, but rarely when they emanate from any other ideological source. An ideologue perceives totalitarianism only in the ranks of his adversaries, never in himself, because he is certain of being in possession of the absolute truth and of holding exclusive rights to the Good. In recent years, intellectual thought police and calumniators have proliferated more on the left than on the far right; but when they engage in persecutory sectarianism, left and right merge into one reality: intellectual totalitarianism. The principles they claim to represent become irrelevant, giving way to identical patterns of behavior that make them indistinguishable.

At the beginning of this chapter I defined the ultra-left as elitist populists. In a contribution to *Le Monde*, Claude Lanzmann and Robert Redeker argue that the notion of populism is not applicable to the new extreme left:

> Nothing gives us cause to think that Bourdieu is a populist. Under the cover of science, he supplies the ideas of the state's *petite bourgeoisie*, a vulgate that covers everything from teaching to journalism, television, economics, and nowadays gender relations. Bourdieu manufactures the readymade ideas for this petit-bourgeois class of functionaries. It is these people (and not the working class—otherwise you could indeed characterize him as a populist) who soak up the books in the "Liber" catalogue. It is these people who feel that everyone, Bourdieu excepted, is conspiring against them.[13]

I concur with this description, merely adding the nuance that you can be populist in the methods you use and elitist in terms of the public you address. Populism boils down to simplistic ideas, unwarranted assertions, erroneous or grossly exaggerated facts, ad hominem attacks on opponents, the art of stuffing the heads of a well-trained audience with delusions of conspiracies by "the real rulers of the world"—whether Jews, capitalists, journalists, television producers, the agents of globalization, or whoever happens to be the current hobgoblin.* Populists never have interlocutors: they see only fanatical partisans or plotting enemies who deserve to be insulted, discredited, caricatured and censored (since, alas,

---

* "Questions aux vrais maîtres du monde" (Questions for the Real Rulers of the World) is the title of a speech given by Pierre Bourdieu in Paris on October 11, 1999, before the International Council of French-Speaking Radio and Television.

they cannot be liquidated—a way of terminating the discussion that has certain legal inconveniences in a democracy).

If there are "new guard dogs," they belong to the ultra-left's security apparatus in general and to Bourdieu's personal body-guard in particular. They launched a ferociously efficient operation to discredit and bury Jeannine Verdès-Leroux's recent book, *Le Savant et la politique: Essai sur le terrorisme sociologique de Pierre Bourdieu*.[14] The methods that had failed against *The Black Book of Communism*—too big a work to destroy and powerful enough to punch through the wall of disinformation—were effective against the book on Bourdieu, clearly a meager subject calling for a more slender treatment. Another troublesome book was Bertrand de la Grange and Maite Rico's *Sous-Commandant Marcos, la géniale imposture*.[15] The authors, journalists for *Le Monde* and *El País*, could hardly be suspected of harboring "fascist" sympathies. But they were guilty of knowing Mexico too well. They had observed the rebellion in Chiapas long enough not to be fooled, as were the crowds of intellectuals and philanthropists who thrilled to the events in the region.[16]

In short, there is a whole cluster of ways of thinking, speaking and acting that are populist in style, even when the audience that succumbs to such obsessive and repetitive vacuities cannot be classified as the "plebs." Jean-Marie Guéhenno, after reading one of Adolf Hitler's speeches, noted in 1940 that the Führer's thinking was "confused but brutal, astoundingly adapted for public consumption. It might well have been a speech by Thaelmann or by Thorez. Any clarity of thought is lost in a mishmash of words. Communism and National Socialism converge in their basest attributes."[17]

This necromancy from the depths has no need for the hypnotized mass audiences of Nuremberg or the Red Square to exert its power. The magnetic effect of crowds, so well described by Gustave Le Bon, can work its marvels in more exclusive circles. It can hold an elite in thrall. I believe, however, that Lanzmann and Redeker are being rather ungenerous when they limit the ranks of ultra-leftist elites to the state-stipended petty bureaucrats. They extend well beyond this spoiled group. The text by

Pierre Bourdieu, "Questions for the Real Rulers of the World," for instance, surfaced simultaneously in *Le Monde, L'Humanité* and *Libération,* no less.

The brand of populism I am describing, which amounts to endless repetition of what its beleaguered elite wants to hear, strives always toward a permanent, overriding goal: to restore belief that Marxism remains true and that Communism wasn't a bad thing—or at least, that it was less of an evil than capitalism. Whence the zeal exhibited by *Le Monde diplomatique* to ensure that Eric Hobsbawm's *The Age of Extremes* was published in French. The English author, an undaunted Marxist and revisionist if ever there was one, goes so far as to deny that the Soviets were guilty of the Katyn massacre, even though Mikhail Gorbachev himself conceded the fact in 1990 and several documents from the Moscow archives have since confirmed it. Various French publishing houses, having drawn the line against bringing out such an absurd hodgepodge as Hobsbawm's, were accused of obeying capitalist marching orders. Note, however, that if these firms had been obedient to the base logic of capitalist profit rather than intellectual honesty and professional integrity, they would have rushed to publish the book, for Hobsbawm's mumbo-jumbo was sure to rake in the cash. Which it did, in fact.[18]

Here is proof, if we need more, that in France we have quite a large and resolute segment of the population that wants to console itself as often as possible for Communism's fall, to hear repeated every day the mantra that actually existing socialism did not fail and that capitalism is still the only demon to be exorcised. For such is the aim of the crusade that sets forth to expel neoliberalism from the Holy Places. Since 1989, this theme has been an extremely profitable publishing and journalistic vein to mine.

* * *

This vision of history, so destitute of knowledge and so gripped by persecution mania, would never wield the influence it does without the vacuity and sclerosis that afflict political thinking in other ways. I am referring to the political thinking of politicians themselves and of the professional commentators whose function it is to mediate between them and us. Even when the latter are as sharp as possible in the questions they ask politicians and in their assessments of them, both groups nonetheless are locked in the same mindset, circulating the same stock of received ideas. It is apparent that their tired, unvarying routine remains innocent of contact with any fresh reading material. Yet the last quarter of a century witnessed in numerous countries a renewal of thinking about history, economics, politics and society in a wealth of original and profound studies, often enough written with engaging literary skill. But these works, which have transformed or broadened our knowledge and understanding of societies, have had little influence on politicians and pundits. Have they been exposed to this literature, or at least to summaries of it? If so, they quickly forget all about it, judging from the way they feebly repeat two or three slogans in place of theory, always concerning some local situation and short-term expediency.

When I wrote "two or three slogans," I was being rather generous. Since the collapse of the Soviet Union, there has been but one basic theme, and that is anti-Americanism. To take the case of France—the paradigmatic laboratory of resistance to the lessons taught by the Communist catastrophe—if you take away anti-Americanism there is nothing left of French political thought. Or very little.

Globalization, for example, is rarely analyzed as such, any more than the workings of the World Trade Organization. Both issues stir up fear. Why? Because they have become synonymous with the American "hyperpower."[19] You might object that the globalization of commerce doesn't unilaterally benefit the United States, which buys more from abroad than it sells, since otherwise the U.S. balance of trade would not be chronically in the red. Or you might suggest that the WTO is not fundamentally harmful to Europeans or to Asians, since otherwise it would be hard to understand why so many countries that are not yet members move heaven and earth to get in (for instance China, whose membership was finally ratified in November 1999). But you would find yourself talking to a brick wall. You would be advancing rational arguments, whereas your audience is standing on its obsessive *idées fixes*. And you would gain nothing by doing so, except maybe to be called a lackey of the Americans. Yet more than half the disagreements between the European Union and the United States have been settled by the WTO in Europe's favor, and the organization has often condemned the USA for hidden subsidies. Far from being a *laissez-passer* free-for-all, the WTO was created to make competition equitable in the global marketplace.

Hatred for the United States is fed by two separate but convergent sources: the U.S. has been the sole superpower since the end of the Cold War; and she is the principal sphere of action and expanding center of the liberal demon. The twin themes of execration merge, since it is precisely because of her "hyperpower" that America is able to spread the plague of liberalism throughout the planet; so consequently she is the major cause of the accursed cataclysm of globalization.

And what would be the remedy for these evils? First, for every country to establish or restore a state-run economy, and then, to seal itself hermetically against international exchange, including, above all, any exchange in the cultural domain. Here we see, in a post-Marxist version, a return of the economic and cultural autarchy desired by Adolf Hitler.

In international politics, America is more detested and disapproved of since the end of the Cold War, even by her allies, than she was by the avowed or covert partisans of Communism during that era. In fact, America incurs the most vindictive anathemas even when she takes actions that are obviously in the interests of her allies as much as they are for herself, and that she alone is capable of doing. Thus, during the winter of 1997–1998, when Bill Clinton announced a possible military intervention in Iraq to force Saddam Hussein to comply with his 1991 commitments, hostility toward the United States rose by several degrees. Only the British government stood in support.

The problem was obvious, however. For several years, Saddam had been refusing to destroy his stocks of weapons of mass destruction and thwarting the efforts of UN inspectors to monitor them, thus violating one of the main conditions he accepted in the peace treaty following his defeat in 1991. Given what this individual was capable of, the danger to international security represented by the accumulation of chemical and biological weapons in his hands could not be denied. But here again, the chief scandal that a large part of international opinion saw fit to denounce was the embargo imposed on Iraq—as if the party culpable for all the privations suffered by the Iraqi people were not Saddam himself, who had ruined his nation by throwing it into a protracted and bloody war against Iran, then into an unprovoked assault on Kuwait, and finally by impeding the implementation of the UN resolutions concerning his armaments. This support for a sanguinary dictator, on account of hatred for the United States, emanated as much from the extreme right as from the extreme left (the National Front and the Communist Party in France), from left-wing socialists (the UK's *New Statesman* or France's minister of the interior, Jean-Pierre Chevènement), and from Russia and some EU countries. So we are dealing with an anti-American common denominator rather than a coherent ideological or strategic stance.

Many countries—France among them—did not deny the threat that Iraqi weapons posed, but said that a "diplomatic solution" was preferable to military intervention. But a diplomatic solution was exactly what was rejected over a stretch of seven years by Saddam, who had many times booted out the UN's representatives. As for Russia, it claimed that any use of force against Saddam would imperil its "vital interests." One doesn't quite see why. The truth is that Russia never gives up a chance to display its spite over the fact that it no longer is the second-ranking superpower, which it was, or believed itself to be, prior to the Soviet Union's collapse. But the USSR succumbed to its own vices, from which Russia still suffers the consequences.

There have been empires and powers with international reach long before the United States in the closing years of the twentieth century. But never before has there been one that achieved preponderance on a worldwide scale—an argument that Zbigniew Brzezinski takes up in *The Grand Chessboard*.[20] To merit the title of global superpower, a nation must hold first rank in four domains:

economic, technological, military and cultural. America is the first nation in history to do so. Economically, from the recovery of 1983 to the beginning of a recession in 2000, she leapt ahead, combining steady growth with virtually full employment, a balanced budget (for the first time in thirty years) and very low inflation. In technology she has enjoyed a quasi monopoly, especially with the lightning progress made in the field of telecommunications. And militarily, she alone can project overwhelming power anywhere in the world, at any time.

The question of cultural superiority is more debatable, depending on whether "culture" is narrowly or broadly defined. In the more limited sense of high culture in the realms of literature, painting, music and architecture, American civilization is certainly outstanding, but it does not stand alone and its influence cannot be compared to that of ancient Greece or Rome or China. One of the reasons is that American artistic and literary culture has a tendency toward provincialism: Since English is dominant globally, fewer and fewer Americans feel any need to read in other languages. And when American universities and critics take up foreign schools of thought, they too often obey the dictates of faddish conformism rather than exercise independent judgment. On the other hand, Brzezinski is indisputably correct when it comes to the broader definition of culture. In the domains of science and technology, there is no question about America's superiority. A sizeable proportion of the political, technological and scientific elites throughout the world have graduated from American universities. English has been the international language of science for a long time and has become the de facto language of the Internet as well. America's popular culture, skillfully advertised, reaches the entire world via the new high-tech media; and American tastes—in dress, music, recreation, fast food— attract young people everywhere. American movies and television shows draw audiences of millions, to the point that some countries (including France, naturally) seek to establish protectionist barriers in the name of "cultural exceptionalism."

Even more decisive (with all due deference to socialists past and present) has been the victory of the liberal-democratic model following from the demise of Communism. American-style federalist democracy is increasingly imitated, starting with the European Union; it serves as the organizing principle of international alliances such as NATO and the United Nations. This is not to deny the flaws of the American system, its lapses or hypocrisies. But the fact remains that Asia, Africa and Latin America have little to teach the United States about democracy. As for Europe, let's not forget that we invented the great criminal ideologies of the twentieth century, forcing the United States to intervene on our continent twice with her armies. America owes her unique superpower status today largely to Europe's mistakes.

Evidently, American ascendancy is indebted only in part to the creativity and determination of the American people; it also sprang by default from the cumulative failures of the rest of the world: the fall of Communism, the ruin of Africa, the Asian and Latin American slowness to evolve toward democracy, and the divisions and blunders of Europe. Not so long ago, for example, France was reproaching the United States for wanting to displace French influence in Africa. But France bears a heavy responsibility for the genesis of the 1994 massacres in Rwanda and the subsequent disintegration of Zaire. France discredited herself without any help from anyone else, creating a vacuum to be filled by a growing American presence.

The European Union is making scant progress toward the realization of a single decision-making center; it can be likened to a choir whose every member takes herself to be a soloist. Lacking unity, how can Europe counterbalance the effectiveness of America's foreign policy when planning the slightest undertaking requires first securing unanimity among fifteen nations? Or what about twenty-seven, and these even more disparate than today's membership?

When NATO intervened in Kosovo, hatred for America heated up several degrees. In the case of the Gulf War, you could at least argue that behind an ostensible crusade to restore peace lurked the hidden agenda of defending petroleum interests (a line, by the way, that ignores the fact that Europeans are much more dependent on oil from the Middle East than are Americans). But regarding Kosovo, even with the worst bad faith in the world it's hard to see how American egoism could have dictated intervention in a region so poor in natural resources and so insignificant as a potential market, a region whose political instability, ethnic chaos and genocidal frenzy were threatening to Europe's equilibrium— but not to that of the United States.

And while NATO was mobilizing for the Kosovo campaign after the failure of the Rambouillet (Paris) conference, which was held in February 1999 on French initiative, it was the Americans who felt they were being dragged into the adventure. The French government had made every effort and committed its prestige to convince Serbia to accept a compromise on the subject of Kosovo. If the Serbs' refusal had incurred no subsequent sanction, it would have been Europe, and above all France, that would have offered a spectacle of pitiful impotence. In fact, the impotence was real, but it was masked and made to seem less urgent by the Americans' participation in NATO's military operations. Out of nine hundred aircraft committed, six hundred were American, as were almost all the surveillance satellites.[21] The United States alone spends twice as much on military equipment and weapons development as fifteen European nations combined, and *ten times* as much on military space technology. If the will to act in Kosovo was European, the means to do so were almost exclusively American. What's more, the barbarism that had to be eradicated was the result of several centuries of inimitable European-style follies, of which the crowning absurdity was to have allowed a Communist dictator turned ardent nationalist to remain in power in Belgrade after the crackup of Titoism.

But since European mistakes must be imputed to the Americans, this constellation of historical antecedents going back almost a thousand years, along with obvious and notorious contemporary factors, was veiled in willful ignorance by many of our intellectual and political cohorts. An imaginary figment was substituted for a realistic appraisal of the situation. The inter-ethnic slaughters in Kosovo were said to be an American invention, a pretext for the United States to step in, controlling NATO and subjugating the European Union. Pascal Bruckner has drawn up an edifying inventory of such idiocies.[22] According o the Greeks and the Russians, for example, America was supporting the Kosovo Muslims as a way of destroying Orthodox Christianity. According to the pro-Arab cheering section, on the contrary, the motive was to create the illusion of being a friend of Muslims the better to deceive them. On display here is obsessive conspiracy-mongering.

Another case in point is the pugilism indulged in by French intellectuals following an article by Régis Debray that appeared in *Le Monde* on April 1, 1999, denying or minimizing Milosevic's racist persecutions. The squabbling that ensued will be completely misunderstood if the reader imagines that Debray was simply concerned with defending the Serbs against accusations he considered ill founded. What lies beneath this revisionist denial of Serb atrocities? By asserting that the Serbs' record in Kosovo did not justify the bombing campaign, Debray wanted to lead us to believe that the only cause of the hostilities was the United States' overweening ambition, a desire to impose her "hyperpower" and hegemony over Europe. This *idée fixe* was repeatedly expressed during NATO's operations, and we heard it from every political direction, from the extreme right to the extreme left, including Communists and numerous Gaullists.

The convergence between the extremes here borders on identity of outlook. Jean-Marie Le Pen is indistinguishable from Régis Debray when he writes, "The spectacle of Europe (and of France!) under the boot of Clinton in this war of cowardly and barbarous moralizers is sickening, ignoble, insufferable. I was for the Croats and against Milosevic. Today, I am for nationalist Serbia and against the dictatorship that the Americans are imposing."[23] For Didier Motchane of the socialist Mouvement des Citoyens, the covert agenda of the Americans was to inflame hostility between Russia and the EU; for Bruno Mégret of the extreme right-wing Mouvement National, it was to create a precedent so that North African immigrants—soon to be in the majority in the south of France—could demand, when the time comes, a referendum on the independence of Provence or even its unification with Algeria. For Jean-François Kahn, editor of the left-wing weekly *Marianne*, the Americans' motive was an equally perverse calculus aimed at inciting a similar *démarche* on the part of the Alsatians, if it ever occurs to them that they might want to become Germans again. And if in this case the French government refuses their wish, Uncle Sam will feel justified in bombing Paris, just as it bombed Belgrade in 1999.

Jean Baudrillard, spelling out his version of the events in *Libération,* said that the hidden scheme was to help Milosevic get rid of the Kosovars![24] And it was the Americans, says Baudrillard, who instigated the financial crisis of 1997 in Japan and the other Asian countries, which were not responsible in the least for their stock market difficulties—just as the Europeans were not responsible in the slightest for the wasps' nest of Balkan hatreds. The moral conscience of these philosophers did not entertain for a moment the hypothesis that the European Union might have been dishonored if it had allowed the Kosovo butcheries to continue in the heart of the continent. According to them, Washington's global project was to "block the road to the slowly emerging worldwide democracy."[25] So the ethnic cleansing in Kosovo marked an "emerging democracy"? With this *passe-partout* in hand, one no longer needs to get a headache studying international relations. Jean-Louis Margolin puts it well: "Reading world affairs becomes simple: Washington is always guilty, inevitably guilty. Its adversaries are always victims, inevitably victims." To which I will merely add: Washington's allies too must be victims. If the Americans show reluctance to engage in a humanitarian mission, they are denounced for their lack of zeal in coming to the aid of the hungry and the oppressed; but when they do put themselves out, they are accused of plotting against the rest of the planet.

Such simplism, which doesn't even merit the term "analysis," further weakens the second- and third-tier powers relative to the American superpower; they are compounding their economic and strategic weakness with a poverty of ideas about the real situation. It is possible to compensate for material inequality by means of intellectual subtlety, sound judgment and impartial analysis. These are the indispensable conditions for improving policies and optimizing possibilities, for overcoming disadvantages. Such disadvantages can only be made worse by faulty rationales that amount to mere compensatory fantasies. By holding ever more stubbornly to their mistakes, which are the indirect cause of American pre-eminence, the Europeans actively contribute to sustaining and reinforcing that pre-eminence.

And if "analysis" deriving exclusively from anti-Americanism is in fact sound, if the United States is at once the instigator of the Asian financial crisis, the Kosovo massacres and the famous French cauliflower slump, then the rest of the world must be peopled by half-wits. With such feeble partners, who are never responsible for their own actions, is it surprising that the United States finds herself at the top of the heap?

It is above all we Europeans who are addicted to projecting onto America the causes of our own errors. The American "uni-lateralism" denounced by the Jospin government's minister of foreign affairs, Hubert Védrine, often comes as a reaction to our own indecisiveness or poor decisions. For France to imagine that it can stand up against this "unilateralism" by selling our West Indian bananas at above-market prices or by outrageously blatant protection of Saddam Hussein is quite simply ridiculous. Likewise, the obsequiousness with which France received the president of China in October 1999 was explained as following from the "grand design" of playing off the giant of China against the giant of the United States. In August of the same year, France had gone so far as to condemn the projected installation of antimissile defenses in the United States and in some Asian countries as "destabilizing for China." That old nag from the barn of pro-Soviet propaganda was being trotted out again: the only threat to world peace was the defensive measures undertaken by the West. After all, they caused pangs of anxiety in the precincts of the Kremlin!

It is certain that China for some years now has been actively building up a nuclear arsenal. If we French are willing to let Beijing conquer Taiwan by force, let us say so loud and clear. Paris's "China gambit" is founded on an economic illusion. For Communist China, despite its demographic immensity, remains an economic dwarf, with a GDP amounting to little more than 3.5

percent of world GDP and a per capita income ranking around *eightieth* on the world scale. China's market absorbs only 1.8 percent of American exports and 1.1 percent of those from France and Germany.[26] Most of the wondrous business deals that Paris brags about after each official visit to Beijing are financed through sweetened loans that we extend and that we always "reschedule." For a long while now, the dream of the "China card" that France keeps tucked up her sleeve to thwart the American superpower has reeked of diplomatic infantilism.

As the twenty-first century begins, the great question that we Europeans must address is whether we can recover the political autonomy that we lost on August 1, 1914—the first day of the First World War. Until that date, Europe had known a restless and troubled history, often barbarous and soaked with blood. But Europeans had always managed to resolve their own crises, finding a more or less lasting equilibrium through negotiations among themselves—for instance, at the Congress of Vienna in 1815 at the close of the Napoleonic episode. The second half of the nineteenth century saw similar accommodations during and after the conflicts that accompanied the unification of Italy and of Germany.

But in 1919, for the first time since the fall of the Roman Empire, the gathered pan-European negotiating powers—whose efforts were destined to remake the political structure of the Old Continent—had for concert leader the president of a non-European power: Woodrow Wilson. This followed from what the winning side owed to America, which by her intervention had altered the course of European history and could impose her own solutions at the Treaty of Versailles. But the treaty was a failure: it did not yield a new equilibrium. The two World Wars were but phases of one and the same protracted conflict, separated by a tense, precarious armistice. It was a vast and suicidal civil war, which twice escalated into global conflict. The powerlessness of the Europeans to resolve their own diplomatic problems was obvious. Moreover, whereas Europe between 1815 and 1914 had slowly but steadily progressed toward more democracy, the years between the World Wars were marked by a sweeping ebb tide of liberty, as large and small totalitarianisms—Europe's great modern innovation—emerged in Moscow, Rome, Berlin, Madrid and Vichy. Although European civilization taken as a whole had managed to escape self-destruction, it nonetheless had shown little aptitude for self-governance.

Once again rescued by the United States' armed forces, Europe was rebuilt economically by infusions of American capital after 1945. And the overriding need to defend what was left of free Europe, this time against Soviet imperialism, conferred on the United States the role of architect and financier of the North Atlantic Treaty Organization, a burden that the European countries were too weak to assume on their own. Today, though, for the first time in eighty years, Europe reluctantly faces autonomy and must bear responsibility for its own destiny. The era of American protection, with its accompanying anti-Americanism, was very comfortable from both the political and the psychological point of view. But that era is gone.

Now that Europe is on its own once again, its spinelessness stands revealed. For half a century the Europeans had become accustomed to gauging their independence by their capacity to resist American hegemony on the one hand and Soviet imperialism on the other—more often than not, by playing off the Soviets against the Americans. It was an independence founded on underdevelopment. Today the pretense is over. Europe is independent, period, and holds its future in its own hands. But we are badly out of practice in the art of standing alone.

Throughout the twentieth century, Europeans have shown themselves slow to understand and respond in timely fashion to the decisive turning points of their own history. We saw this failure splendidly on display again in 1989, when the Eastern Europeans urgently advanced the question of German reunification. The leaders of Western Europe (with the exception of Helmut Kohl) not only had failed to see what was coming, but had completely missed what had already happened.

So on November 9, 1999, at the ceremony held in the Bundestag to commemorate the tenth anniversary of the fall of the Berlin Wall, it was not surprising that the only heroes of the occasion were Helmut Kohl, Mikhail Gorbachev and George H. W. Bush. From the European Union, no other head of state or government, past or present, had been invited. The EU, formally absent at the celebration of the continent's return to democracy! And there was a reason for this lack of representation, for Europe's leaders had participated hardly or not at all in the reunification process; indeed, some of them, particularly Margaret Thatcher and François Mitterrand, had been vociferous in their opposition. For Italy's Giulio Andreotti, hostility took the form of passive indifference. Once again, the principal European powers failed to comprehend and control a watershed in modern history; in their desire to maintain a German Communist enclave in a de-Communized Europe, they were exhibiting a moral blindness bordering on insanity.

The two pilots of the reunification were first and foremost the Soviet president and the West German chancellor. But they needed international guarantees and foreign backing against the possibility that elements within the Soviet power structure, most threateningly from the generals, might decide to throw their weight against Gorbachev and intervene militarily in order to prolong the GDR's lifespan. It was the United States that provided the guarantees and gave the support from abroad, with the U.S. president sending unambiguous signals to potential warmongers in Moscow that a reprise of the Prague Spring intervention in East Germany would this time run up against an American response. Having grasped neither the importance nor the meaning of the events that plucked central Europe from the clutches of Communism, and having played no positive role in these events, Western Europeans have earned no right to deplore the American *hyperpuissance*.

The unpalatable truth is that it was Americans once again who had to make up for the Europeans' political and intellectual vacuity, even in circumstances that primarily affected Europe's vital interests and future. To belong to Europe—to be allied with France, the United Kingdom and Italy—was of no help to Helmut Kohl in 1989 and 1990, when he oversaw the riskiest and most consequential operation in his nation's post–National Socialist history. In contrast, to be allied to the United States allowed him to effect the reunification peacefully while completing the de-Communization of central Europe. What's more, George Bush *père* was wise enough to abstain from the sort of triumphalism liable to have pushed the Soviet opponents of Gorbachev over the edge; he refused to follow his advisors' recommendation that he visit Berlin on the day after the Wall was brought down. He had the tact to respect the purely German resonance of the populations' reunion.

Oneiric anti-Americanism stems from two distinct sources, which combine and reinforce each other. The first of these is the wounded nationalism of the old European powers; the second is the hostility toward liberal society harbored by Communism's erstwhile partisans, including those who, without approving of the sanguinary Soviet or other totalitarianisms, had gambled that Communism could one day be democratized and humanized.

The syndrome of wounded nationalism goes back well before the end of the Cold War, making its appearance after the Second Word War. Its outstanding, most adamant spokesman was General de Gaulle. In 1963 he told Alain Peyrefitte, "Western Europe has become, without noticing it, an American protectorate."[27] For the Fifth Republic's first president, Washington's relationship with Western Europe was equivalent to Moscow's with central and Eastern Europe: "The decisions are made more and more in the United States.... It is the same in the Communist world, where the satellite countries are used to having decisions made in Moscow." Unfortunately, Western Europeans—France excepted—"rush to Washington for their orders," and "the Germans are becoming the Americans' houseboys." Already during the war, "Churchill toadied up shamelessly to Roosevelt," and "the Americans were no more concerned about delivering France than were the Russians about liberating Poland."

De Gaulle publicly developed this thesis at a press conference on May 16, 1967. He claimed that since 1945 the United States had treated France exactly as the USSR had treated Poland and Hungary. Nothing could persuade him otherwise. In 1964, President Johnson sent a memorandum to the Department of State and the Department of Defense telling them that he would approve of no defense-related measures that had not been reviewed beforehand with the French. De Gaulle's reaction, recorded by Peyrefitte: "Johnson is trying to muddy the waters" (*noyer le poisson*). Yet if Johnson had not taken this step, he would thereby most certainly have given proof of his "hegemonism." The familiar mental tic is here on full display: the United States is always in the wrong.

A nationalist's thoughts circle endlessly in a labyrinth of wounded pride. For such people, their nation's backwardness even in the realms of science and technology cannot be imputable to wrong roads taken or a chronic inability to identify pathways leading forward—on account of statist rigidity, for instance. If a competing nation takes advantage of opportunities and leaps ahead, then it can only be out of malevolence and a will to dominate. Intelligent adaptability and a sound economic system have nothing to do with it. In 1997, Jacques Toubon, the French minister of justice, told the American weekly magazine *U.S. News and World Report* that "the dominance of English on the Internet is a new form of colonialism." Naturally, the technological blindness of a country like France, obstinately clinging to her nationalized Minitel, played no role in this depressing situation. In 1997, we had one-tenth as many computers linked to the Internet as the United States, half as many as Germany, fewer even than Mexico and Poland. But the fault lies always with the other, who has the impudence to see more clearly and earlier than we do and whose liberal flexibility allows for the initiative of private innovators.

In France we bear the millstone of the Centre National de la Recherche Scientifique, which bureaucratizes science and distributes public funds to unproductive researchers who know their way around the corridors of power. Jean Cluzel, president of the Comité Français de l'Audiovisuel, in a 1999 text titled *Pour l'exemption culturelle*, persists on the path of timid protectionism: "Faced with the shattering invasion of the new technologies in the service of the dominant American culture, French cultural sovereignty is being seriously threatened." A shattering invasion, is it? Then we should study the reasons for its effectiveness, and look for remedies. Instead, we set up quotas, subsidize our film and television industries, and demand that everyone speak French—meanwhile remaining deaf to the debasement of our language in our schools and in the media.

When wounded egos project the causes of their own setbacks on others, we are likely to hear deranged interpretations that are inherently contradictory. On the one hand, the French are supposed to hate the United States; but on the other, if someone ventures to protest against the needless Americanisms that are infecting the vocabulary of our mass media, the complainer is immediately labeled an old fogey, a narrow-minded purist and pedant ridiculously hanging on to the past. We are pulling off an especially French tour de force: the uniting of Francophonic imperialism with linguistic hara-kiri. We are eager to impose a language on the world that we ourselves speak less and less well and that we consciously hold in contempt.

Contradiction reigns with the same brio in the heart of the left's anti-Americanism. But their obsession is ideological rather than nationalistic, although in severe cases it can be both. When the Green deputy Noël Mamère and the ARTE television reporter Olivier Warin joined forces for a book, *Non, merci, Uncle Sam,*[28] the title they picked could mean only one thing: the authors would have preferred to see Europe under the thumb of Hitler or Stalin rather than under American influence. America is reviled by the left because it is a robbers' den of liberalism. In the socialist view, liberalism, if you scratch the surface a bit, is still "fascism"—an assimilation the ultra-left makes openly. And you don't have to push an interlocutor of the "moderate" left very far before you uncover the same driving idea. In these pages, we have already seen several examples of the expression "totalitarian liberalism" and other equivalents, used by speakers who in other respects display no sign of alienation. This verdict on liberalism would seem to imply a call for restoring Communism, for returning to the roots of socialism with the abolition of property and free trade. Herein lies the contradiction: the left's most ardent apologists may yearn for this outcome, yet the left simultaneously shies away from calling for it, given the actual record of Communism and even of the French-style social statism of the 1980s.

No responsible government would implement such a policy any longer, so it is mostly left-wing intellectuals who, faithful to their historic mission, remain ever eager to trumpet the glories of socialism.

Günter Grass, for instance, in his novel *Ein weites Feld,* nostalgically sings the alluring charms of the German Democratic Republic, with only harsh words for West Germany.[29] Reunification in his eyes was nothing but a "colonization" (a term we have already encountered in this context) of the GDR by the West and therefore an invasion by "imperialist capitalism." It ought to have been the other way around, says Grass: we should have let East Germany shine forth like the sun, bringing socialism to life throughout the German lands. As a crowning touch to this elegant argument, the hero of Grass's novel is an individual whom you and I might naïvely consider to be ignoble and sickening, since he has spent his days spying on his fellow citizens and informing on them, first for the Gestapo, then for the Stasi. But Grass has other ideas. The 1999 Nobel Prize winner for literature reveals the soundness of his historical and moral judgment when he pronounces his protagonist altogether respectable: after all, hasn't he been inspired by the ancient Prussian virtues, doing loyal service to antiliberal states?[30] From the perspective of "resistance" to American influence, Grass's position is logical, because the only political inventions of the twentieth century that were original to Europe and owed nothing to "Anglo-Saxon" thought were Nazism and Communism. So let's remain true to our traditions of terror!

The ideological anti-Americanism of the left in no way rests on a balanced perception of American social realities. The United States deserves numerous criticisms; all the more need, then, that such critiques be founded on a serious study of American society's unique characteristics and the way it actually works. It won't do just to condemn failures wholesale without also acknowledging successes. The phobic total rejection of the United States—archincarnation of the Great Liberal Satan—tells us little about the civilization inveighed against, but much about the mental state of the enraged prosecutors, who carefully avoid gaining any knowledge of it.

It is a good thing that politicians dare not allow themselves to follow the intellectuals in their follies perpetually, being more constrained by the reality principle. Returning from an official trip to the United States in July 1998, Lionel Jospin accurately skewered a tall tale about America that has gained currency in France, one of those clichés that serve as consolation for subsidized sterility.[31] France's prime minister straightforwardly admitted that "contrary to what we have maintained, and perhaps believed, job creation in the United States does not consist solely—or even mostly—of low-skill, minimum-wage positions."

Between 1974 and 1994, why did the United States, with 258 million inhabitants, manage to create 40 million new jobs, while the twelve nations of the EU, with their combined population of 270 million and inundating their economies with massive subsidies and "structural funding," created only three million? This is the question that Lionel Jospin did not neglect to ask. He went so far as to say, "We would like to see not a welfare society, but a working society." Does this sound like a turn toward "fascism"? Is it another step along the road to *l'horreur économique* and liberal dictatorship?

CHAPTER FOURTEEN

Hating Progress

The most challenging task before the international left today, and one that will continue to preoccupy it for years to come, is that of obstructing all discussion of its active participation in, or passive adherence to, Communist totalitarianism. The left has only reluctantly and half-heartedly, at best, repudiated the Total State. It refuses to examine whether or not socialism in itself is fundamentally a sound concept, fearing that such an enquiry will reveal that the essence of socialism is totalitarian—and that it will be forced to concede this reality. Socialist parties in free countries are democratic in inverse proportion to their degree of socialism.

In trying to block any effort to evaluate its past errors—which might result in squelching the stealthy, hypocritical perpetuation of those errors in new dress—the left deploys various strategies, of which only the most important have been discussed in this book.

One of these strategies is to inundate the public square with virtually nonstop denunciations of Fascism and Nazism. We have seen that the left's assimilation of Italian Fascism to the Nazi phenomenon has functioned as camouflage for the latter's essential kinship with Communism. But however much this assimilation might be justified, the denunciations concern two political systems that were defeated, eliminated, judged and condemned more than half a century ago. So the constant, deafening refrain about the "duty to remember" a past that is already well behind us seems at least partly like an effort to enforce a "duty to forget" when it comes to Communism.

After all, which of these two systems began earlier and held sway longer? And which survives today, dominating large areas of the world and seducing susceptible minds everywhere? The socialist partisans silence those who invoke the Nazi/Communist parallel, if necessary claiming that such scandalous talk about Communism indicates sly complicity with Nazism.

If the democratic left had sincerely and genuinely reflected upon its past and broken every tie with the Communist tradition, would Mme Mitterrand have said, at the tenth anniversary commemoration of the Velvet Revolution in Prague, that the disappearance of Communist totalitarianism had opened the way for an even worse scourge, that of "liberal totalitarianism," imposed worldwide? Here is another favorite way for the left to evade its past: admitting the reality of the totalitarian phenomenon—but in democratic societies only.

The left has critically examined its ideological prejudices far less than is generally admitted; if it had done so in any significant measure, would the socialist Ministry of the Arts in 1999 have subsidized—that is, made the taxpayer underwrite—a French edition of *The Age of Extremes,* a product of the elder statesman of Britain's remaining incurable Stalinists, Eric Hobsbawm? That this manifesto should come out in France is all very well: in a free country, the press must be free. But for a Socialist government to provide financial support for such a book—a piece of pure propaganda from another era, disguised as serious scholarship—shows how little the left has examined the basis of its ideology, unless it is to project its own characteristics onto the liberal adversary. The incomparable Ignacio Ramonet, *Le Monde diplomatique*'s editor-in-chief, echoes a leftist commonplace when he writes, "The *pensée unique* is a new totalitarianism . . . the only ideology authorized by the opinion police, invisible and omnipresent." Here Ramonet is giving a nice thumbnail description of the police state that is dear to him—the Communist regime.[1] One would like to ask him: Was the failure, for example, of the 1999 World Trade Organization conference in Seattle, which was shut down by the antiglobalist left, a proof of this liberal "dictatorship"?

For leftists, Communism is like a phantom limb, an arm or a leg that is gone but which the amputee still feels as though it were present. And while we have seen Communism disappear as a global ideology molding every aspect of daily existence in those countries where it was established, this doesn't mean that it has ceased to dominate various aspects of our societies and cultures. This is what Roland Hureaux, in his book *Les Hauteurs béantes de l'Europe*, calls "an ideology in bits and pieces." He points out that an ideology need not be monolithic: "Phenomena of an ideological nature can be operative in such-and-such a sector of political, administrative or social life, without society as a whole for that reason being totalitarian."[2]

A good example of such a fragmentary ideology is the current of negative emotions aroused by the globalization of commerce. The guerrilla warfare unleashed in Seattle against the WTO, which was even more ferocious than similar "demonstrations" the previous year in Genoa, authentically embodied the totalitarian madness. Confronted by such a degrading spectacle, you can hardly even say totalitarian "ideology," for this word implies at least a passing bow to rationality. In Seattle, the spectacle was provided not by revolutionaries but by primitives, yelling a hodgepodge of irrelevant grievances and incompatible demands.

The protests were irrelevant because the WTO, far from advocating completely free and unregulated international trade, was created in order to organize, regulate and codify it—to surround it with legality. The protesters were therefore attacking an imaginary foe: "savage" globalization, which revealed itself to be far less savage than the protesters themselves. In fact, it was a clinging to subsidy-fed protectionism on the part of some major players in the negotiations that set up the conference for failure.

Another leftist complaint—that the rich nations are imposing free trade and capital circulation on developing countries in order to exploit poorly paid and socially unprotected local workforces—was the fruit of Communist thought that survives in paranoid form. In Seattle, it was the developing countries that refused to adopt social measures such as a guaranteed minimum wage or prohibition of child labor; they argued that the advanced nations' motive was really to curtail Third World competitiveness, since it's the low production costs in Third World countries that offer them their best chances for economic takeoff and a higher standard of living. Contrary to leftist prejudices, "savage capitalism" is a state of affairs desired by the poorest countries, because free trade works to their advantage in some important sectors where they have the most competitive products. In these sectors, the wealthy countries, handicapped by higher production costs, fear globalization. The rich countries, moreover, are divided among themselves on the issues of trade globalization, which shows that the notion of a liberal *pensée unique* dominating the stage is not tenable. It does so only in the imaginations of those who are prey to an obsession.

Likewise, and contrary to the slogans of the Greens (who also were vociferous among the Seattle rioters), it isn't the multinational corporations who gripe the most about being obliged to protect the environment, it's the least developed nations that do so. Developing nations must provisionally put environmental considerations aside—as did the advanced nations when they made their first steps toward industrialization. But when this argument was proffered by Indian and Indonesian shrimpers to justify their use of a certain type of fishing net, they became a target for the "ecos" who complained that their traditional practices entailed the capture of a threatened species of tortoise.

A comic spectacle indeed—well-fed bawlers from the great American universities doing their utmost to deprive fishermen at the world's antipodes of their age-old livelihood! Why didn't our Greens pick on the protected "savagery" of European fishermen, who persist in using narrow-mesh nets that massacre immature fish and threaten to exhaust the resources of our seas? (Admittedly, confronting the marine fishermen of Lorient or La Carogne might be a risky business.) And to cart along vengeful placards against freedom of international commerce in a city like Seattle, where a substantial proportion of workers are employed by Microsoft or Boeing and are therefore active contributors to America's export trade, likewise has a ridiculous side.

Another amusing point: the fanatics who violently display their hostility to free trade are the same people who campaign, with equal ardor, for canceling the United States' embargo on Cuba. Why should free trade, that diabolical manifestation of world capitalism, suddenly become a blessing when it works in favor of Cuba or Saddam Hussein's Iraq? If international free trade is indeed such a curse, wouldn't it be advisable to extend the embargo to every country on earth?

It would be hard to explain such a tissue of contradictions collectively displayed by people who individually are doubtless of normal intelligence without invoking the spell cast by the lamented specter of Communism, which has conditioned certain political attitudes and behaviors for a long time and will continue to do so. According to these Communist residues, capitalism remains the absolute evil, and revolution the only means of combating it—even if socialism is dead, and revolution is pretty much confined to smashing windows and then perhaps making off with what lies behind them.

Such comfortable simplism dispenses with the need for intellectual effort of any kind. Ideology does your thinking for you; without it, you are obliged to study for yourself the complexities of democracy and the free market—those sworn enemies of revolution. Unfortunately, the detritus of ideology and the "revolutionary" pantomimes it inspires function as screens for well-defined interest groups. Behind the yelling mobs at Seattle marched the forces of the old protectionist pressure groups of the rich countries' agricultural and industrial unions, which knew exactly what they wanted: the continuance of their subsidies, privileges and export advantages—all under the guise of a principled, noble war against the "inequality-generating market."

The cries of joy by this so-called "citizens' uprising" of the NGOs, the anticapitalist ultra-left, the environmentalists, all the herds of activists hostile to the global free market, all claiming the glory of the Seattle fiasco—this noisy triumph amounted to a carnival of inconsistencies. It bears repeating that what caused the WTO failure was not at all the supposed "ultraliberalism" of the European Union and the United States of America, but on the contrary their excessive protectionism, notably in the agricultural domain—a protectionism that caused resentment among the emerging economies of the world, and especially in the Cairns Group of countries that are or would like to be major exporters of agricultural products. The victor at Seattle was the protectionism of the rich countries—whatever the fanatics, obsessed with stigmatizing the liberalism of rich countries, have to say about the matter. The developing countries scored a point by rejecting the social-justice and environmental clauses that the WTO wanted them to accept. By its support of these proposed policies, the left found itself in the position of applauding child labor, starvation wages, pollution, and slavery in the Chinese, Vietnamese and Cuban gulags. Rarely has the intrinsically contradictory nature of ideology been manifested with such blind fatuity.

The antiglobalizers' posturing graphically illustrates another property of the ideological mindset, aside from its deliberate ignoring of facts and its cult of inconsistencies: a penchant for accomplishing, under the banner of progressivism, the exact opposite of its proclaimed goals. It declares and believes itself to be working toward an egalitarian world—but in fact sets inequality in concrete. Another disparity between intentions and results can be seen in the area of education after thirty years of collectivist policies in France.

In 1997, I published a rather modest editorial titled "Wrecking Our Schools."[3] It didn't broach any original themes. For years, lamentations had been heard from every side about the constant lowering of standards, about the ever-increasing illiteracy and classroom violence, and about what has been prudishly euphemized as "academic failure"—apparently a kind of natural catastrophe with no connection whatsoever to the methods followed or imposed by those in charge of France's public education.

The day after my editorial came out, I received a missive under the letterhead of the Ministry of National Education, signed by one Claude Thélot, "director of evaluation and forecasting." While ironically addressing me as "Monsieur l'Académician" and "Cher Maître," this consequential personage deigned to notify me that my piece displayed a rare intellectual poverty and was, in a word, "unfortunate." Obligingly, the magnanimous director was entirely at my disposal to furnish me with basic knowledge about our secondary school system that I was clearly lacking.

Yet the very next week, the press published a study by the same government "Department for Evaluation and Forecasting" that revealed, among other appalling facts, that 35 percent of students entering *sixième* (roughly equivalent to sixth grade in America) have little reading comprehension and that 9 percent do not even know the alphabet. Looking over these widely reported and devastating statistics, I couldn't help but ask myself if M. Thélot had done likewise. Was he merely an idiot—self-confessed, obviously, since the very same bureaucracy he presided over had corroborated my assertions? Or was he just a hopelessly lazy individual who hadn't even bothered to glance at his agency's reports?[4]

I rejected these hypotheses and came around to the view that Thélot's arrogant blindness was due to the omnipotence of ideology, which had completely parasitized his mind. Just like the apparatchiks of yesteryear, who couldn't imagine that the low yields of Soviet agriculture were the inevitable result of collectivization, our educational bureaucrats are incapable of grasping that the ideological treatment they have been inflicting on French schools for thirty years could be responsible for their breakdown. If decades of practice yield the opposite of the intended result, the ideologue can never accept this as proof that his principles could be wrong or his methods faulty. The educational fiasco is a good example of an often-encountered phenomenon: that of a "totalitarian sector" in the heart of an otherwise democratic society.[5] Such ideological flotsam, mostly of Communist affiliation, continues to float around in various places throughout the world.

In these pages I have frequently drawn attention to three characteristics of the totalitarian mindset, and in particular of Communist ideology: a voluntary ignorance of the facts; an ability to live with contradictions that refute its own principles; and a refusal to analyze the causes of failure. How and why did these salient traits emerge, and how can we explain their ability to survive, as it were, posthumously? Any answer to these questions must not rule out an apparent paradox: the socialist hatred of progress.

In the previous chapter, we saw how Communist Party theoreticians and those of the Marxist ultra-left sweepingly condemn all modern means of communication as "commodities" manufactured by "cultural industries." The progress they supposedly represent is said to have the ulterior goal of boosting capitalist profits and enslaving the masses. In this view, publishing, television, radio, journalism, the Internet—perhaps even the printing press itself?—were never means of disseminating knowledge and freeing minds, but rather means to deceive and control.

We should not forget that this excommunication of modernity, of scientific progress and technology and of cultural free choice, has its roots in the origins of the contemporary left and was glaringly apparent in the writings of a principal founding figure: Jean-Jacques Rousseau. The work that made Rousseau an instant celebrity was a virulent manifesto against scientific and technical progress, which he considered to be regressive insofar as it takes us away from the state of nature. This is the first thing that most people learn about Rousseau's beliefs, but few draw the appropriate conclusions. *The Social Contract* flies against everything the Enlightenment thinkers stood for: the advancement of rational knowledge, of science and its practical applications, which could only lead to the improvement of humanity's lot in every way. So the hostility that the philosophes—and notably Voltaire—were quick to manifest toward Rousseau did not derive solely from personal animosities (as is routinely maintained), but from profound doctrinal differences. In opposition to the main intellectual current of his time, Jean-Jacques regarded civilization as noxious and degrading to humanity. He constantly preached the merits of a return to ancestral ways of living: small rural communities, with the peasantry dispersed around the countryside in hamlets of two or three families. And he hated cities. After the Lisbon earthquake of 1755, which killed sixty thousand people, he loudly proclaimed that there would have been fewer victims if only no one had been living at that site—if Lisbon had never been built. The enemy, from Rousseau's omni-optic point of view, is the very institution of the city itself, which corrupts its inhabitants and exposes them to catastrophes that wouldn't affect them if they were still living in caves or huts. Clearly we would have been much better off, culturally and physically speaking, if Athens, Rome, Alexandria, Isfahan, Fez, London, Seville, Florence, Venice, New York or St. Petersburg had never been built.

Once again, the rural protectionism and reactionary fantasies of certain leftist currents—those that gave rise to totalitarianism—coincide with the "return to the sources"* theme of the traditionalist extreme right. This convergence can still be seen in the fiercest debates at the end of the twentieth century: some of the left's invectives against "ultraliberalism" and "imperialist globalization" are so close to *souverainiste*** productions of the right that their bylines could be switched without betraying their authors' thinking in the slightest.[6]

Rousseau's hostile brief against civilization, which he held to be intrinsically corrupting, establishes him as the inventor of cultural totalitarianism: his *Letter to D'Alembert and Writings for the Theater* prefigures Stalinist "socialist realism" and the "revolutionary" performances of the Beijing Opera under the directorship of Madame Mao. For him, as for the hardest-line ecclesiastical authorities of the seventeenth and eighteenth centuries, theater was a prime source of moral corruption, inciting to vice by its depictions of passion and undermining social discipline by provoking controversy. The only performances that accorded with his taste were those edifying little comedies improvised on evenings of the grape harvest in Swiss

---

* *Translator's note:* "Return to the sources" in the sense of going back to a simpler, more authentic life, closer to nature.

** *Translator's note: Souverainiste* refers to the Euroskeptics who want to retrieve French autonomy from the EU.

cantons. If Jean-Jacques had practiced the aesthetic that Rousseau preached, he would not have allowed himself to put the *Confessions* to paper—thus depriving French belles-lettres of a masterpiece.

With regard to political institutions, *The Social Contract* guarantees democracy in exactly the same way that the Stalinist constitution of 1937 did for the USSR. Both documents derive the authority of the state from the "general will" of the "entire people," stipulating that not the slightest manifestation of individual liberty will be tolerated after the formal constitution of the state. In *The Social Contract* we find a prefiguring—*avant la lettre* and couched in a different vocabulary, of course—of "democratic centralism" and the "dictatorship of the proletariat." And a telltale symptom stands revealed: Rousseau unfailingly exalts Sparta to the disadvantage of Athens. In the eighteenth century and until the time of Maurice Barrès, this preference for Sparta was virtually a coded signal, a rallying cry for the adversaries of pluralism and liberty.

Benjamin Constant* shows clearly how a penchant for Spartan-inspired, permanent re-education camps—on display in the work of the formidable Abbé de Mably, one of the most rigid precursors of totalitarian ideologues—was shared by the well-intentioned Jean-Jacques:

> Sparta, which united republican forms with the subjugation of the individual, awakened in this philosophe's soul an even livelier enthusiasm. The vast monastery that was Sparta seemed to him like the model of a perfect republic. For Athens he had nothing but scorn, and he would readily have said of that nation, the foremost of Greece, what a prominent *académicien* and nobleman said of the Académie Française, "What a frightful despotism! Everybody does what he wants."

As Bertrand de Jouvenel ironically noted, Rousseau has for two centuries been touted as the forefather of ideas completely

---

* *Translator's note:* Benjamin Constant (1767–1830) was a French-Swiss political writer and novelist of literary merit, who in principle espoused liberal constitutionalism.

opposed to those that were actually his. Rousseau preferred "the countryside over the city, agriculture over commerce, simplicity over luxury, custom over novelty, citizen equality in a rudimentary economy rather than inequality in a complex one . . . and, most important of all, traditionalism rather than progress." In this respect, if Jean-Jacques cannot be understood as an intellectual forebear of liberal democracy, his legend notwithstanding, he was well and truly a man of the totalitarian left.

Echoing Rousseau, Friedrich Engels in his celebrated *The Condition of the Working Class in England* (1845) depicted industrialization and urbanization mainly as destroyers of traditional moral values, and of family values above all. In the new industrial cities, he said, women have to work away from home. Thus they are denied the role that nature has conferred on them— that of "watching over children, keeping house, and preparing meals." Worse still: if the husband happens to be thrown out of work, then such menial tasks will devolve—horrors!—upon *him*. "In the city of Manchester alone, hundreds of men are thus condemned to household work. One can easily understand the justified indignation of workers who are made into eunuchs. Family relations are turned upside down." The emasculated husband is reduced to struggling in the kitchen, while the wife, left to her own devices in the big city, is exposed to every sort of temptation. It will not escape the reader's notice that this sermon by the Reverend Engels can hardly be considered an early manifesto for women's liberation.

The societies created by actually existing socialism were in fact the most archaic that humanity had experienced for millennia. This "return to Sparta" moreover characterizes all utopias. Socialist societies are oligarchic. The ruling minority assigns to each individual his or her place in the production system, including place of residence. Above all, the official doctrine must be made to penetrate into everyone's mind as the exclusive intellectual fare. As for art, the only justification for its continued existence is to promote the edifying ends of the revolution, and artists are required to restrict themselves to the comically vacuous project of portraying a society that swims in egalitarian bliss and reflecting the ecstatic, admiring gratitude felt by the people toward the Supreme Tyrant. Forbidden to travel freely, even in their own country, without the authorization conferred by an "interior passport," the population is cut off from all foreign influences, effectively realizing that dream of isolation so beloved by our homegrown French intellectual and artistic protectionists ever since they felt threatened by the "danger" of cultural globalization—which they routinely denounce as an engine of uniformity.

The reality is that cultural uniformity has always been overwhelmingly the hallmark of "closed" societies, in Karl Popper and Henri Bergson's sense of the word; and diversity has always been the natural fruit of cultural exchange. It is in societies where actually existing socialism has prevailed that camps proliferate to re-educate citizens who dare to think politically forbidden thoughts—a policy that has the added advantage of providing the state with a cheap, readymade workforce. At the turn of the century, for example, one-third of China's workforce was made up of slaves. It's hardly surprising how such vast quantities of that nation's exports, produced at negligible cost, can flood international markets at unbeatable prices.

It may seem incredible that there could still today be large numbers of people who harbor nostalgia for societies of this type, wholesale or piecemeal. The long tradition, going back two and a half millennia, of utopian ideas—of writings that are astoundingly similar, down to the smallest detail, in their prescriptions for the Ideal City—confirms this truth: the totalitarian temptation, lurking beneath the demon mask of the Good, is a constant of the human mind. It has always been in conflict with our aspirations for liberty, and it always will be.

APPENDIX A
La Pensée Unique

The expression is attributed to Ignacio Ramonet, editor-in-chief of *Le Monde diplomatique*. Here is a translation of his editorial for the January 1995 issue.

Mired. In the democracies, this means that more and more citizens feel themselves to be stuck in a sort of viscous doctrine that is imperceptibly closing in on those who rebel—inhibiting, confusing, paralyzing and stifling counterarguments. The doctrine in question is *la pensée unique,* the one and only way of thinking authorized by an invisible and omnipresent thought police.

Since the fall of the Berlin Wall, the collapse of the Communist regimes and the demoralization of socialism, this new gospel has reached such a height of arrogance, pride and insolence that one may, without exaggeration, describe it as an ideological mania, a modern orthodoxy.

What is *la pensée unique?* An ideology with universal pretensions, it is a translation into ideological terms of the interests of an ensemble of economic forces—in particular those of international capital. It was formulated, so to speak, as early as the international Bretton Woods Agreements of July 1944. Its principal sources today are the great economic and monetary institutions: the World Bank, the International Monetary Fund, the Organization for Economic Cooperation and Development (OECD), the General Agreement on Tariffs and Trade (GATT), the European Commission, the Bank of France, and the like. With their financial power, these institutions enlist the worldwide services of numerous think tanks, universities and foundations, which work to refine and disseminate the gospel.

An anonymous discourse, it is picked up and amplified by the main organs of economic information, notably by the bibles of the investors and stockbrokers: the *Wall Street Journal, Financial Times, Economist, Far Eastern Economic Review, Les Échos,* Reuters, etc., which are often owned by giant industrial or financial entities. Almost everywhere, economics faculties, journalists, essayists and politicians adopt the central commandments of these new Tablets of the Law and repeat them ad nauseam over the mass media. They know full well that repetition, in our media-dominated societies, is as good as proving your case.

The first principle of *la pensée unique* is all the more powerful in that an absent-minded Marxist might not reject it: Economics trumps politics. Hewing to this concept, such an important instrument as the Bank of France, in the hands of the executive branch of government, was able to make itself autonomous in 1994—allegedly "beyond the vagaries of politics." This *démarche* was accomplished without notable opposition. "The Bank of France is independent, apolitical and transpartisan," claimed the bank's governor, M. Jean-Claude Trichet, who nevertheless added, "We are asking that public deficits be reduced . . . [and] we are pursuing a policy of monetary stability."[1] As if these two goals were not political! But at headquarters, in the name of "realism" and "pragmatism," the economy takes first place, in accordance with a rule that M. Alain Minc reduces to: "Capitalism cannot collapse: it is the natural state of society. Democracy is *not* the natural state of society; the market is."[2] Of course, it is an economy relieved of the social burden—an encumbering straitjacket whose weight would cause regression and crisis.

The other key concepts of *la pensée unique* are well known: the market, that idol whose "invisible hand tends to correct the sharp edges and malfunctions of capitalism," and in particular the financial markets, whose "signals orient and determine the general direction of the economy"; competition and competitiveness, which "stimulate and energize businesses, so that they constantly and beneficially upgrade"; unlimited free trade, "agent of uninterrupted commercial growth, and hence of societies"; globalization with respect to manufactured goods as well as capital flow; international division of labor, which "curbs union demands and lowers wage costs"; a strong currency, which "makes for stability"; deregulation; privatization; liberalization, etc. Always "less government," and always arbitration in favor of capital earnings to the detriment of labor. And indifference with regard to the ecological costs.

The constant repetition of this catechism in all the media,* and by practically all politicians across the spectrum,** is so intimidating that it stifles every attempt at unfettered thinking and makes resistance to this new-fangled obscurantism very difficult.***

One might almost conclude that the 17.4 million Europeans out of work and the rising tide of those whom society has rejected, the urban disasters and *banlieues* on fire, the prevailing insecurity and corruption, the ecological destruction, the return of various forms of racism, religious fundamentalism and extremism—all these are merely mirages, inadmissible hallucinations that are highly discordant in this world, this best of all worlds, enlightened by *la pensée unique* for our anesthetized consciences.

---

* A typical example of the dominant mode of thinking: *La France de l'an 2000: Rapport au premier ministre* (Paris: Éditions Odile Jacob, 1994).

** M. Dominique Strauss-Kahn, the Socialist minister for industry, was asked, "What's going to change if the right carries the day?" His reply is notorious: "Nothing. Their economic policies will not be very different from our own." *Wall Street Journal Europe*, March 18, 1993.

*** Could this be the reason why several intellectuals, among whom was Guy Debord, have chosen to commit suicide in recent weeks?

Lionel Jospin
and *The Black Book*

Jean-François Revel was interviewed by Jean-René Van der
Plaetsen for *Le Figaro* (November 14, 1997) concerning Lionel
Jospin's irritated response to a question about *The Black Book of
Communism*. See Chapter 5, pp. 91–92.

Le Figaro: **What was your reaction to Lionel Jospin's statement?**
Jean-François Revel: First, I'd like to say that the prime minister's statement contains two historical errors. In his speech,
Lionel Jospin refers to the Popular Front, to the Resistance and to
the Coalition of the Left (Cartel des Gauches), implying that the
French Communist Party has participated in all the struggles of
the French left. Well, in 1924 the CPF stood against the Coalition
of the Left, which had formed a Radical-Socialist government. So
it is false to assert that the CPF has always been on the side of the
Socialists. I can only say that I'm astonished that the first secretary
of the Socialist Party is so ignorant of the history of the left.

The prime minister commits a second error in saying, "When Nazi Germany was our adversary, the Soviet Union was our ally." Everyone knows that the USSR was not always our ally, and that initially it was allied with the Nazis. Stalin would never have commenced hostilities against Germany. It was only because Hitler attacked the Soviet Union that the latter entered the war. Here again, I find it very curious that a Socialist prime minister should skate over the Hitler-Stalin Pact, just like the Communists in 1945. Lionel Jospin is doing a makeover of history. Which suggests that the Socialist Party's conversion to historical truth is happening even more slowly than the Communist Party's.

In this era of "repentance," should we expect the prime minister to pay homage to the victims of Communism?
I am staggered that Lionel Jospin, by ignoring the crimes committed in the name of Communism, is encouraging the French CP to persist in its denial of past mistakes. Instead of pointing out that Communism, wherever it has been in power, has given rise to barbaric and criminal phenomena, the prime minister has opted to conceal the totalitarian character of Communist ideology. In this respect, our Socialist Party is way behind the Italian Communist Party, which was able to engage in self-criticism after 1968 and the events in Prague, going even further after 1989.

Do you think, like Lionel Jospin, that we should distinguish between Marxism, Leninism, Stalinism and Communism?
The distinction between Leninism and Stalinism was refuted more than twenty years ago. For years, we heard so-called historians say that Stalinism was a betrayal of Leninism. Today, it is well established that the principles of terror and of totalitarianism were set forth and put into practice by Lenin himself. And a book such as Christian Jelen's *L'Aveuglement* shows that the French Socialist Party, from 1918 onward, was aware of the totalitarian character of the Bolshevik revolution. It was precisely because some French Socialists of the period recognized Leninism's real nature that the

SFIO* split into two at the Congress of Tours in 1920. So again, by drawing a distinction between Stalinism and Leninism that is no longer tenable, the prime minister is showing that he hasn't been keeping up with his reading.

Lionel Jospin has refused to "put an equals sign between Nazism and Communism." Ought there be a hierarchy?

One would hope that the French left had finally understood that there is no difference between "good" and "bad" executioners. Is it better to be murdered by Pol Pot than by Hitler? There are no grounds for drawing distinctions between victims of the Red and the Black totalitarianism. The Nazis never made any secret of their intentions: to eliminate democracy, to rule by force, and to engage in systematic racial persecutions. We are told that Communists had an ideal. I am tempted to think that this makes them even worse, because it means that millions of people were deliberately deceived. Because, in addition to the crimes, there was the most abject mendacity.

According to the prime minister, the French Communist Party "has never laid hands on our freedoms" . . .

That's because it never had the opportunity. The distinctive feature of the French Communist Party is that for a long time, along with the Portuguese CP, it was the most Stalinist of all the European CPs. The Portuguese party ended up disappearing. But not the French CP, which, thanks to the Socialist Party, continues to play a political role. That's why we might have hoped that Lionel Jospin would put pressure on the Communists to make a genuine acknowledgment of their errors. These days, the question of Communism's history is no longer merely political— it is a moral problem. And it is on this level that Lionel Jospin's words disappointed me.

---

* *Translator's note:* SFIO was the "Section Française de l'International Ouvrière" (French Section of the Workers' International), a predecessor of the Socialist Party.

The Little Red Writer

This short piece appeared in *L'Express*, August 28, 1968. It briefly assesses *Le Petit Livre rouge* (Seuil, 1968), the selection of quotations from Chairman Mao Zedong, and Mao's *Écrits choisis*, 3 vols. (Maspero, 1967).

In 1930, Mao Zedong wrote a pamphlet titled *Against the Cult of the Book*. Today he is the center of the most obscurantist cult of a book that has ever gripped a civilization since the promulgation of the Qur'an.

Recited by rote, commented upon, publicly displayed by millions of Chinese, used as a breviary and reread countless times, this year *The Little Red Book* has become a bestseller in France. The political reasons for its success are obvious. Many are the French readers—if not voters—who think that only America benefits from peaceful coexistence and that a global transition to socialism cannot be achieved without violent revolution.

What, then, is the intellectual value, the philosophical substance of this book, which people acclaim as the "Chinese version" of Marxism-Leninism?

To ascertain whether Mao is an original thinker, it is preferable to refer to the unabridged texts rather than rely on *The Little Red Book*. Important though it is as a historical document, the book is a brief compendium of quotations vaguely linked by topic, in no chronological or logical order. It makes no demands on the reader's critical intelligence. It reads like stripped-down Marxism-Leninism, sprinkled with moral adjurations of the most banal character, and often redundant as well.

For example: "Modesty leads to progress." Or: "The difficult thing in life is to act well." Or: "An uneducated army is an ignorant army." Or: "Unilateral analysis means not knowing how to consider questions from every point of view."

A multilateral analysis of Mao's texts reveals that he cannot be considered a theoretician and he is hardly original. His rare theoretical expositions—"Concerning Praxis" or "Concerning Contradictions," for example—are limited to simplifying and vulgarizing Lenin's *Materialism and Empirio-Criticism*. Moreover, these excursions into theory, like all his writings, are occasional pieces produced in the context of struggles within the Chinese Communist Party or outside it, designed to bring political pressure to bear on this or that faction. Mao adopted Marxist-Leninist ideology wholesale and never attempted to rethink it. When he appears to be dealing in ideology, he is really bent on tactical maneuvers.

On the other hand, like all Communists, he dresses up the merest details in abstract phraseology. For example: Should the Red Army soldiers in 1929 spend their free time amusing themselves in the cities or stay in the countryside, where they are more useful? Mao expounds a solution: "Elimination of erroneous concepts within the Party." Among these erroneous concepts— alongside "subjectivism" and "remnants of 'putschism'"—is "individualism," the chief component of which is the "taste for pleasure," which manifests itself mainly in the phenomenon of "our troops heading for the big towns."

Even the Hundred Flowers theory—so florid in its formulation!—scarcely amounts to bona fide theory. It was intended to placate those who in 1957 were demanding more freedom of discussion within the party, who were invoking recent events in Hungary in order to condemn authoritarian tendencies. Mao approves of the brutal treatment meted out to the Budapest uprising. He makes rhetorical concessions to the malcontents, but then immediately withdraws them and reverts to orthodoxy. In the Hundred Flowers speech, titled "On the Correct Handling of the Contradictions among the People," as in earlier texts such as "On Popular Democratic Dictatorship" (1949) and "Oppose Stereotyped Party Writing" (1942), the line of argument Mao uses, always the same, is this: Freedom of discussion is certainly permissible within the party. But in practice, objections to the party come from two sources—from enemies of the revolution, who should not have the right to express their views, and from sincere supporters of the revolution, who are never really in disagreement with the party. Therefore, authoritarian methods amount to "democratic centralism" and are altogether legitimate; for among the people, "liberty is correlative to discipline."

The same schema applies in philosophy. May one criticize Marxism? Of course, because "Marxism is not afraid of criticism," and if Marxism "could be demolished by criticism, it would no longer be good for anything." Hence, Marxism is invulnerable, and you argue against it in vain. That being the case, why bother to try?

In art and literature also, the Hundred Flowers can bloom intellectually, but since it's important not to let "poisonous weeds" grow alongside "fragrant flowers," Mao quickly reverts to a doctrine of cultural *dirigisme* identical to that of Stalin's cultural commissar Andrei Zhdanov. Mao's hobbyhorse of a "cultural army" is far from new: culture always reflects political and social realities. Once the economic revolution has been accomplished, culture must be brought into alignment with it. This is the standard analysis, entirely in conformity with militant Leninism and without the slightest personal alteration.

Let me be clear: Here I am not passing political judgment on China. But if you turn to the texts themselves, you will have to admit that there is no such philosophy as a "Chinese version" of Marxism. There is no such thing as Maoism.

Genocide Defined: French Criminal Code, 1992

Felonies and Misdemeanors against Persons
Title I. Crimes against Humanity: Genocide

Article 211-1
Genocide occurs where, in the enforcement of a concerted plan aimed at the partial or total destruction of a national, ethnic, racial or religious group, or of a group determined by any other arbitrary criterion, one of the following actions is committed or caused to be committed against members of that group:

- willful assault on the right to life;
- serious attack on mental or physical integrity;
- subjection to living conditions likely to entail the partial or total destruction of that group;
- measures aimed at preventing births;
- forced relocation of children.

Genocide is punished by imprisonment for life. . . .

Article 212-1

Deportation, reduction to slavery, or the massive and systematic practice of summary executions, of abduction of persons followed by their disappearance, of torture or inhuman acts, inspired by political, philosophical, racial or religious motives, and organized in pursuit of a concerted plan against a group of a civilian population, are punished by imprisonment for life. . . .

Article 212-2

Where they are committed during wartime in execution of a concerted plan against persons fighting the ideological system in the name of which are perpetrated crimes against humanity, the actions referred to under article 212-1 are punished by imprisonment for life.

Article 212-3

The participation in a group formed or in an agreement established with a view to the preparation, characterized by one or more material actions, of one of the felonies defined by articles 211-1, 212-1 and 212-2 is punished by imprisonment for life. . . .

. . .

Article 213-4

The perpetrator or the accomplice to a felony under the present Title is not exonerated from his responsibility on the sole basis that he performed an act prescribed or authorized by statutory or regulatory provisions, or an act ordered by legitimate authority. A court shall nevertheless take this circumstance into account when deciding the nature and extent of the sentence.

Article 213-5

Criminal liability for the felonies set out under the present Title is imprescriptable, as are the sentences imposed.

Adapted from the English translation at Legifrance: http://www.legifrance.gouv.fr/ html/codes_traduits/code_penal_soman.htm, *made with the participation of John Rason Spencer, Professor of Law, University of Cambridge.*

APPENDIX E

Cambodia:
The Occupation

Jean-François Revel's review of Esmeralda Luciolli, *Mur de bambou, ou le Cambodge après Pol Pot,* with a preface by François Poncahaud (Médecins sans Frontières, Régine Deforges, 1988), from *Le Point*, November 28, 1988.

One of the most richly enrolled clubs on the planet is the Enemies of Past Genocides. Its only competitor is Friends of Genocide in Progress. Membership in these groups often overlaps. When pro-Soviet Vietnam invaded pro-China Cambodia in 1979 in order to chase out the Khmer Rouge, the Western media stopped being concerned with the fate of the unhappy Cambodians. Their country was going to be occupied by a foreign power from now on, and that was regrettable, but (this was the general reaction) at least the invaders had put a stop to the massacres of the frightful years between 1975 and 1979.

Certainly, the Vietnamese and the collaborationist Khmer government that serves them have not killed two million Cambodians, or a quarter of the population, as did Pol Pot. But their indirect methods of extermination and enslavement, less visible and more insidious, are no less terrible. The Soviet-Vietnamese censorship apparatus has succeeded in hiding the new Cambodia behind a rampart of silence. As more films and books about the Khmer terror regime continue to emerge,* firsthand accounts of Vietnamized Cambodia remain hard to come by.

Hence the importance of Esmeralda Luciolli's revelations. A thirty-four-year-old French woman, born of Italian parents in the United States, Luciolli took part in a Médecins sans Frontières mission and was one of the few Western physicians admitted into Cambodia. She sojourned there for fifteen months, from 1984 to 1986. Her account is personal and lively, informed by direct experience. In addition to the exceptional advantage of having actually lived in Cambodia, the author happens to be familiar with the Khmer language, which she studied at the National Institute for Oriental Languages in Paris.

Ideologically, the new regime differs so little from its predecessor that most of the present party cadres are former Khmers Rouges. Moreover, the official radio station inveighs only against Pol Pot, never against the Khmer Rouge in general. Like all Communist regimes, the authorities hope to create a "new man" by means of protracted political indoctrination sessions that consume so much work time as to suppress the country's already low productivity levels. Repression of suspected dissidents, of the recalcitrant and the half-hearted, results each year in thousands of arrests, "disappearances" (as in Argentina, but not so frequently mentioned!) and cases of torture. Aid from Western organizations and governments in the form of food, construction and medical supplies is embezzled by the nomenklatura—for their own use or to be sold at exorbitant prices on the black market, or to be exported to Vietnam or the USSR. The West's brilliant technique of "gorging the executioners so as to feed the victims," as William Shawcross put it, is working perfectly here.[3]

---

* Among the most shattering of these is: Molyda Szymusiak, *Les Pierres crieront, ou un enfance cambodgienne*, with a preface by Jean-Marie Domenach (La Découverte, 1984).

But worse was to come in the story of the Vietnamese occupation. In 1984, a terrible decision was taken in Hanoi (and not in Phnom Penh, a fact which underscores the typically Communist character of the relations between the two governments) to construct a new Great Wall of China along the entire length of the eight-hundred-mile frontier separating Cambodia from Thailand. This structure, however, is a simple palisade, a frail "bamboo wall" of no strategic value. Its purpose is to prevent Cambodians from fleeing to Thailand. Two or three times annually, 120,000 men—called "volunteers"—spend months doing the labor. They are decimated by the working conditions, by malaria and undernourishment, for neither the quinine nor the food supplies sent by the West reach these unfortunate convicts, who fall victim to what is referred to there as "clearances."

The chapter that Esmeralda Luciolli devotes to the spineless complicity of UN agencies, several NGOs and even the Red Cross deserves a prominent place in the annals of human cowardice. You must read the details of these evasions to understand the Khmer people's despair when they see how those who are supposed to come to their aid are in league with the forces that have undertaken to exterminate them. After that, we can resume our high-minded perorations about human rights.

Our heads of state should be concerned. But indeed they go a step further: To save Hanoi from failure, they are flooding it with our money.

Endnotes

Chapter 1: *La Grande Parade*

1. "Catastroika intellectuelle," *Le Point,* July 2, 1990.

2. *Manual del perfecto idiota latinoamericano* (Plaza y Janés, 1996); in English, *Guide to the Perfect Latin American Idiot* (Madison Books, 2000).

3. To fill in the details: The hysteria directed at Octavio Paz was mostly precipitated by two speeches. The first was given at Frankfurt in October 1984 on the occasion of the writer's being awarded the Peace Prize of the German Book Trade by the president of West Germany; it was a very general discussion on the topics of war and peace, on international affairs and the Cold War. The words that provoked the rage of the ideologues were the following: "It is clear that the United States supports armed groups that are opposed to the Managua regime. It is equally certain that the USSR and Cuba are sending military advisors and weapons to the Sandinistas. And it is also true that the roots of the conflict are deeply buried in Central American history." These remarks are unobjectionable—a moderate statement of the obvious. But the hatred for Paz had a more unforgivable cause: his longstanding refusal to be a fellow traveler of Communism.

In the second speech, delivered in Valencia on June 15, 1987, Paz was commemorating the congress of antifascist intellectuals held in that city in 1937 during the Spanish Civil War. He made the mistake of recalling the role of Stalin and his henchmen in the defeat of the Republican side, a role that has since been abundantly documented by all serious historians.

4. *Libération,* April 9, 1999.

5. *Economist,* September 20, 1997.

Chapter 2: Evasion . . . Then Counterattack

1. At an international symposium on "Les Défis démocratiques, de l'Amérique latine aux pays de l'Est," held at Lausanne University, April 26–27, 1991.

2. Danièle Sallenave, "Fin du communisme: l'hiver des âmes," *Les Temps modernes,* March 1992.

3. Danièle Sallenave, *Passage de l'Est* (Gallimard, 1993).

4. By 1999, the transfer of wealth from West to East Germany still amounted to seventy billion dollars annually.

5. Paul Noirot, *Le Trou noir du communisme après le naufrage,* Panoramiques no. 4 (Arléa-Corlet, April 1992).

6. *Le Regain démocratique* (Fayard, 1992); in English, *Democracy Against Itself: The Future of the Democratic Impulse,* trans. Roger Kaplan (Free Press, 1993). See in particular Chapter 6, "The Predictable and the Unexpected," and Appendix 1, "On the Reversibility of Communism," a reprint of an article first published in 1988.

7. *La Tentation totalitaire* (Robert Laffont, 1976); in English, *The Totalitarian Temptation,* trans. David Hapgood (Doubleday, 1977).

8. *Ni Marx ni Jésus* (Laffon, 1970); in English, *Without Marx or Jesus: The New American Revolution Has Begun* (Delacorte Press, 1972).

9. The *New York Times* saw fit to print two articles about my alleged volte-face: Alan Tonelson, "Very Well, He Contradicts Himself," November 11, 1993; and Michiko Kakutani, "Contradicted by Events, a Pundit Plows Ahead," December 17, 1993.

10. *La Croix,* February 10, 1990.

Chapter 3: The Real Culprit

1. Jean-Christophe Rufin, *La Dictature libérale* (Hachette, 1995).

2. Philippe Séguin, speaking in Brussels, January 6, 1997.

3. Philippe Dagen in *Le Monde*, February 15, 1997.

4. *Time*, July 7, 1997.

5. For example, in "The Capitalist Threat," *The Atlantic*, February 1997.

6. Viviane Forrester, *L'Horreur economique* (Fayard, 1996); in English, *The Economic Horror* (Polity Press, 1999).

7. Alain Cotta, *Wall Street ou le miracle américain* (Fayard, 1999).

8. Jean-Denis Bredin, "Est-il permis?" *Le Monde*, August 31, 1991.

9. Immanuel Wallerstein, *L'Après-libéralisme* (Éditions de l'Aube, 1999); in English, *After Liberalisme* (New Press, 1995).

10. *Memoires: Le Voleur dans la maison vide* (Plon, 1996).

11. Frédéric Martel, *Le Rose et le Noir* (Seuil, 1996).

12. *Politique internationale*, no. 76, Summer 1997.

13. *Le Regain démocratique* (Fayard, 1992); in English, *Democracy Against Itself: The Future of the Democratic Impulse*, trans. Roger Kaplan (Free Press, 1993).

14. Alain Touraine, *Comment sortir du libéralisme?* (Fayard, 1999). This publisher nevertheless remains one of the best.

15. "Sandinista estranguló a su esposa por simpatizar con los liberals," *Diario las Americas*, February 22, 1998.

16. Karel von Wolferen, *The Enigma of Japanese Power* (Macmillan, 1989); published in French by Robert Laffont, 1990.

Chapter 4: A Rigged Match

1. *Le Monde*, April 20, 1999.

2. *Jeune Afrique*, June 1999, reprinted from *New York Review of Books*.

3. *Le Figaro*, May 27, 1999.

4. Quoted by Pierre Lemieux in *Du libéralisme à l'anarcho-capitalisme* (PUF, 1983).

5. Nicolas Baverez, *Les Trente Piteuses* (Flammarion, 1997).

6. Guy Sorman, *La Nouvelle Solution liberal* (Fayard, 1998).

7. Jacques Lesourne, *Le Modèle français* (Odile Jacob, 1998).

8. *Le Figaro*, May 31, 1999.

9. Francis Fukuyama, "The End of History?" *National Interest*, Summer 1989. Fukuyama developed his theme further in *The End of History and the Last Man* (Free Press, 1992).

Chapter 5: From Illusion to Accountability

1. *L'Événement du jeudi,* February 9, 1995. Having published *The Totalitarian Temptation* twenty years earlier, I can confirm the accuracy of Furet's diagnosis. I experienced such annoyances and gave a full account of them, with documentary evidence, in *La Nouvelle Censure* (Robert Laffont, 1977). Here I would like to take the opportunity to thank François for his friendship and encouragement during this episode; he used to congratulate me heartily for having been promoted to the rank of guinea pig in "an unparalleled sociocultural experiment."

2. Stéphane Courtois et al., *Le Livre noir du communisme* (Robert Laffont, 1997); in English, *The Black Book of Communism: Crimes, Terror, Repression,* trans. Jonathan Murphy and Mark Kramer (Harvard University Press, 1999).

3. *Le Point,* January 14, 1995. The article was reprinted in my collection *Fin du siècle des ombres* (Fayard, 1999).

4. François Furet, *Le Passé d'une illusion: Essai sur l'idée communiste au xxe siècle* (Robert Laffont/Calmann-Lévy, 1995); in English, *The Passing of an Illusion: The Idea of Communism in the Twentieth Century,* trans. Deborah Furet (University of Chicago Press, 1999), ch. 8, "The Antifascist Culture."

5. *L'Histoire,* November 1997.

6. *L'Humanité,* November 7, 1997.

7. *Témoignage chrétien,* November 28, 1997; *Le Monde,* November 9, 1997.

8. *Le Journal du dimanche,* November 2, 1997; *L'Humanité,* November 7, 1997.

9. Pierre Vidal-Naquet, *Critique communiste,* February 1998.

10. *Le Monde,* November 27, 1997.

11. See Chapter 1, pp. 20–21.

12. *Le Monde,* April 1998.

13. Jean-François Bouthors in *La Croix,* November 13, 1997.

14. Among the most recent works devoted to this politico-intellectual suicide, I will mention Christian Jelen, *L'Aveuglement* (Flammerion, 1984); and Pierre Rigoulet, *Les Paupières Lourdes* (Éditions universitaires, 1991). There have been many others, in every language, over many years.

15. François Furet, *Penser la Révolution française* (Gallimard, 1978); in English, *Interpreting the French Revolution* (Cambridge University Press, 1981).

Chapter 6: Panic among the Revisionists

1. Régine Deforges in *L'Humanité*, November 18, 1997.

2. Andrei Gratchev, *L'Histoire vraie de la fin de l'URSS*, trans. Galia Ackerman and Pierre Lorrain (Éditions du Rocher, 1992). The television broadcast took place on December 4, 1997.

3. Jacques Rossi, *The Gulag Handbook: An Encyclopedic Dictionary of Soviet Penitentiary Institutions and Terms Related to the Forced Labor Camps* (Paragon House Publishers, 1989); in French, *Manuel du Goulag: Dictionnaire historique* (Le Cherche-Midi, 1997); first published in Russian in 1987.

4. Romain Rolland, *Voyage à Moscou* (Albin Michel, 1992).

5. Boris Souvarine, *Staline: Aperçu historique du bolchévisme* (Plon, 1935); in English, *Stalin: A Critical Survey of Bolshevism*, trans. C. L. R. James (Longmans, Green & Co., 1939).

6. Quoted in Annie Kriegel and Stéphane Courtois, *Eugen Fried, le Grand secret du PCF* (Seuil, 1997), p. 87.

7. Jean-François Delassus and Thibaud d'Oiron, *Hitler-Staline, liaisons dangereuses*, France 3.

8. *Le Journal du dimanche*, November 2, 1997. See also *L'Humanité*, November 7, 1997.

9. Jean Lacouture, *Survive le peuple cambodgien* (Seuil, 1978).

10. *Le Monde*, October 15, 1997.

11. Juan Benet in *Cuadernos para el Diálogo*, March 27, 1976.

12. Interview for *Evénement du jeudi*, February 9, 1995.

13. With regard to the history of the relations between French Socialists and Communists (among other subjects), the reader can do no better than go to Michel Winock's scholarly and illuminating study, "La culture politique des socialists," in *Les Cultures politiques en France*, ed. Serge Bernstein (Seuil, 1999).

Chapter 7: The Intellectual and Moral Origins of Socialism

1. Alain Besançon's speech was published in *Commentaire*, January 1998. Besançon develops the same theme in *Le Malheur du siècle: Sur*

le *nazisme, le communisme et l'unicité de la Shoah* (Fayard, 1998); in English, *A Century of Horrors: Communism, Nazism, and the Uniqueness of the Shoah,* trans. Ralph C. Hancock (Intercollegiate Studies Institute, 2007).

2. George Watson, *The Lost Literature of Socialism* (The Lutterworth Press, 1998). The author is a fellow in English at St. John's College, Cambridge, and editor of *The New Cambridge Bibliography of English Literature.* Several passages in this chapter have been drawn from my preface to the French edition of Watson's book, *La Littérature oubliée du socialisme* (Nil Éditions, 1999).

3. Ibid., p. 85.

4. Otto Wagener and Henry Ashby Turner Jr., *Hitler aus nächster Nähe: Aufzeichnungen eines Vertrauten, 1929–1932* (Ullstein, 1978); in English, *Hitler: Memoirs of a Confidant* (Yale University Press, 1985).

5. Ludwig von Mises, *Omnipotent Government: The Rise of the Total State and Total War* (Random House, 1969), a collection put together during the war and published in the United States.

6. Louis Dupeux, *Le National-Bolchevisme allemand sous la République de Weimar* (Librairie H. Champion, 1976).

7. Louis Dupeux, "Lecture du totalitarisme russe via le national-bolchevisme allemand (1919–1933)," *Revue d'Allemagne,* July–September 1998.

8. François Furet to Louis Dupeux, Letter dated August 16, 1996.

9. Adapted from Hermann Rauschning, *Hitler Speaks* (Thornton Butterworth, 1939), p. 185.

10. See ibid., pp. 220–21.

11. Luce Irigaray, "Le Sujet de la science est-il sexué?" *Hypatia,* Fall 1987.

12. Quoted by Alain Laurent, *Histoire de l'individualisme* (PUF, 1993). See also the same author's *L'Individu et ses ennemis* (Hachette-Pluriel, 1987).

13. Laurent Cohen-Tanugi, *Le Droit sans l'état: Sur la démocratie en France et en Amérique* (PUF, 1985).

14. Quoted by George Watson in *The Lost Literature of Socialism.*

15. Quoted in Mikhail Geller, *La Machine et les rouages, ou la formation de l'homme soviétique,* trans. Anne Coldefy-Faucard (Calmann-Lévy, 1985).

16. André Gide, *Retour d'USSR* (Gallimard, 1936).

17. Vladimir Lenin, "The Proletarian Revolution and the Renegade Kautsky," *Pravda*, October 11, 1918.

Chapter 8: Truncated Memory

1. *Le Monde*, July 18–19, 1999.

2. Alain Besançon, *Le Malheur du siècle: Sur le nazisme, le communisme et l'unicité de la Shoah* (Fayard, 1998); in English, *A Century of Horrors: Communism, Nazism, and the Uniqueness of the Shoah*, trans. Ralph C. Hancock (Intercollegiate Studies Institute, 2007).

3. This anecdote comes from a book by Beria's son, Sergo Beria, recounting memories of his father: *Beria, mon père*, trans. with preface and notes by Françoise Thom (Plon/Criterion, 1999); in English, *Beria, My Father: Inside Stalin's Kremlin*, trans. Brian Pearce (Duckworth Publishers, 2003).

4. See Jean-Louis Margolin's essay in Stéphane Courtois et al., *The Black Book of Communism: Crimes, Terror, Repression*, trans. Jonathan Murphy and Mark Kramer (Harvard University Press, 1999). And above all see Jasper Becker's *Hungry Ghosts: Mao's Secret Famine* (Free Press, 1996).

5. "Revelations on Mao's Famine: The Great Leap into Death," *International Herald Tribune*, July 18, 1994.

6. Reuter's dispatch from Beijing, December 23, 1998. See also *International Herald Tribune*, December 25, 1998.

7. Laogaï Research Foundation, PO Box 361375, Milpitas, California 95036, USA.

8. See *Le Figaro* and *International Herald Tribune* for December 19 and 20, 1998.

9. Disclosed by the *Washington Post*, January 1, 1999.

10. Jean-Claude Chesnais, "Les comptes fantastiques de la Chine," *Annales des Mines*, March 1999.

11. Vladimir Bukovsky and Wei Jingsheng, "Les crimes impunis de la Chine," *Libération*, April 24–25, 1999.

12. Li Zhisui, *The Private Life of Chairman Mao* (Random House, 1994).

13. Christopher Patten, *East and West: China, Power and the Future of Asia* (Times Books, 1998).

14. This *idée fixe* produced its ravages from the beginning of the occupation in 1950–51; and these ravages continue, or rather reach their perfection, today. See John Pomfret, "Tibetans Struggle for Identity," *International Herald Tribune,* July 22, 1999.

15. *International Herald Tribune,* January 4, 1999. See also *Life and Human Rights in North Korea,* Summer 1999. This quarterly publication, financed by contributions from Japanese and Korean citizens, comes out in Japanese, Korean and English.

16. Hélène Carrère d'Encausse, *Lénine* (Fayard, 1998).

17. Dominique Colas, *Le Léninisme* (PUF, 1987).

18. Jacques Baynac, *La Terreur sous Lénine* (Le Sagittaire, 1975).

19. Christian Jelen, *L'Aveuglement: Les Socialistes et la naissance du mythe soviétique* (Éditions Flammarion, 1984).

20. Olivier Todd, "The Ho Chi Minh Myth," in *Hô Chi Minh, l'homme et son heritage,* ed. Duông Moï (La Voie Nouvelle, 1990). Reprinted in *Commentaire,* Summer 1990.

21. *L'Histoire,* November 1989. Quoted by Olivier Todd in "The Ho Chi Minh Myth."

22. Sophia Quinn-Judge, *Ho Chi Minh: New Perspectives from the Comintern Files,* as quoted in *The Black Book of Communism.*

23. *Apostrophes,* with Bernard Pivot.

24. One of these prisoners, Claude Baylé, has described his experiences in *Prisonnier au camp 113, le camp de Boudarel* (Perrin, 1991).

25. Crimes against humanity are not granted immunity from prosecution by the 1966 amnesty law.

26. *Commentaire,* Winter 1993–1994. I am grateful to M. Moracchini for the valuable insights relating to these problems that he as a legal scholar has been able to provide me.

27. *Le Monde diplomatique,* March 2, 1999.

28. The documentary was shown on December 30, 1998. The executions took place on July 13, 1989. *Translator's note:* For an inside account of the whole affair, see Jorge Masetti, *In the Pirate's Den: My Life as a Secret Agent for Castro* (Encounter Books, 2002).

29. *Translator's note:* For an account of one prisoner's eighteen-year internment in Castro's worst camps, see Armando Valladares, *Against All Hope: A Memoir of Life in Castro's Gulag,* trans. Andrew Hurley (Encounter Books, 2001).

30. In particular, see Pascal Fontaine's chapter on Latin America in *The Black Book of Communism.*

31. Manuel Lucbert, "La RDA, cinquième puissance d'Europe," *Le Monde diplomatique,* May 18–19, 1976.

32. *Le Figaro,* November 5–6, 1995.

33. *Granma International,* November 8, 1998.

34. Quoted in Jean Guisnel, *Les Pires Amis du monde: Les Relations franco-américaines à la fin du XXᵉ siècle* (Stock, 1999).

35. See Yuri Orlov, *Un Socialisme non totalitaire est-il possible?* (1975), which appeared in French translation in *Les Cahiers du Samizdat,* no. 37, July–August 1976. It is reprinted as an appendix in my book *La Nouvelle Censure* (Robert Laffont, 1977).

36. Jacques Rossi, *The Gulag Handbook: An Encyclopedic Dictionary of Soviet Penitentiary Institutions and Terms Related to the Forced Labor Camps* (Paragon House Publishers, 1989); in French, *Manuel du Goulag: Dictionnaire historique* (Le Cherche-Midi, 1997).

37. From an interview in the *International Herald Tribune,* January 30, 1995.

38. These works, unobtainable for a long time now, deserve to be reissued. I thank M. Jacob Sher for having drawn my attention to the work of Franck and Richter, as well as to his own remarkable essays—as yet unpublished, alas—about those authors.

39. Karl Jaspers, *Three Essays: Leonardo, Descartes, Max Weber* (Harcourt, Brace & World, 1964).

Chapter 9: The "Most Favored Totalitarian State" Clause

1. David Bosc, *Ombre portée: Notes sur Louis Aragon et ceux qui l'ont élu* (Éditions Sulliver, 1999).

2. Mario Vargas Llosa, *A Fish in the Water: A Memoir,* trans. Helen Lane (Farrar Straus & Giroux, 1994).

3. I thank Xavier Zeegers for sending me a recording of this conversation.

4. Pierre Daix, *J'ai cru au matin* (Robert Laffont, 1976).

5. *Le Nouvel Observateur,* August 26, 1995.

6. Ibid., under Catherine Marconnet's byline. There is a full account of Burchett's career in my *La Nouvelle Censure* (Robert Laffont, 1977).

7. *Le Figaro,* January 6, 1999. Replying to the same questionnaire, Alain Besançon and Pierre Daix were in general agreement with Ladurie. But Alain Krivine, secretary-general of the (Trotskyist) Revolutionary Communist League, deplored how *L'Humanité* had indulged in "a distressing mea culpa."

8. Jean-Jacques Marie, *Le Goulag* (PUF, 1999), part of the *Que sais-je?* series. See Pierre Rigoulot's review of this production in *Cahiers d'Histoire sociale,* Summer 1999.

9. This document is reproduced in *La Nouvelle Censure.*

10. Quoted by Yves Santamaria, "Ethiopia, Angola, Mozambique," in Stéphane Courtois et al., *The Black Book of Communism: Crimes, Terror, Repression,* trans. Jonathan Murphy and Mark Kramer (Harvard University Press, 1999).

11. *Le Nouvel Observateur,* November 5, 1997.

12. André Glucksmann and Thierry Wolton, *Silence, on tue* (Grasset & Fasquelle, 1986).

13. See Chapter 5, p. 87, for Jean Lacouture's analysis.

14. Ben Kiernan, *Race, Power, and Genocide in Cambodia under the Khmer Rouge, 1975–1979* (Yale University Press, 1996). But Kiernan is not exempt from wanting to exonerate the Communists from the charge of genocide.

15. *Le Monde,* June 24, 1997.

16. *International Herald Tribune,* December 29–30, 1998.

17. *Le Monde,* July 29, 1999. Report by Jean-Claude Pomonti from Phnom Penh.

18. See especially Jean Montaldo, *Les Finances du PCF* (Albin Michel, 1977).

19. "Robert Hue menacé de correctionelle," *Le Parisien-Aujourd'hui,* August 18, 1999. This short piece was mischievously buried in the "News in Brief" section.

20. Vladimir Bukovsky, *Reckoning with Moscow: A Nuremberg Trial for Soviet Agents and Western Fellow Travelers* (Regnery, 1998); in French, *Jugement à Moscou.*

21. Victor Kravchenko, *I Chose Freedom: The Personal and Political Life of a Soviet Official* (Transaction Publishers, 1988); in French, *J'ai choisi la liberté.*

22. Thierry Wolton, *L'Histoire interdite* (Jean-Claude Lattès, 1998).

Chapter 10: A History without Meaning?

1. Pierre Vidal-Naquet, preface to Arno Mayer, *La "Solution Finale" dans l'histoire* (Découverte, 1990); in English, *Why Did the Heavens Not Darken? The "Final Solution" in History* (Pantheon, 1988).

2. I owe these figures to two of the most reliable experts on the period: Henri Amoureux and the American historian Herbert Lottman.

3. Emmanuel Todd, *Le Destin des immigrés* (Seuil, 1994).

4. *Le Point,* no. 1283.

5. From the preface by Françoise Thom to Sergo Beria, *Beria, mon père*, trans. Françoise Thom (Plon/Criterion, 1999); in English, *Beria, My Father: Inside Stalin's Kremlin,* trans. Brian Pearce (Duckworth Publishers, 2003).

6. *Le Monde,* January 25, 1997.

7. In an interview with Agence France-Presse, April 13, 1997. A few days later, Mme de Gaulle-Anthonioz, a member of the Conseil Économique et Social, repeated the same words before the National Assembly.

8. This text is quoted by Stéphane Courtois, "PCF: l'impossible redressement," *Les Cahiers d'Histoire sociale,* Spring–Summer 1997.

9. Marc Lazar, "L'idéologie communiste n'est pas morte," *Esprit,* March–April 1997.

10. Ibid.

11. In English, Jean Valtin, *Out of the Night* (Kessinger Publishing, 2005).

12. *L'Humanité,* December 26, 1995.

13. See *International Herald Tribune,* December 26, 1998, and September 23, 1999. The author of the *Protocols* was one Mathieu Golovinski; see Victor Loupan's article in *Le Figaro Magazine,* August 7, 1999. Golovinski was named People's Commissar by Lenin in 1917 and remained in Lenin's close circle until his death.

14. Editorial, "Les Placards du PCF," *Le Monde,* November 21, 1998.

15. See, notably, Annie Kriegel and Stéphane Courtois, *Eugen Fried, le grand secret du PCF* (Seuil, 1997). Born in Slovakia, appointed by Stalin, Fried was the covert patron of the French CP during the 1930s and 1940s. An earlier portrait of this individual and his role may be found in Maurice Thorez's 1974 biography. The archives make the case against Fried unassailable.

16. Marc Lazar, "L'idéologie communiste n'est pas morte."

17. "Les pétards mouilles du libéralisme," *Le Figaro,* July 22, 1999.

18. *Le Monde,* August 16, 1999.

19. Olivier Duhamel, Jérôme Jaffré, Sofres, *L'État de l'opinion* (Seuil, 1997).

Chapter 11: The Highest Stage of Democracy?

1. *Commentaire,* Autumn 1979.

2. Pierre Milza, *Mussolini* (Fayard, 1999).

3. The late Renzo De Felice is the author of a four-volume book on Mussolini and various other works whose publication between 1965 and 1997 have renewed our understanding of Fascism.

4. Indro Montanelli, *Storia d'Italia* (Rizzoli, 1975).

5. See L. S. Dawidowicz, *The War against the Jews: 1933–1945* (Penguin, 1987), p. 480. See also Emmanuel Todd, *Le Destin des immigrés* (Seuil, 1994); and Renzo De Felice, *Storia degli ebrei italiani sotto il fascismo* (Einaudi, 1961); in English, *The Jews in Fascist Italy: A History* (Enigma Books, 2001).

6. See especially Renzo De Felice, *Intervista sul fascismo, a cura di Michael Ledeen* (Laterza, 1976). Serious contemporary historiography has exposed the superstitious character of some myths. See H. A. Turner Jr., "Le grand capital et la montée de Hitler au pouvoir," in David Schoenbaum, *La Révolution Brune: La Société allemande sous le IIIᵉ Reich* (Robert Laffont, 1979); trans. from English, *Hitler's Social Revolution: Class and Status in Nazi Germany, 1933–1939* (Doubleday, 1966). Turner notes that "The great majority of German industrialists neither wished for a Nazi victory [at the elections] nor contributed financially in order to bring it about." On the other hand, "Hitler received considerable assistance from small and medium-sized businesses." We know that the sensationalist book attributed to Fritz Thyssen, *I Paid Hitler* (Weidenfeld & Nicholson, 1941), was padded with inventions by the American journalist Emery Reves. A refugee in France, the industrialist was handed over to the Nazis in 1940. As far as Fascism is concerned, among other works, Piero Melograni's *Gli Industriali e Mussolini: Rapporti tra Confindustria e Fascismo dal 1919 al 1929* (Longanesi, 1972) may be consulted. Here we learn that Italian employers defended elected workers' committees against the "corporations" that the Fascists wanted to impose on the fac-

tories, and how growing public-sector interventionism in the economy was institutionalized under Mussolini by the creation of the Istituto per la Ricostruzione Industriale.

7. Luigi Pirandello, *Il Fu Mattia Pascal;* in English, *The Late Mattia Pascal* (Eridanos Library: Marsilio Publishers, 1995). Quoted by Michel Ostenc, *Intellectuels italiens et fascisme: 1915–1929* (Payot, 1983).

8. Paolo Simoncelli, *Cantimori, Gentile e la normale di Pisa* (Franco Angeli, 1994).

9. Vasily Grossman, *Life and Fate* (HarperCollins, 1987); first published in Switzerland under the title *Vie et Destin* (L'Age d'homme, 1980).

10. Claude Lefort, *La Complication: Retour sur le communisme* (Fayard, 1999); in English: *Complications: Communism and the Dilemmas of Democracy* (Columbia University Press, 2007).

11. Quoted by Nicolas Werth in Stéphane Courtois et al., *The Black Book of Communism: Crimes, Terror, Repression,* trans. Jonathan Murphy and Mark Kramer (Harvard University Press, 1999).

12. Already by 1911, Beveridge, as director of labor exchanges, had influenced Lloyd George and helped put into place the National Insurance Act, Britain's first unemployment and health insurance.

13. Here I have taken this point further than I might otherwise have done had I not read Claude Lefort's *La Complication: Retour sur le communisme,* which I encountered while I was writing this book.

14. *Commentaire,* Spring 1998. I also am happy to count myself among them.

15. *Caractères,* February 14, 1992.

16. Maurice Merleau-Ponty, *Les Aventures de la dialectique* (Gallimard, 1955); in English, *Adventures of the Dialectic* (Northwestern University Press, 1973).

17. Claude Lefort, *La Complication: Retour sur le communisme.*

18. Ibid.

19. Francois Furet and Ernst Nolte, *Fascisme et Communisme* (Commentaire-Plon, 1998).

20. *International Herald Tribune,* August 19, 1999.

21. Karl Marx, *Misère de la philosophie, Oeuvres complètes* (Éditions de la Pléiade), vol. 1, p. 89. The first English edition was published in 1900 under the title, *The Poverty of Philosophy* (Twentieth Century Press).

22. Leon Trotsky, *Their Morals and Ours* (Pathfinder Press, 1973); first published 1938.

23. Karl Marx, *Oeuvres complètes,* vol. 1, p. 1623.

Chapter 12: Fearing Liberalism

1. The TV drama, aired on October 1, 1999, was an adaptation of a detective thriller by Manuel Vasquez Montalban, which apparently is much better than the ARTE travesty.

2. In my *La Connaissance inutile* (1988); in English, *The Flight from Truth: The Reign of Deceit in the Age of Information* (Random House, 1992); and *Le Regain démocratique* (1992); in English, *Democracy Against Itself: The Future of the Democratic Impulse,* trans. Roger Kaplan (Free Press, 1993).

3. Daniel Bell, *The End of Ideology: On the Exhaustion of Political Ideas in the Fifties* (Free Press, 1960).

4. From a talk given over Europe 1 on September 17, 1991. See *Commentaire,* no. 56.

5. Quoted in "100 Years Ago," *International Herald Tribune,* April 21, 1990.

6. Pierre-Jean Martineau in *L'Histoire,* writing about the strikes of 1995–1996.

7. *Translator's note: Répartition* ("sharing out") is a French pension system. Violaine Messager writes: "There is cultural opposition as highlighted by the following analysis: The English expression 'Pay-as-you-go' has no French equivalent. French people use the technical and more neutral term *répartition* or the positive term *solidarité,* which evokes social goodwill and strength through unity. Contrariwise, the positive English expression 'funded,' which gives an impression of seriousness and security, is translated in French by the word *capitalisation,* which evokes capitalism, a word that in many minds remains linked with nineteenth-century exploitation of workers. In theory, *répartition* and *capitalisation* are quite equivalent. Pensions, when paid, are scaled with respect to productivity. In France, rights are settled with respect to future earnings on interest, to the market prices of shares. . . . If the economy collapses, the worth of these rights collapses too. [*Répartition* schemes] do not need to be funded because they are national and compulsory, as is the social security system. Centralization of this sort is also a French

characteristic. In order to maintain the *répartition* system, there is a need for either increasing the duration of contributions, or decreasing pensions. The government proposes a bit of both." Adapted from http://goinside.com/03/5/strike.html.

8. Alain Peyrefitte, *C'était de Gaulle*, vol. 2 (Éditions de Fallois-Fayard, 1997). *Translator's note*: De Gaulle actually uses the word *veaux*, plural of *veau*, "calf," in its argot sense of "lazy dolt."

9. Found in *Les Échos*, October 12, 1999.

10. Pierre-Patrick Kaltenbach, *Associations lucratives sans but* (Denoël, 1995). On the subject of the state's corrupt wastefulness, see also Louis Bériot, *Abus de bien public* (Plon, 1998).

11. *Le Point*, June 4, 1999.

12. Michèle de Mourgue, *Projet d'avis du Conseil économique et social sur la conjoncture*, June 19, 1997.

13. *Revue de métaphysique et de morale*, October–December 1922.

14. The details can be found in the monthly publication *Capital*, July 1999.

15. *International Herald Tribune*, October 14, 1999.

16. *Le Nouvel Observateur*, October 7, 1999.

17. *Les Échos*, October 6, 1999.

18. Alain Madelin, ed., *Aux sources du modèle libéral français* (Perrin, 1997).

19. *Commentaire*, Spring–Summer 1998.

20. On this subject, see Jacques Lesourne, *Le Modèle français, grandeur et décadence* (Odile Jacob, 1998). Also Richard Kuisel, *Le Capitalisme de l'État en France, modernization et dirigisme au XXe siècle* (Gallimard, 1984).

21. *Le Figaro Économie*, October 12, 1999.

22. The title of an article by Paul-Marie de la Gorce in *Jeune Afrique*, August 31, 1999.

23. Quoted by Seymour Martin Lipset, "The Death of the Third Way," *National Interest*, Summer 1990.

24. Ibid.

25. On February 26, 1985, the dollar reached a record exchange rate of 10.61 francs. It had stood at 5.50 francs in 1981. The franc's value had been cut in half . . . but this was the Americans' fault, naturally.

26. *Le Nouvel Observateur*, June 24, 1999.

27. *Les Temps modernes,* October–November 1998.

28. To the left were those loyal to the old Marxist Oskar Lafontaine, the finance minister who resigned in March 1999. As for the Greens, they suffered even worse setbacks than the SPD.

29. The PASOK party of Greece was an exception.

30. Louis Althusser, preface to Dominique Lecourt, *Lysenko: Histoire réele d'une science proletarienne* (Maspero, 1976).

31. *Corriere della Sera,* September 12, 1999.

32. *Corriere della Sera,* January 27, 1999.

33. *Le Point,* November 19, 1999. See also "Le chaumage en France: le trucage des chiffres," *Société civile,* November 1999, a publication of the Institut Français pour la Recherche sur les Administrations Publiques.

34. *La Stampa,* October 16, 1999.

35. In a broadcast on RMC-*Le Figaro,* October 24, 1999.

36. A detailed assessment of this debate can be found in Philippe Baillet, "La réception italienne du *Livre noir du communisme,*" *Les Cahiers d'Histoire sociale,* Summer 1999 (Albin Michel).

37. The phrase is from Pierre-Patrick Kaltenbach, *Associations lucratives sans but* (Denoël, 1995).

Chapter 13: The Ultra-Left and Anti-Americanism

1. The Zapatista Army was named after Emilio Zapata, the peasant hero of the 1911 Mexican Revolution.

2. Pierre Bourdieu, *Sur la television: Suivi de l'emprise du jornalisme* (Liber-Raisons d'agir, 1996); in English, *On Television,* trans. Priscilla Parkhurst Ferguson (New Press, 1999); and *Contre-feux: Propos pour servir à la résistance contre l'invasion néo-libérale* (Liber-Raisons d'agir, 1998); in English, *Firing Back: Against the Tyranny of the Market* (Verso, 2002). Serge Halimi, *Les Nouveaux Chiens de garde* (Liber-Raisons d'agir, 2005). Halimi's title alludes to Paul Nizan's 1932 pamphlet attacking "bourgeois" philosophers.

3. Daniel Schneidermann, *Du journalisme après Bourdieu* (Fayard, 1999).

4. Pierre Bourdieu and Jean-Claude Passeron, *La Reproduction: Éléments pour une théorie du système d'enseignement* (Minuit, 1970); in English: *Reproduction in Education, Society and Culture,* trans. Richard Nice (Sage Publications, 1990).

5. Jean-Paul Jouary, Guy Pélachaud, Arnaud Spire, Bernard Vasseur, *Giscard et les idées: Essai sur la guerre idéologique* (Éditions sociales, 1980). Éditions sociales is the publishing house of the French Communist Party.

6. *Le Pouvoir intellectuel en France* (Ramsay, 1979); in English: *Teachers, Writers, Celebrities: The Intellectuals of Modern France* (Schocken Books, 1981).

7. Pierre Boncenne, *Les Belles Âmes de la culture* (Seuil, 1996).

8. *Esprit*, July 1998.

9. Serge Halimi, *Les Nouveaux chiens de garde* (Liber-Raisons d'agir, 2005).

10. *Le Monde diplomatique*, December 1996.

11. Daniel Schneidermann, *Du journalisme après Bourdieu* (Fayard, 1999).

12. Marc Fumaroli, *Heros et Orateurs: Rhétorique et dramaturgie cornéliennes* (Droz, 1990); Jean Tulard, *Napoléon, ou, le mythe du sauveur* (Fayard, 1986). On this affair, I have an article titled "L'index au XXe siècle" in my collection *Fin du siècle des ombres* (Fayard, 1999).

13. *Le Monde*, September 18, 1998. Redeker belongs to the editorial board of *Les Temps modernes*, whose editor-in-chief is Claude Lanzmann.

14. Jeannine Verdès-Leroux, *Le Savant et la politique: Essai sur le terrorisme sociologique de Pierre Bourdieu* (Grasset, 1998).

15. Bertrand de la Grange and Maite Rico, *Sous-commandant Marcos, la géniale imposture* (Plon/Ifrane, 1998).

16. For an analysis of this book by Mario Vargas Llosa, see "L'autre visage de l'utopie," *Le Point*, June 20, 1998; the article originally appeared in *El Pais*.

17. Jean Guéhenno, *Journal des années noires (1940–1944)* (Gallimard, 1947). Ernst Thaelmann was the Communist candidate in the German presidential election of 1932.

18. *L'Âge des extrêmes* came out in France in October 1999, under the Éditions Complexes imprint. It was on the Bestseller list published by *Le Point*, November 12. English first edition: *The Age of Extremes: The Short Twentieth Century, 1914–1991* (Michael Joseph, 1994).

19. See the poll results in *Les Échos*, November 2, 1999.

20. Zbigniew Brzezinski, *The Grand Chessboard: American Primacy and Its Geostrategic Imperatives* (Basic Books, 1997).

21. See Pierre Beylau, "Défense: l'impuissance européenne," *Le Point*, May 14, 1999.

22. Pascal Bruckner, "Pourquoi cette rage antiaméricaine?" *Le Monde*, April 7, 1999. And "L'Amérique diabolisée," interview in *Politique internationale*, Summer 1999.

23. In *National Hebdo*, the National Front weekly, April 22, 1999.

24. *Libération*, April 29, 1999.

25. Denis Duclos, *Le Monde*, April 22, 1999.

26. See Gerald Segal, *Foreign Affairs*, September–October 1999. Segal is director of the London-based International Institute for Strategic Studies. The economic statistics furnished by the Chinese are absolutely not to be trusted. On this topic of falsified Chinese statistics, see Jean-Claude Chesnais, *Les Annales des mines*, March 1999.

27. Alain Peyrefitte, *C'était de Gaulle* (Éditions de Fallois, 2000).

28. Noël Mamère and Olivier Warin, *Non, merci, Uncle Sam* (Ramsay, 1999).

29. Günter Grass, *Ein weites Feld* (Steidl, 1995); in English: *Too Far Afield* (Harcourt, 2000).

30. See Rose-Marie Mercillon's review, "La nostalgie de Günter Grass," *Commentaire*, Winter 1995–1996.

31. Such clichés are innumerable and are triumphantly resistant to all the well-documented books that have demonstrated their inanity. Three of the most recent of these are: Christian Gérondeau, *Candide au pays des libéreaux* (Albin Michel, 1998); Alain Cotta, *Wall Street ou le miracle Américain* (Fayard, 1999); and Philippe Manière, *Marx à la corbeille* (Stock, 1999). The *corbeille* in the last title refers to the stock-brokers' trading floor in the Paris Stock Exchange.

Chapter 14: Hating Progress

1. See Jean-Claude Casanova, "Les Habits neufs du progressism," *Le Figaro*, November 24, 1999.

2. Roland Hureaux, *Les Hauteurs béantes de l'Europe: La Derive ideologique de la construction europeenne* (Éditions François Xavier de Guibert, 1999).

3. "Le Naufrage de l'École," *Le Point*, September 20, 1997.

4. In *Le Point*, September 27, 1997, Luc Ferry, president of the Conseil National des Programmes, made a lengthy analysis and com-

mentary on this report. See also Claude Imbert's editorial in the same issue.

5. See Liliane Lurçat, *La Destruction de l'enseignement élémentaire* (Éditions François Xavier de Guibert, 1998). In November 1999, at the first meeting of the "Education Salon" organized by the Ministry of Education (it is easier to organize an Education Salon than actual education), Mme Ségolène Royal, minister for secondary education, "declared war on illiteracy" (*Journal du dimanche,* November 28, 1999). If she has declared war on illiteracy, that's because—whatever M. Thélot imagines—illiteracy is a real problem.

6. This convergence was manifested in the simultaneous publication, on December 8, 1999, of two exquisitely interchangeable opinion pieces. In *Le Monde,* Charles Pasqua, president of the Gaullist political party Rally for France (Rassemblement pour la France), titled his piece "La mondialisation n'est pas inéluctable" (Globalization Is Not Inevitable). In *Libération,* Alain Krivine and Pierre Rousset, both members of the Revolutionary Communist League, came out with "Encore un effort, camarades!"

Appendices

1. *Le Monde,* December 17, 1994.
2. *Cambio 16,* Madrid, December 5, 1994.
3. William Shawcross, *The Quality of Mercy: Cambodia, Holocaust and Modern Conscience* (Simon & Schuster, 1984); in French, *Le Poids de la pitié* (Balland, 1985).

Index

LAST EXIT TO UTOPIA

Sudre, Alfred, 141
Suhartos, 47
Sur la télévision (Bourdieu), 250
Survive le peuple cambodgien (Lacouture), 87
Sweden, 6–7, 32, 252; Palme in, 73; privatizations in, 238, 239

Taiwan, 118
Ta Mok, 160
Télérama, 132–33
Témoignage chrétien, 66
Temps modernes, 240
Terreur sous Lénine, La (Baynac), 124
Thailand, 48
Thatcher, Margaret, 4, 9, 33, 54; on German reunification, 274
Their Morals and Ours (Trotsky), 209
Thélot, Claude, 287
Third Way, 54, 183, 238–39
Thorez, Maurice, 200
Thyssen, Fritz, 324
Tibet: censorship on, 120; cultural destruction in, 87, 121–22; as "subversive," 118; torture in, 117
Tillon, Charles, 202
Tintin au pays des Soviets (Hergé), 151
Tocqueville, Alexis de, 233, 234–35
Todd, Emmanuel, 170
Todd, Olivier, 125
Togliatti, Palmiro, 194, 200
Tolstoy, Leo, 143
Totalitarian Temptation, The (Revel), 24n, 27, 62n, 205, 314; on Burchett, 148
Toubon, Jacques, 126–27, 276
Touraine, Alain, 43–44, 57
Tournier, Michel, 136

trade/labor unions, 232; American, 23–24; legal status of, 38; politicization of, 197; socialist/Communist opposition to, 38–39; subsidies of, 39; suppression of, 196; teachers', 6
Trahison des clercs, La (Benda), 191
Treaty of Maastricht, 184, 242
Trichet, Jean-Claude, 294
Trotsky, Leon, 209
Trotskyists, 65, 78, 182, 228, 251, 320; and Stalinists, 202–3
Tulard, Jean, 259
Turgot, 56, 231
Two Treatises on Civil Government (Locke), 231

Ukraine, 116, 176
Unesco: on Ho Chi Minh, 124–27; and Mengistu, 157
Ungaretti, Giuseppe, 190, 194
Union for French Democracy (UDF), 37
Unité, L', 149
United Kingdom. *See* Great Britain
United Nations, 235, 267; and Cambodia, 309; and China, 121; and Cuban aid, 138; Human Rights Commission, 134; and Iraq, 212, 264–65; and Khmer Rouge, 161
United States: academic left in, 24–26, 175–76; and Africa, 267; and Blair, 239; and Cold War, 25–27, 28, 153, 264; Communist Party in, 23–24; and Cuban embargo, 137–38, 177–78; culture in, 266; Democratic Party, 24, 38, 239; economic growth